Becoming a Restorative Lawyer

How to Transform Your Legal Practice for Self, Client, and Community Growth

Brenda Waugh

Foreword by
Howard Zehr

Photography by
Howard Zehr

goodmedia PRESS

GoodMedia Press

An imprint of goodmedia communications, llc

Book cover and book layout design by Longevity Marketing, LLC

The text in this book is set in Fanwood and Montserrat.

Manufactured in USA

10 9 8 7 6 5 4 3 2 1

Publisher's Cataloging-in-Publication Data

Names: Waugh, Brenda, 1958-, author. | Zehr, Howard, foreword author.

Title: Becoming a restorative lawyer : how to transform your legal practice for self , client , and community growth / Brenda Waugh; foreword by Howard Zehr; photography by Howard Zehr.

Description: Includes bibliographical references and index. | Dallas, TX: GoodMedia Press, 2025.

Identifiers: LCCN: 2025941332 | ISBN: 979-8-9852429-8-0 (paperback) | 979-8-9852429-9-7 (ebook)

Subjects: LCSH Restorative justice. | Criminal justice, Administration of--Moral and ethical aspects. | Cause lawyers. | Public interest law. | BISAC LAW / General | LAW / Alternative Dispute Resolution | LAW / Arbitration, Negotiation, Mediation | LAW / Civil Law | LAW / Criminal Law / General | LAW / Criminal Law / Juvenile Offenders | LAW / General Practice

Classification: LCC HV8688 .W38 2025 | DDC 364.6/8--dc23

Contents

Foreword

I have been waiting for this book for a long time.

During five decades working with people involved in the criminal legal system, I have encountered many lawyers who are frustrated, demoralized, and overwhelmed by their work. Some have given up the profession or resigned themselves to living with their discomfort. Some have developed serious health issues. Others, on their own or in collaboration with others, have found ways to become healers for their clients as well as themselves through the application of restorative justice, therapeutic justice, conflict transformation, or other approaches. I have long wished for more focused resources to aid such seekers on their journeys.

This book addresses that need, based not only on theory and ideas but on concrete experiences: real-life case stories from the author's own career. Attorney Brenda Waugh has been on a journey of discovery and healing herself, and in these pages, she shares what she has learned in ways that will be of immense help to others who wish to find more life-giving ways to lawyering for the sake of their clients as well as themselves.

Although some may find this surprising, I have found that the practice of law has space for real creativity. Formal restorative justice programs are wonderful when they are available, but what if your community doesn't have one? What if a formal program doesn't fit the needs of the situation? I have worked with dozens of restorative justice programs over the years, but my real enthusiasm is for the way restorative justice principles and values can be brought to bear creatively in a variety of situations, regardless of whether a program is available or appropriate. As Waugh demonstrates here, the practice of law itself can provide an excellent opportunity if practitioners learn to look beyond what Norwegian criminologist Nils Christie has called the "trained tunnel vision" of legal education and practice. This book offers a restorative justice lens tailored to a legal practitioner's context.

I am confident that this resource will be a source of inspiration and guidance for experienced practitioners. I'm also hopeful that it will be adopted as part of law curricula.

I dream of a day when lawyers will see themselves not only as legal analysts and strategists but as agents of transformation and healing.

Howard Zehr, Ph.D.
    Distinguished Professor of Restorative Justice
    Center for Justice & Peacebuilding
    Eastern Mennonite University

Introduction

Finding Healing Power Within the
Practice of Law

Every day, in every moment, you get to exercise choices that will determine whether or not you will become a great person, living a great life.

— Jeff Olson, *Slight Edge*

1.

"This is worse than going to a funeral," the young girl's uncle explains to me as we walk up the steep marble courthouse steps. I listen to his proclamation as we climb upwards — upwards toward justice, I assume. But do these sagging steps create obstacles to justice? Do they direct us to a source of shame or even the site of recurring tragedy?

"Worse than going to a funeral."

On that crisp October morning, we walk side by side. The victim's middle-aged uncle wears a brown polyester suit, the pants hemmed to break over his cowboy boots. He looks back at me without expression.

"Worse than a funeral?" I ask him and then ramble on. "It's going well. It's a hard case. We don't have any physical evidence; it's her word against her grandfather's. But the jury seems like they are going along with me. The opening went well. Our witnesses are good. A funeral?"

"Yes. Worse."

We open the double doors into the oldest courthouse in the state. We walk past the tiny hexagon-tiled vestibule, past the plaques lining the entrance that honor the local fallen soldiers, and up the stairs; we open the double doors leading to the courtroom.

I am acutely aware of where I am, who I am, and what I'm doing here. I'm just over forty, married, with three kids under fifteen. I've been practicing law for twelve years, advocating for children and women. I'm in court prosecuting a tough case. We have no corroborating physical evidence. The community respects this church-going eighty-year-old lifetime resident. Today, I am prosecuting Darrell Walters for five counts of sexual abuse against his great-granddaughter, Anna.

By now, Darrell had abused three generations. When he molested his daughter, the family denied the abuse, shamed the victim, and moved on. When his granddaughter disclosed the molestation, the family believed her and sent him to a counselor to be "fixed." Today, the jury hears the case of his offenses against his great-granddaughter. I remind myself: "The jury will serve justice."

The funeral analogy distracts me as we open the heavy, oak double doors and walk down the center aisle of the courtroom. I try to dismiss it.

I have work to do. And I like — no, I love — my work. I also love this courtroom — it reminds me of the courtroom in *To Kill a Mockingbird*. I walk past the jury box into the well of the court. It's like a basketball court or boxing ring. The well is framed by two jury boxes, the judge's bench, and a carved wooden railing that separates the court professionals and named parties from the empty pews. In a few hours, spectators, including family, friends, church members, and the press, will fill them. I spread my trial notebook, evidence labels, and other materials out on counsel table, concentrating only on the task before me. I've learned to ignore most of my grievances with the system. However, I cannot ignore what victims articulate as their needs. In the past year, I've prosecuted two defendants. They both pled guilty and offered public apologies as conditions of their sentences. Their victims wanted both an apology and for the defendant to accept responsibility.

Darrell's victims, all three generations, want him to take responsibility. They want an apology. And they want an assurance that he cannot do this to anyone else. Darrell denies everything. I can only satisfy one of their requests, keeping the community safe, by incarcerating this octogenarian. And even that will not be easy.

I look back at the uncle. Worse than a funeral. I had never thought of being in a trial like that. Worse?

"Why isn't his name in the paper?" Leah asks. She is Anna's aunt, Darrell's granddaughter, and one of Darrell's victims. She sits on a 1920s Art Deco chrome-framed sofa reupholstered in the 1960s in green pleather. A group of women talk, sitting in the comfortable, quiet lounge attached to the women's bathroom. The frosted glass window in the door says, "Women's Witness Room."

"The press doesn't identify the victim of sexual crimes. Especially when it's a child," I answer. Leah often sits on that green pleather couch during recesses from the trial, sometimes breastfeeding her baby. One day, she outlined for me her recovery from drug addiction. Another time, she described never feeling worthy.

Anna sits on the sofa, too. I look at her, fourteen years old. Alone in the room with me, she explains how, when her great-grandfather kissed her, it felt like "dog slobber." In another breath, she asks me to promise not to tell her mother that she is having sex with her boyfriend. I listen, and I learn. I learn how abuse changes victims. Couldn't I do something to change them back? Couldn't I make Leah feel worthy? Couldn't I give Anna the strength to decide not to have sex when she doesn't want to?

Across the hall, the courtroom tells its own story — a different narrative, a diverse cast of characters, and an all-male jury.

The defendant is eighty-two years old. He reminds me of a ventriloquist's dummy dressed in a shiny black suit. He sits erect beside his defense attorney – a man my colleague nicknamed "Rooster" after watching him strut around the courtroom during a trial a few years ago. Rooster appears calm this morning.

"All rise." The jury files out of the deliberation room and into the jury box.

"Has the jury reached a verdict?"

"Yes, your honor."

It takes a few moments for the bailiff to walk from the foreperson to the clerk. The clerk hands the jury verdict form to the judge, who then passes it back to the clerk. These moments feel like eons.

"As to the charge contained in Count 1 of the indictment, we find the defendant, Darrel Walters, not guilty." My heart sinks. The clerk continues, "Count 2. Not guilty." I turn to see Leah's reaction, but it is too painful, and I turn to look at the clerk. "Count 3. Not guilty." I close my eyes; afraid I may cry. "Count 4. Not guilty."

"As to the charge contained in Count 5 of the indictment, we find the defendant, Darrell Walters, guilty." Darrell turns around and looks at the women seated behind me. He mouths, "WHORES" and turns back. Moments later, his eighty-three-year-old wife faints. She remains unconscious as EMTs carry her out of the courtroom on a stretcher.

Two weeks later, on my last day as an assistant district attorney, the judge sentences Darrell to an indeterminate prison term of one to five years. It feels good. Finally, someone recognizes the tiny man in the shiny black suit for who he is. Someone sees the pain he caused. It feels good.

At the same time, it does not feel good. To win, I brought this family into a process that was "worse than a funeral" that produced a shallow outcome. Darrell never apologized or accepted responsibility.

I like doing trials. I tell the story — expose injustice. And, of course, I like winning. But what does one victory mean to everyone else? Sometimes, when we win, we lose.

2.

Walking up the steps to the courthouse that fall morning, my fate became intertwined with Leah and Anna's fate. Their pain rippled into my underlying fear that working for justice within our legal system may be impossible. Even on the first day of law school, I questioned whether lawyers promote justice or merely prop up an ailing system. As a district attorney, I found that this framework failed to meet the needs of the victims, the offenders, and their families. They often find themselves tangled up in a dark, incomprehensible system within our powerful courts. Looking for answers, I stumbled upon restorative justice, therapeutic justice, and mediation. However, my academic inquiry gained a physical form once my life intertwined with Anna and Leah's lives.

Despite my skepticism, I had enjoyed my role as a kind of director and producer, creating the *mise-en-scène*. I'd strategically developed my theory of the case. I had scrambled with "Rooster" about jury instructions and maneuvered to get Leah's 404(b) testimony about Darrel's other acts into evidence. I had orchestrated "a view" of the crime scene. At the same time, I'd begun to understand that I did not operate in isolation, and neither did my colleagues. Trials are not academic exercises. We routinely place ourselves smack dab in the middle of the most devastating human tragedies.

Like every other lawyer who finds themself in the middle of human tragedy, I learned we do not easily escape the pain. We are invited into countless stories that expose our clients' untreated wounds. And I go with them into those stories and their pain. In those days, when my pain grew too strong, I distracted myself by strategizing case theories. I planned cross-examinations and played a game theory of litigation. My diversion obscured the aches, but the suffering lingered.

Suffering: mine, the clients', witnesses', community members', and offenders'. Our court system prevents lawyers from overcoming the deep hurt. It interrupts the potential for lawyers to become healers. This system causes lawyers themselves to suffer recurring wounds. The same goes for judges, probation officers, police officers, court reporters, clerks, and everyone else who encounters the system.

Decades have passed since I walked up the bowed steps on that brisk October morning. I am now stitching together what I've learned as a spectator of both hideous pain and miraculous healing. My viewpoint is so close that sometimes I cease being a bystander and find myself in need of restorative healing.

At first, my wounds would heal, only to reopen. I came to see that the pain I suffered as a lawyer emerged from bearing witness and seeking recompense for the troubled. Their troubles had been caused by preventable and unpreventable events, circumstances created through acts of God, tragic misunderstandings, and poverty. My futile attempts to respond constructively sometimes only compounded the pain. Finding ways to manipulate this unruly machine, our legal system, consumed my efforts. Ready to give up and move on to a new career, I stumbled onto restorative justice (RJ), a different approach to harm and wrongdoing. I learned that bringing RJ principles to my work created new possibilities. They provided a new structure to this chaos. They also let me focus on harm and healing.

I don't pretend that I share this or any experience with every other lawyer. I don't presume to have encountered the same things that each of my professional colleagues may witness. I've found no perfect answers. I've written this interactive memoir of several decades in the courtroom as a lesson and guide. I write from within the pain of my clients' tragedies and within the shared world I inhabit with my brethren: other lawyers. Our collective wisdom, viewed through a restorative lens, may create a new practice of law.

This new practice of law may rely on lawyers, but it will depend on clients, judges, and the community to support the role of the lawyer as a healer. We will refuse to segment our lives and identities in the new practice. We will strive to create satisfying personal and professional relationships. We will create opportunities to bring restorative practices into every part of our home and work lives. My idea of a restorative justice-based practice of law is based on a common-sense approach to conflict. It roughly accepts concepts, principles, values, and elements of restorative justice identified by the early scholars and adopters of restorative justice.[1]

In sharing these stories and their lessons, I do not consider myself an expert. I don't have answers. Dolly Parton once remarked, "I don't give advice, I just give information, and if you can use any of it, that's good."[2] I want to share my stories and that information. In doing so, I want to hear more stories. I want to discover how to create a way to practice law based on the principles and values of restorative justice — a practice that will create the opportunity to heal our clients and ourselves.

I'm going to share the stories that I've been invited into and that I've lived. This is not a *how-to* or *advice* book. I won't propose any single solution. Fixing the court system will take more than one solution anyway. It will involve both success and failure. The system is focused on procedures and laws, not relationships.

Although this book cannot be a *self-help* book, I hope it can be a community-help book. I'm not trying to construct or celebrate the self as the essential part of our work life — much less how to make that self better. I want to improve our communities by finding the values we share and allowing them to be active guides in our work.

I most want to share the healing lessons wonderful clients have taught me. In this, my experience has been like Annie Dukes', a champion poker player who keeps her eyes open for teachers. "At the Crystal Lounge, I found myself becoming more open to being with different kinds of people ... I came to realize that ... you need to take people for who they are. And they can often teach you some pretty amazing things."[3]

My friends, clients, and colleagues are my gifted teachers. In sharing our stories, I want to share the lessons they taught me while respecting the confidentiality of our interactions. I have changed their names, locations, and identifying information. I have decided to tell the stories in the present tense and have recreated our conversations. My accounts reflect the essence of the interactions, but they are based only on my memory and may not be entirely accurate. The stories I share are not uncommon, but our modern law practices rarely stimulate the self-reflection needed for profound personal and professional growth.

I suspect that if we can learn to listen to clients, their families, witnesses, lawyers, paralegals, and the people we encounter daily, we may collectively find opportunities to address harm and reduce conflict. I have tried to bring my understanding of restorative justice and conflict transformation theory into my work to help create a type of healing in my practice. Although I experienced many failures, there were many more successes. I'm learning to meet my clients' complex needs, extending far beyond ordinary legal remedies, as well as my own needs for a satisfying, rewarding, and peaceful career. As a work in progress, I thank you for joining me in my quest to become a restorative lawyer.

Chapter 1

My Heart Is Broken

OR YOU CAN'T STOP A TRAIN WRECK WITH A CASE BOOK

All that you have is your soul.

— Tracy Chapman, "Crossroads"

I.

I STARTED my career as a restorative lawyer in West Hollywood, California, in April 1982. I'd gone to California to be a costume designer and wanted to do socially relevant work with the potential to create change. I accepted both profit-oriented and less-commercial projects. One of the less commercial was Center Stage's production of *In the Matter of J. Robert Oppenheimer* (starring Alan Arbus).[1] This production, about creativity, intention, exploitation, and destruction, provides a good foundation for a story worth telling. J. Robert Oppenheimer was a brilliant physicist. He was recruited to run the Los Alamos Laboratory during World War II. On July 16, 1945, the project detonated a nuclear device at Trinity site, New Mexico. Two weeks later, the United States dropped nuclear bombs on Hiroshima and Nagasaki. Oppenheimer became "the father of the atomic bomb." Nine years after that, a committee created by the Atomic Energy Commission held a trial to revoke Oppenheimer's security clearance. The revocation was due to his social connections with communists before World War II and his opposition to the hydrogen bomb.

∿

I ARRIVE at the costume shop one morning to organize the dozens of vintage men's suits I'd scoured Santa Monica Boulevard thrift shops to find.

Suffering from morning sickness, I move slowly. I meticulously organize the suits in preparation for the actors to file through for fittings. The actors portraying John Landsdale, Ward V. Evans, and J. Robert Oppenheimer arrive. They move in and out of the fitting room. I am making notes and tacking them to suit jackets, ties, and hats. "Hem the pants, switch the tie." The actor portraying Edward Teller shows up late. Teller is not sympathetic — being the only member of the scientific community to testify against Oppenheimer retaining his security clearance. This actor adds more dislike to the character as he moves with a heavy, lumbering gait, circling around the room and complaining about his costume. I try to ignore him. His suit is not new. It's not perfect. We are working on a low-budget show, and Teller's suit is fine. He continues, grunting, complaining. I try to make some suggestions, but he'll have none of it.

"I said..." He looks at me, his loud voice filled with impatience and disdain. I calmly continue in my work as I listen, rehanging a suit and selecting a tie for the next fitting. Teller trudges towards me, his face slightly contorted as he intentionally slams into me, "I don't like it."

"Look, it's all I have. We don't have much of a budget — the suits need to be period." I ask myself, "What am I doing here?" I think I'm working for justice, but I'm merely trying to please an actor who has just assaulted me, holding absolute disregard for anything beyond his own ego. I am pouring my heart into getting this group of great actors well-suited to deliver a powerful message. But will it be delivered? Is this even the way to do it? I rehang his suit, tie, and shirt and finish the morning.

We open a week later. Critics, colleagues, and audience members praise the production. Allan Arbus receives accolades for his portrayal of Oppenheimer. I am grateful to work with the outstanding production company (despite Teller) on this show. Sitting in the audience, I am proud of our effort to bring social justice into the theater. But as I watch this well-executed production, I become distracted. Worried. My silent internal soliloquy drowns out Allen Arbus' poignant monologue. "What am I doing here? I picked this life in the theater to create social change. You know, to expose corruption, disrupt power imbalances, and bring positive reform. But it's not happening. I murmur aloud by accident. "I'm in the wrong profession."

As Teller shoved Oppenheimer's career out of one trajectory, the actor portraying Teller shoved me in a new direction. I'd move beyond exposing injustices and strive to prevent them. I'd go to law school. I'd learn to fight for justice. I'd create a better world. I'd be an instrument of social change. I'd shut the next big guy down before he slams into the vulnerable person trying to help him.

2.

A few months later, my husband, Chris, and I packed our one-year-old daughter, our tailless Manx cat, and five houseplants into our Buick Opel to travel across the country to start law school. We made one last stop, a visit with a college friend, Ann, in Davis, a few hours' drive from the campus. Ann attended law school directly after college and had recently graduated. After dinner, she handed me a book, telling me I'd need it and that she didn't need for me to return it.

I opened the book *One L* by Scott Turow. I skimmed the preface, "I am a law student in my first year at the law, and there are many moments when I am simply a mess."[2] I was surprised. A mess? What could that mean?

Six weeks later, Chris and I moved into married student housing. We found childcare, the organic health food store, and a tiny independent bookstore downtown. We showed up for class, printed our names on seating charts, bought case books, and committed to *thinking like a lawyer*. Within the first week, I felt sure that, like Scott Turow, I would have many moments when I was simply a mess.

Classes started, and we were assigned to Section One of the Class of 1987. Each of the two sections had about fifty students. Each had five classes: Civil Procedure, Torts, Contracts, Property, and Criminal Law. Each student occupied a plastic chair anchored to the floor in a stadium-style arrangement and behind long

Formica tables, also anchored to the floor, spanning the room's length. Law professors structured the classes the same in each of the five courses. They read out the name of an appellate case. They stared at a legal-sized sheet of typing paper. The paper contained the seating chart identifying the anchored plastic chair that each student occupied. "Ms. Waugh, state the case."

Resembling well-trained circus poodles, each student stood when identified and recited critical case summaries printed in our $60 per copy, twelve-point font, fake leather, and gold-lettered casebooks. We listed the plaintiff's name, the defendant's name, the scant facts contained in the casebook, and the rule that emerged from the case: the holding.

I wondered: Who are these people? Mrs. Pennoyer, Mrs. Palsgraf, Mr. Pierson, and Mr. Post. Did they have a life story beyond the singular event described in these case books? Does the deeper narrative of their lives matter as we dissect the excerpts for the holding? Like Mrs. Palsgraf, I have no part in my story as I stand and perform. No dialogue, no discussion, and no context. I am no longer a wife and mother, a transplant from out-of-state, an artist, or a good seamstress; I'm another One L.

"Ms. Waugh, please state the case."

"Defendant helped to push a man aboard a train. The man's package fell. The firecrackers inside exploded, causing some scales to fall and injure Plaintiff Palsgraf."

Confused about these people's lack of identity, the absence of an examination of the power dynamics at play, and the institutional infirmity creating the court rulings called "holdings," I struggled. This process of "learning the law" created more questions than answers.

Having a husband also in law school provided advantages; we saved hundreds of dollars by sharing our fake leather casebooks and saved time by sharing notes. We shared questions and a quest for answers outside of casebooks, hornbooks, and Gilbert's outlines.

One afternoon, Chris came home from running errands. The baby was asleep, and I was reading a casebook.

~

> The question submitted by the counsel in this cause for our determination is, whether Lodowick Post, by the pursuit with his hounds in the manner alleged in his declaration, acquired such a right to, or property in, the fox, as will sustain an action against Pierson for killing and taking him away? The cause was argued with much ability by the counsel on both sides and presents for our decision a novel and nice question. It is admitted that a fox is an animal feræ naturæ, and that property in such animals is acquired by occupancy only. These admissions narrow the discussion to the simple question of what acts amount to occupancy, applied to acquiring right to wild animals?[3]

MY HUSBAND SITS down beside me to read. A few minutes later, he reads aloud from a book he purchased from the tiny bookstore downtown. This book has a red cardboard cover, not fake leather. The title, *Legal Education and the Reproduction of Hierarchy,* is in black ink, not fake gold font. I open it to a random page.

> Law schools are intensely political places despite the fact that they seem intellectually unpretentious, barren of theoretical ambition or practical vision of what social life might be. The trade-school mentality, the endless attention to trees at the expense of the forests, the alternating grimness and chumminess of focus on the limited task at hand — all these are only a part of what is going on. The other part is ideological training for willing service in the hierarchies of the corporate welfare state.[4]

We are not alone in our critique of this experience. And I am not alone in wondering if the law is an instrument of justice, especially for the powerless.

3.

After three years of preparation, I entered the practice of law. Everything changed. Suddenly, I was bearing witness firsthand to unimaginable tragedy. I began to suspect that I may never be able to understand, much less communicate, the complicated narrative of my clients' lives. I may never gain sufficient skill to undo the harm and find healing. I may never participate in a process free of gross power imbalances.

The obnoxious actor playing Edward Teller will always knock over every vulnerable woman in his path. The reported cases I learned to state with precision take shape in real people who live in unique communities and have lives that are more than the single event that changed them forever. And these "cases" can't be stated. And these "cases" break my heart. After a couple of years, I experienced the big heartbreak. All lawyers and many other helping professionals, I suspect, never recover from that first big heartbreak.

Working for legal services in rural Camden County, I spent much of my time representing abused women, enforcing the Domestic Violence Protection Act. My husband and I had two children and lived in the city, an hour away. Every other week I "rode the circuit," traveling the crooked mountain roads to the courthouse that had been built over a hundred years ago in the county seat of Camden County.[5]

⁓

ONE MORNING, I am sitting at my desk. The office is in the old courthouse building, in what was once the jail. My desk sits beyond the reception area, a few abandoned jail cells, and several unoccupied desks. I only have one hearing later in the afternoon and a few appointments this morning. Ella Riley walks into my tiny office across the street from the modern judicial building. She fills out an intake form, signs it, and describes the event that changed her life. The one that brought her to see me today. The one that will intertwine our lives.

Ella is a beautiful, simple, country woman wearing dress pants to attend our appointment. She doesn't wear makeup and speaks practically as she explains this situation. The welfare department has placed her two grandsons, Chris and Michael, with their paternal grandparents and has scheduled an emergency hearing in three days. Ella wants custody of the children or at least the ability to visit with them.

It's only been a week since Ella's daughter, Valerie, died. Ella explains that Billy, Valerie's husband, had abused her for years. Ella felt relieved last month when Valerie got a protective order and moved to the battered women's shelter in the city with the boys. Last week, Valerie's friend gave her a ride back to Camden County to pick up a few things. Her sons were riding in the back seat.

Billy intercepted them and shot the driver and Valerie, who both died immediately. Billy put the boys in his car and drove back to his parents' house in Camden County. Hours later, the sheriff arrested Billy and left the children with Billy's family. The welfare, as Ella calls them, filed paperwork with the court. Ella hands me documents that confirm the basic outline of the story, as she told it.

I accept her case and adjust my schedule to attend the hearing.

∿

AT THE EMERGENCY HEARING, the paternal grandparents retained custody, and the judge ordered that Ella could visit her grandchildren. I attended the next hearing and the one after that. The matter proceeded along the typical course that included dozens of hearings, meeting the basic requirements demanded by "due process." Everyone had a lawyer: the State, Billy, the paternal grandparents, Gail (Billy's sister from out-of-state), and the maternal grandmother. The children had a court-selected and state-funded lawyer, a *Guardian Ad Litem*. We participated in full-blown adversarial hearings with testimony, exhibits, experts, motions, and memorandums of law.

4.

In all that due process, I witnessed little effort to address the harm this family sustained. I spotted scant attempts to meet the needs of any of the people lined up on the benches. Me? What was I doing? Was I working to address harm and meet needs? Hell no. I struggled to match legal rights and points of law to facts. I didn't think about identifying unmet needs. I had never heard of "interest-based negotiation." The folks on the other side of the courtroom became opposing parties and opposing counsel. We were in battle, and they were the enemy.

The details of Valerie's murder confirmed my suspicion that we were in battle, and that Ella and I were at a disadvantage. The day Billy murdered her, Valerie was coming to Ella's to pick up a textbook she'd forgotten. The friend driving her was a male classmate, Todd Mason, whom Billy imagined to be Valerie's boyfriend. Billy stalked them after they left Ella's, forcing Todd's car to the road's shoulder. Billy imagined that Todd and Valerie were taunting him. He shot Todd in the head two times. Valerie jumped out of the car, trying to run away. Billy gripped her arm and threw her to the ground, shooting her in the median. Billy grabbed the children, put them into his car, and drove to his parents' house. A few hours later, the police went to Billy's parents' house and arrested Billy, put him in the cruiser, and took him to jail. The police left both children with their paternal grandparents and explained that the children could stay there until social services filed a petition and scheduled an emergency hearing.

That night set the stage, and as the case progressed, Ella became everyone's "opposing party." The alliances that began the evening Billy murdered Valerie and the police left the boys at the paternal grandparents' house intensified. With a slightly better economic situation and superior status in the community, the Lawson family attracted the police, social services, and the district attorney's support. The court-appointed children's lawyer gushed over Billy's sister, Gail's stable home life in a neighboring state supported by her superior financial resources.

Many hearings were scheduled over the next year, compounding the harm of the arduous process. The presiding judge, Donnie Casey (nicknamed "old elephant ears" for his over-sized ears that could hear every utterance in the courtroom) "rode the circuit." He conducted court in multiple counties on different days of the week. He presided over criminal cases, contested divorces, boundary line disputes, and almost everything else. For Ella Riley, this meant the court scheduled the five-day custody trial when full days opened on Judge Casey's circuit-riding calendar. It took us over a year to get to the final witnesses and closing arguments.

I kept my regular schedule in Camden County that year, seeing clients every other Wednesday and battling in Ella's custody trial every other month. Near dawn on most trial dates, I left for the hour-long ride from my house in the city to this rural county seat. When I turned off the interstate onto the winding back road, zigzagging to the new judicial complex, a familiar gut-wrenching pain would set in as I anticipated the upcoming hearing. I worked to ignore an undeniable sensation that my head was squeezed in a vice. (I didn't know it, but I was living in fight or flight mode every single one of those days.)

~

My DRIVE HOME un-does the day, first reversing course on the swerving roads as I try to find a way to believe everything will be okay. It will work out; this grandmother will not be robbed of the relationship with her dead daughter's children. I can't pick up a radio signal in this remote area until I get to the interstate, so I play the same CD stuck in the player. "Hunger for a taste of justice, hunger only for a world of truth." I turn south, entering the same interstate where Billy chased Valerie and shot her in front of their children. "All that you have is your soul."[6]

When I get home, I rush to change clothes and meet my friend Eugene for a run. Eugene is a therapist in private practice and is familiar with the case. "I get sick every time I go up there," I tell him. "The lawyers all treat Ella like she doesn't matter. They don't even ignore or avoid her. And Billy's family, they sneer and laugh. It's unbearable."

"It's a dynamic," Eugene explains. "In this situation, the Rileys are a victim family and the Lawsons are offenders. And now, they've found another tool." I don't understand what he means. "Our court system," he clarifies. "The Lawsons are using the court system to victimize the Rileys."

I drive the few miles from the running trail back to my house. I'm lost in thought, pondering if the legal system might not actually function as the neutral arbiter of legal conflicts, as I assumed. I wonder if the system itself could be an offender, creating wrong-doing rather than manifesting justice. I question my efforts. Am I protecting Ella, or am I complicit in deepening her pain? The CD player turns on, the same disc playing that has been the theme song for months. "All that you have ... is your soul." I turn the CD off and go inside my house. I have dinner to make, clothes to wash, and homework to help with. I try to focus on my family.

~

JUDGE CASEY CONVENED hearing after hearing, following a familiar pattern. Each party's lawyer questioned Ella's ability to raise her grandsons. Did she even have running water? What would she do about their education? Would they have their own bedroom? Ella sat alone, proud and pained, behind the railing separating the well of the court from the galley. I sat alone at counsel table.

During pauses, questions ran through my head: "Am I the only person she has in the entire world? Why don't these people believe in her? Her daughter is dead. Ella wants the chance to love her grandsons."

Meanwhile, district attorneys in the neighboring county, where the shootings occurred, prepared for trial. My close friend, Barb, was one of Billy's defense lawyers. Her theory of the case was that Valerie was dead because she spent the night in a hotel with Todd and with Billy and Valerie's children. Billy saw them on the interstate the next day and "snapped" when they kissed, mocking him. That's why he shot them. It is not challenging to decipher Barb's "theory of the case."

Billy created this narrative that Barb circulated, published, and amplified in a public trial. I was confused by Barb's work. As a lawyer, how could she parrot Billy's ridiculous story, with all the earmarks of an abuser, as a defense? How could she allow Billy's mother to call Valerie a slut in front of Ella? Eventually, I unraveled an explanation. We were both cast in roles as "zealous advocates," creating arguments and developing the theory of a case with no insight into the trauma that both we and our clients were surviving. We were both protecting our client as best we could without deep insight into the harm they suffered and what could make things right. We quit going to lunch together, meeting for coffee, or laughing at parties. Our friendship became another casualty of this tragedy.

The series of hearings to determine if Ella's relationship with the children would be preserved is finally scheduled to end a little over a year after Valerie died.

5.

On court dates, after my drive from the city, I park behind the old jail. I meet Ella and walk across the street to the new judicial center. Today, like every other court day, Ella and I go into the windowless courtroom with wall-to-wall, thin piled carpet. I take my seat at the 1980s modern-styled counsel table. Ella feels uncomfortable in the spotlight of the well of the court. She sits tall in the pew behind me.

I am alone. The other lawyers cluster around another blond oak 1980s counsel table on the opposite side of the courtroom. The Lawson family lines up behind them. It's time for the closing argument. I listen.

Chris Barnes, the children's court-appointed attorney, the *Guardian Ad Litem*, emphasizes the testimony provided by Billy's sister, Terry. Years ago, she escaped the alcoholism and poverty of her upbringing and now lives more than six hours away in another state. He moves photos of her tidy 2300-square-foot vinyl-sided home, situated in a subdivision far from Camden County, into evidence. He explains that the boys will have their own bedrooms if they live with Terry. They will attend a good school. They will have a fresh start.

The others march up to the podium: Billy's lawyers, Terry's lawyers, and the district attorney. One after another touts the positive attributes of Terry's house and minimizes the importance of Ella, Valerie's family, and the community where the boys had grown up. They unilaterally line up, concluding Terry and her husband should receive custody. Ella has a broken heart. I have a broken heart. Maybe everyone in the room has a broken heart. How could we heal? Who was going to be our healer? I feel like anything except a healing lawyer.

Waiting for the court's decision, I hope Judge Casey recognizes the importance of Michael and Chris's extended family and tight-knit community. I naively trust our legal system to be wise. I trust that a judge couldn't separate the children, who lost both parents, from everything remaining in their world.

"All rise."

We stand as the judge returns and is seated on the bench. We sit. We wait.

"I understand the complexity and importance of decisions such as this one. The court has no greater burden than finding a way for these boys to have a normal life." I stop hearing anything, but I know he's talking.

"The court rules that it is in the children's best interest to reside with their paternal aunt and her husband." I think okay, fine. We'll appeal. The kids can't move six hours away. "The court finds that Terry Lawson Moore shall be granted sole legal and physical custody of the children." Now, I hear him clearly. I am going to cry. A lump feels bulky in my throat, my eyes water a bit, and unseen sharp blades puncture my gut. It is happening. Tears begin to drip down the sides of my face.

Stop! I can't cry. It is impossible for me to cry in this courtroom. I would be unprofessional. I would be acting like a woman. I would be acting like a sore loser. I would be immature. I would be thin-skinned. I would be admitting that a lawyer's heart could be broken. I would be recognizing that a lawyer could absorb human pain. I would be announcing that I witnessed a process that was supposed to confer justice but instead compounded suffering. I would be saying with my tears that I felt responsible for Ella's loss and misery. I turn around. Ella sits stoically. The gloss in Ella's eye does not form a tear.

My heart is broken.

Most lawyers can recount the first time their heart was broken. Many remember standing at the bar before the court and holding back tears. We can't ignore the crushing pain of the vulnerable person sitting beside us. Sometimes, this person is someone spending the rest of their life in prison, a parent who will never see their child again, or a victim of a crime that no one believes. Often, they would be standing alone if their lawyer wasn't beside them.

6.

After Ella's case, I never wanted to feel this heartbreak again. I pledged to myself that I would never let it happen again. I would be a better advocate, a better warrior. I would fight harder, citing better authority and calling more qualified witnesses. I would argue louder. And another thing: I would stop loving my clients. I would create more distance between my client and myself. I would protect myself. I wouldn't cry.

But it didn't work. The pain wasn't as bad, but the heartbreaks kept coming. Belinda, suffering from mental illness, lost custody to Martin, who beat her children. Calvin decided to dismiss his case against Mike, the neighbor who sexually abused him for five years as a child, because the process was destroying him. Rocky was convicted over and over, beginning at age fifteen, and spent his life in prison. The state removes Warren's baby from his custody based only on his physical limitations.

The heartbreak did not stop.

Our legal system positioned Belinda, Warren, Calvin, and Rocky as spectators in incomprehensible proceedings that produced the biggest losses of their lives. The same system positioned me as a lead actor or even director. And, like a director, I felt responsible. I felt like a failure. And I felt like I let them down. Belinda, Warren, Calvin, and Rocky needed me in the most challenging time of their lives, and I failed them.

Eventually, after years of watching precedent and argument disappointing, neglecting, and slighting me, I decided to try something else — healing. I came to wonder what potential might rest there. Could I stop seeing clients as legal problems and meet them as people who needed to be healed? Instead of seeing myself as only an advocate, a champion, a warrior, could I also see myself as a healer? Are we (my clients and myself) concurrently people needing to be healed and healers?

Physician Rachel Naomi Remen describes a mutual healing relationship with her patients. "One of my patients once defined a healer as someone who can see the movement toward wholeness in you more clearly than you can at any given moment."[7]

Remen posits that one reason physicians feel drained is that "they do not know how to make an opening to receive anything from their patients."[8] Could all lawyers also receive healing from clients? Could an opening provide us with guidance on how to meet clients' needs? How does one grow from being an advocate to being a problem solver to being a healer? We can't define healing only by winning a judgment or ruling. We must be vulnerable to the openings, listen to our clients, and learn to identify opportunities for mutual healing.

What if we changed the questions we ask? Without a case to state and no dominating narrative to tell, can we look wider for healing opportunities? We lawyers can be so involved with how the case started (the precipitating event or the legal problem) and how it will end that we miss how the case is. What if a verdict or settlement does not contain or limit the legal problem?

Can we imagine the people we work with, clients, opposing counsel, judges, and mediators, as partners? Could we work with them to create healing processes — to find better resolutions? Resolutions that would be grounded not in the facts of the case but in working through the harm and strengthening relationships.

In my restorative practice of law, I now try not to begin by charging into developing a theory of the case, researching precedent for rights, or looking at sentencing guidelines. Instead, I stop and look at who is seated before me. I explore how experiences have impacted them. Are they afraid? Why? Do they fear loss? Has something happened to a meaningful relationship? What can I do today and tomorrow and the next day to try to right the wrongs? What can we do together to meet my client's needs, those of the opposing party, and those of the community? Can I create a collaborative environment to involve all stakeholders in meeting needs and healing the harm?

But I'm getting ahead of myself. Years after Ella schooled me on what it means to be a lawyer, a few more events shook my world, and I realized my underlying assumptions about the law (and being a lawyer) needed to be re-examined. And perhaps even ditched. Only then could I begin, in earnest, to endeavor to become a restorative lawyer.

Chapter 2

My Jealous Mistress
AND MY LOST SAINTS

The law is a jealous mistress and requires long and constant courtship. It is not to be won by trifling favors, but by lavish homage.

— Justice Story, *The Miscellaneous Writings of Joseph Story*

I.

WHAT HAPPENED to put me in the well of the court that day, separated from Ella by a ten-foot by three-foot wooden set of railings? What moved me to escape to a narrow hall behind the judge's bench, seeking sanctuary to succumb to my outburst of regret, dread, and aching? Why had safe assumptions about justice and the law that I'd lived with since childhood abandoned me? Over the next two decades, I questioned the premises underpinning my beliefs. Do lawyers and judges work for law, justice, order, or peace? In describing the relationship of law to justice, Howard Zinn noticed, "I was acutely conscious of the gap between law and justice. I knew that the letter of the law was not as important as who held the power in any real-life situation."[1]

I wondered what could possibly keep me here, in the well of the court. Mortgage payments, student loans, car payments, and childcare costs. I continued to practice law, notwithstanding the nagging questions and lack of answers. I accepted jobs as an assistant district attorney, legislative attorney, and court clerk. Eventually, I entered the private practice of law and began hearing about new ways of approaching legal disputes: restorative justice, collaborative law, therapeutic jurisprudence, and holistic law. I continued to search for a way to be a lawyer, working for justice and peace. I continued to believe I would succeed in finding it in this framework of filing, responding, negotiating, and resolving. I clung to the scraps of my unraveling faith in a legal system I'd once revered — my saints.

Until I didn't.

That was on the morning of April 16, 2007.

My son, Dashiell, had just returned to college after spending a year in an internship off campus.

∽

AT 7:30 A.M., he calls. A sniper shot someone on campus. Dash promises he is safe, locked in at a fraternity house. I continue my day, thinking that things will soon return to normal. But soon, I know that nothing will ever be normal again; the shooting continues, the death toll rises. Dash calls frequently to assure me of his physical safety. I stream Roanoke television news in the background as I try to work. I answer calls from family and friends. By the afternoon, we learn that thirty-three people are dead in the "Virginia Tech shooting." I watch helplessly.[2] A few days later, professor and poet Nikki Giovanni speaks at the convocation. "We do not understand this tragedy, and we did nothing to deserve it."[3]

Hours, days, and weeks pass, and I find little comfort. Charitable contributions pour into the university, politicians promise an investigation, and families demand legislative reform. With the offender dead, the law seems unfocused in search of a remedy.

At the end of the semester, my son, a creative writing minor at Virginia Tech, invites me to a departmental program. Professor Lucinda Roy speaks first. She had been the shooter's teacher. The university's administration ignored her reports of his bizarre behaviors. Her words embrace my pain. Professor Roy recognizes that she needs to choose the end words for her sestina.

> By their laughter, I know my students hear the voices of an unarmed choir. We teach peace in the stuttering light, reconcile silence with the world's residual, clamorous beauty.[4]

I listen, wondering if healing flows more naturally from revelations within a poem than from the arguments or positioning on legal rights. Student Heather Lockwood walks to the front of the room and places a piece of paper on the podium. She announces that she will read "a love poem" for us. She identifies her poem as a "look in two by millions because we see them," and she promises, "to learn to hold and hope and accept and take the hands of another."

I am beginning to understand the limitations of positional argument—advocacy. I am witnessing the potential of embracing multiple visions and diverse possibilities. David Orr, a columnist, describes the nature of poetry when he examines competing interpretations of Frost's "The Road Not Taken." He says, "Poems, after all, aren't arguments — they are to be interpreted, not proven, and that process of interpretation admits a range of possibilities, some supported by diction, some by tone, some by quirks of form and structure."[5] What might the law learn from how we experience a poem? Can we inhabit a world with a range of possibilities and abandon the burden of persuasion?

My son, Dash, walks to the podium. He speaks of what we lost, "not only our people and our souls but also the innocence and simplicity."

~

WITNESSING the healing power of this poetry created questions for me. How might the healing in that room accompany our work for justice? Could the law admit a range of possibilities? Promote healing without proving anything?

The poetry revealed the shortcomings of a legal response to this type of tragedy. The law creates a framework seeking to make sense of the events and create responses within the confines of that understanding. The law then decides who the stakeholders are, their losses, and how much they deserve. After the tragedy in Blacksburg, the law offered nothing to the shooter or his grieving family; he was dead. The law offered little to the surviving families of his innocent victims. The law offered nothing to stop this from happening again. The law ignored most of the evolving needs of the dead, the wounded, their families, and the traumatized community. No one received what they needed or deserved.

What did the law do? It created a fund to hold charitable contributions. It sets up a process. Lawyer Kenneth Feinberg, who designed the September 11 Victims Compensation Fund, designed a similar fund for the Virginia Tech victims. He allocated shares to families of the dead and wounded students. He parceled out the shares based on his evaluation of what each deserved in accordance with a schedule allocating funds based on the victims' proximity to trauma and catastrophic loss. The law created structures for bureaucrats to order investigations and draft reports. The law created opportunities to draft more laws; some passed the legislatures in two or ten years, and others always failed to pass. Yet, nothing has been repaired. Healing stalls and harm cycles continue reverberating throughout our community, state, and nation.

My own healing process led me to inquire further into the relationship between justice and law. I wondered if the law could ever create a justice as powerful as poetry. I'd never questioned whether becoming a lawyer was my path to working for justice and to making lives better, so I decided to broaden my search for answers.

Less than two months after the shootings, I returned to school. I registered for the summer courses at the Center for Justice and Peacebuilding at Eastern Mennonite University.

~

ON THE FIRST morning of the Summer Peacebuilding Institute, I walk alone into the welcome ceremony in Martin Chapel. I sit in a pew, watching more than 400 people from seventy countries file in. I am reminded of the courtroom pews I've sat in for the last twenty years, waiting for my case to be called. Rows: full of colleagues thumbing through files, scrolling through their phones. Rows: packed with voluntary and involuntary litigants who stare ahead, watching one case after the other being called. Rows: full and empty.

Today, the pews are filled with my new colleagues — singing and reading poetry. We share our hope to expand our ways of working for peace. I am overwhelmed to be in this spot with unfamiliar faces, sharing this passion. I also feel overpowered. I fear my faith in our legal system won't survive the rigorous challenges that may evolve from a novel perspective. Then what? Will I be left permanently orphaned, untethered? Once I stop thinking like a lawyer, will I have nothing to ground me? How will I pay for my kids' college if I can no longer love the law?

Struggling with what justice means, much less restorative justice, I show up for class. I walk into a classroom and select a comfortable-looking chair from those arranged in a circle. I introduce myself to the guy sitting next to me, who is also a lawyer. Our instructors, Howard Zehr, and Lorraine Stutzman Amstutz, are also seated in the circle. Three theater students act in a role-play. It portrays parties in a situation when a young man dies while riding in a friend's car when he is drunk. In this dramatization, I see, for the first time, how the principles of restorative justice might create healing. I watch, listen, and ask a lot of questions. The role-play includes the victim-offender encounter. They examine the community's needs, including the victim's and offender's family and friends. In identifying stakeholders, they look far beyond those participating in the conference. The participants seek healing from within the circle of those harmed and their community. They place the judicial and governmental institutions in a secondary role.

During our discussion, I begin to see potential for healing in our legal institutions. The shift will require power to be shared with the stakeholders, the community, and those outside the institutions. I suspect the principles providing the foundation for restorative responses demonstrated in this role-play could provide the groundwork for many processes and outcomes. These extend beyond criminal wrongdoing into civil misunderstandings and other legal disputes. The principles provide a foundation for proactive management of relationships within a community.

I'm challenged by questions that demand both courage and imagination. Could restorative justice also create a foundation to reframe how we think about justice and how we practice law?

What changes in our work as advocates may spring from adopting the restorative approach? I begin to understand the potential for attorneys to be guided by restorative justice as agents for healing.

2.

What is restorative justice? Some believe that the term *restorative justice* was first used by Albert Eglash in articles he wrote in 1958. He described three kinds of criminal justice: retributive (based on punishment,) distributed (based on therapy to the offender,) and restorative (based on restitution.)[6] Many scholars cite indigenous practices as the basis of our contemporary view of restorative justice.[7] These practices often focus on maintaining community peace by addressing wrongdoing. Community members value relationships, inclusivity, and reintegration as goals in working to create justice after wrongdoing. Restorative justice scholar and educator Dan Van Ness identifies a group of early adopters of restorative justice, including Howard Zehr, Mark Umbreit, and Ron Claassen.[8] Professor Zehr often describes restorative justice by comparing the questions that conventional processes ask to those posed by restorative justice. This table adapts these questions to illustrate how we might compare restorative justice responses to conventional responses.

Looking at some practices associated with restorative justice helps to understand how the principles and values might inform a process. Restorative justice explorers Daniel Van Ness and Gerry Johnston include the "encounter" as a critical point in the restorative justice process. The dialogue brings the victim and offender together for a meeting.[9] Facilitated by a trained practitioner, the participants are prepared and then engage in conversation. The meeting is more inclusive than a criminal proceeding. It allows those most affected by wrongdoing to openly communicate the harm and their needs. Van Ness indicates that the purpose of the encounter is to identify injustice, make things right, and set future intentions.

TABLE 1

A Comparison Between the Questions Asked by the Conventional
Judicial System and Restorative Justice

CONVENTIONAL JUDICIAL SYSTEM	RESTORATIVE JUSTICE
What Happened?	What did each person experience happening? How do they describe it?
Who did it?	Who is affected and how?
What rule was broken?	How were you (and others) feeling at the time?
What is the penalty for breaking the rule?	What might be done to make it right? What might you do to make it right?
How will the offender be punished?	What do you need (and others) need for the next time this could happen?

These questions are modified from *Howard Zehr, Changing Lenses, A New Focus on Crime and Justice*, (Herald Press: Scottdale, PA, 2005) 29.

The encounter can be a discussion between the victim and offender (Victim Offender Conference), or it can be a discussion between a youthful offender, their family, friends, and community (Family Group Conference). The meetings are structured to allow for multiple coexisting narratives to develop. They provide a forum for the healthy expression of emotion. Some meetings focus on providing the opportunity for dialogue to provide the victim with an opportunity to have their questions answered. The dialogue also provides an offender with a chance to apologize outside of the public eye. Other conferences are focused on identifying needs and creating a plan to meet them.

The other process often associated with restorative justice is the talking circle. In a talking circle, the participants pass a desig-nated object, "a talking piece," around the circle. Everyone has an equal opportunity to speak since only the person with the talking piece speaks. Circles have been used in the United States as part of re-entry programs and in the U.S. and Canada for sentencing.

Circles of Support and Accountability (CoSA) have been developed in some areas to decrease the potential for re-offending, particularly by sex offenders.

RESTORATIVE JUSTICE

The principles of restorative justice articulated by Howard Zehr in *Changing Lenses*

HARMS & NEEDS	OBLIGATIONS	COLLABORATIVE	STAKEHOLDERS	MAKE RIGHT THE WRONGS
Focuses on harms and consequent needs.	Addresses obligations resulting from those harms.	Uses inclusive, collaborative processes.	Involves those with a stake in the situation.	Seeks to put right the wrongs.
(Of victims, but also communities and offenders.)	(Offenders' but also communities' and society's)		(Victims, offenders, community members, society)	

These processes are often linked to restorative justice. Zehr describes restorative justice not as a specific practice or a program but instead as a group of principles and values. They can be applied to many practices and situations. In *Changing Lenses*, he articulates the principles that underpin restorative justice.[10] This perspective is broad enough to guide the healing work of a restorative lawyer. These principles allow us to abandon a binary, oppositional-based approach to addressing conflict, defined by taking sides and adopting assumptions about the parties' needs. Inclusive processes based in restorative justice permit uncertainty while celebrating our collective ability to imagine resolutions beyond a fixed, predetermined capacity. Restorative justice-informed processes create opportunities to increase community resilience by involving the larger community in encouraging responses beyond punishment tied to a presenting conflict.

My developing concept of a restorative practice of law is rooted in a common-sense approach to disputes and conflict. This approach roughly accepts Zehr's principles alongside the concepts, values, and elements of restorative justice identified by the early

Western adopters.[11] These practitioners generally promoted a restorative justice approach to criminal wrongdoing. I propose a broader application that allows for a more expansive definition of harm and a more exhaustive search for consequential needs.

Many Western restorative justice practitioners consider restorative justice as an alternative to retributive and distributed criminal justice processes. A far broader application of the principles, unrestricted by whether the state elects to be a party in the conflict, may also guide a response to wrongdoing. Restorative justice principles provide a well-reasoned way to respond to both wrongdoing and to harmful civil misunderstandings. Broadening restorative justice beyond what is identified as criminal wrongdoing may be more consistent with the original applications of restorative justice. Most restorative justice practitioners believe that restorative justice has roots in indigenous processes. I've found nothing in the indigenous processes that creates the division between civil and criminal matters. Early historical traditions of Western courts also do not delineate this division so rigidly. Our modern way of partitioning the law as civil or criminal and demanding expertise in substantive knowledge of the rules may overshadow how clients are impacted by wrongdoing or misunderstanding and what is necessary to repair the harm, sustain relationships, and improve well-being.

3.

Where do lawyers fit in? How do we describe a lawyer's work? How do these principles and this concept of repairing harm and meeting needs change how we view our job? The new lens through which I view wrongdoing and harmful misunderstandings challenges me to examine the lawyer's role as an agent to help resolve conflict. Lawyers have many roles. They are the ones who hear the stories from clients and other witnesses, weaving them into another story — the theory of the case. They are the ones who translate the complicated language of the law for clients, jurors, and judges. Indeed, a lawyer is not only a storyteller, a journalist, or a translator of complicated legal language. Lawyers are advocates. And within this adversarial process, they become gladiators. Brave and well-armed with reason.

If a practice of law can be constructed with the principles and values of restorative justice, the lawyer's role will necessarily change. What might the role be if lawyers are no longer focused on battling in the courtroom to have their story adopted? How would a lawyer's practice shift if consequential needs are no longer limited to those identified within the legal remedies? An ordinary afternoon at work helps me consider these questions.

Occasionally, I volunteer at the pro bono clinic at the courthouse, about an hour's drive from my house in the city. Volunteer attorneys sit in small cubicles as community members come through the doors with questions and forms.

～

JAMES HOOVER WALKS in and is greeted by the person sitting at the desk who asks him to sign in. He waits a few minutes and then meets with me in my semi-private cubicle. James explains that his children are now twelve and fourteen. Their mother doesn't supervise them appropriately. He wants to change custody so that he'll have the authority to make medical decisions and travel out of the country with the children.

I locate the *pro se* form for him to complete to request the change of custody. I finish his case by filling out the form and giving him directions to the clerk's office to file it. I suspect Mr. Hoover will have his order in a month or two, but what will happen to this family's relationships? Did I provide them with access to justice? Two more clients come in — a woman from Poland with a contested custody case and a grandmother trying to transfer her grandchild's custody while her daughter is incarcerated. We fill out their forms and send them to another reception desk down the hall. I leave my cubicle. My long ride home gives me time to ponder these simple exchanges.

~

WHAT WAS MY ROLE TODAY? I did not feel like a gladiator helping Mr. Hoover slay the enemy by filling in forms. I also did not feel like a healer handing him a map of the courthouse with the clerk's office highlighted. The law is a complex system of rules that purport to improve his life by creating expectations around rules. Without an opponent, I escorted Mr. Hoover through a myriad of confusing legal mandates and rewards. My role became less of a gladiator and more of a navigator. Is there any other potential in my work?

Nothing in the laws, rules, or my work today provided Mr. Hoover with an opportunity or duty to improve his family's well-being. I did nothing to help create stronger relationships for this family or this community to sustain them as they face life's challenges. I volunteer for this center to create access to justice. But what is *justice* without healing? Without making things right? Without providing an inclusive process that creates stronger relationships?

4.

A few years ago, I attended a program that explored improving access to justice. The underlying theme was that a lack of lawyers to provide legal services to "the poor" deprived them of justice. I question this assumption. Why are lawyers and direct representation in litigation the focus of our access to justice? Why can't justice focus on meeting unmet needs? Access to justice must not be limited to providing gladiators for battle. We cannot assume that access to a lawyer equates to access to justice.

It's easy to see how this assumption fails. Lawyer/gladiators cannot prevent further harm arising out of the process. I learned that having a lawyer did not equal access to justice when I watched Ella learn that her grandchildren were moving out of state forever. Going to court perpetuated harm and victimization to this bereaved mother and grandmother. Lawyers/gladiators operate in a legal system that tends to narrowly define stakeholders and remedies. Access to justice requires looking broadly at those impacted and providing remedies beyond dollars and days. Hiring a lawyer does not guarantee to be included in a legal process or to have standing. Hiring a lawyer does not provide access to meeting needs beyond the narrow remedies listed in statutes.

A belief that hiring a gladiator gives access to justice perpetuates the idea that fervently employing weapons in adversarial processes is "doing everything possible," which basically means engaging in aggressive litigation. I've watched lawyers and clients in custody cases perpetuate that fiction. One family I worked with in mediation involved a mother, a father, and two adolescent daughters. The girls wanted to live with their father. Yet, the oldest daughter also voiced fears about her deteriorating relationship with her mother.

During mediation, the mother refused to consider any option that would not give her what she called "full custody." When we ended in an impasse, she told me she had no choice but to suspend mediation. This mother told me she could have peace with her future only if she felt she'd "done everything." To her, "doing everything" meant exhausting all legal remedies within the adversarial system. Many litigants, and lawyers, underestimate the power in remedies adjacent to and external to the legal systems. The young girls left my office with nothing being done to attend to their dissolving parental relationships. They left feeling more abandoned than when they arrived. Months later, I learned that the mother and her lawyer litigated the issue and lost. They "did everything" except give the relationship the priority it deserved.

Access to justice requires that we imagine justice not as a *thing* to access but as a *place*, an environment, or an opportunity. Justice is not an object we can hold. It's not something we can paint, salute, or create. Justice embraces a state of equity — equilibrium in relationships. To imagine justice as something we can do for or do to other people is faulty and oppressive. Restorative justice-based processes create environments, situations, and conditions to allow those in the relationship to create this state of equilibrium — a place where justice grows into peace. Herein lies the work of healers.

How can lawyers work to create these environments? How do we grow from gladiators and navigators into healers? Where do we begin? Should we trust a court system that allocates rights, duties, and roles based on a complex system of rules that operates to sustain the powerful institutions that support the court system?

We can't blindly trust legal (or any other) institutions. We must keep asking questions and change the lens through which we examine legal problems. In the restorative practice of law, consistent with the principles of restorative justice, we change the questions we ask. What, if any, wrongdoing contributes to the legal problem? What are the needs that have arisen? How can we collaborate to meet needs? Our communities may build and maintain peace only when those who experience wrongdoing are involved in preventing further harm and providing opportunities to heal.

In the restorative practice of law, we examine the legal problem with a view that looks not only at the facts but also at the relationships of the parties and those we are working with to address unmet needs. Our modern American judicial system describes crime as an offense against the government and adopts prevention, rehabilitation, and deterrence goals. The legal system functions in a very formalized way to preserve the rules but fails to value relationships. Restorative justice is relational, seeking to repair or restore the damaged relationships within the community.

With the restorative lens, we design inclusive processes to identify resources creating resolutions. The early adopters differentiate
restorative justice from the conventional process by rejecting an
exclusionary hierarchical way to address conflicts in exchange for a
more inclusive and equal process for victims, offenders,[12] and
communities. We look for opportunities for creating encounters,
opportunities to make amends, and safe, healthy means for reintegration. Most legal processes separate the parties and structurally
limit how they communicate, restricting the potential for collaboration and healing. As restorative lawyers, we bring them together
and expand ways of communicating.

In bringing the restorative principles and values to our work,
we recognize that justice requires healing. We undertake a challenge to function as healers. Since crime, under any concept,
creates injuries, it is natural that justice should create an environment for healing. Agents of the institutions, when relieved of their
role to do battle as gladiators, can become healers.

This newly formed role of the lawyer as a healer is not tethered
to philosophical assumptions embedded in our legal systems that
create the foundation of our laws: rights and ancillary duties, individual responsibility, or social contract.

6.

In many religions, "saints" are those who have reached the
highest level of religious teaching and have special holiness and
reverence. In the law, philosophers such as Aquinas, Hobbes,
Hume, Rousseau, Kant, Bentham, Austin, Mill, Pound, Rawls, and
others developed theories that set them apart as nearly saint-like.
The theories create a philosophical base (embedded with Western
assumptions and values) that provides the bedrock upon which our
everyday statutes and precedents are constructed. As I explored a
new practice based on a new restorative justice lens that sees less in
rights and more in needs, less in procedures and more in conversa-

tion, I feared abandoning these philosophers who contribute so much to western jurisprudence — our saints. I feel a bit like Elizabeth Barrett Browning in Sonnet 43 when she admits to losing devotion to her "lost saints." Would this new view demand that I abandon hundreds of years of deep, well-reasoned thinking contained in the body of law, jurisprudence, and legal theory that I understand as our foundation? What will happen to my philosophical road map with the comfortable logic of legal positivism, naturalism, and the social contract?

The authors of these theories were mere mortals with flaws, implicitly including values like individualism and competition. However, they further the discourse, the process, and the search for healing. Well-worn philosophies like these have often changed through time. They may still be integrated into processes in a healthy way to be part of the story, but not the whole story. In the next chapter, I will describe a different philosophical approach to support a restorative practice of law.

Chapter 3

Being a Good Lawyer

IS NOT GOOD ENOUGH

You come in here with a skull full of mush, and you leave thinking like a lawyer.

— Scott Turow, *One L*

I.

KATE, the assistant district attorney, calls.

"We have a case that I think would be good for restorative justice."

"Why?"

"I don't know what else to do with it."

Great. Today is not the first time a district attorney has called me with this dilemma. I often get referrals when the lawyers are stumped. I'm the option of last resort.

"It's a juvenile case. Maybe the parties can reach an agreement. The state will pay the costs. Can you do it?" I call my former professor and co-facilitator, Lorraine Stutzman Amstutz who agrees to co-facilitate. We schedule the preparatory meetings.

The day arrives for us to meet separately with the victim and the offender. Lorraine and I visit for a few minutes until the meeting is scheduled to start. Travis Marshall, an innocent, kind-looking young man, walks in with his parents. He describes himself as an A student, an Eagle Scout, and a school basketball team member. His father, David, takes over when Travis struggles to describe what happened.

"We were on our way to a basketball game— a few hours away. Travis had his learner's permit, and I thought it was a good opportunity for him to practice on the highway. It's a two-lane highway, without much traffic." He pauses and continues. "It was a sunny afternoon, and Travis was catching on. I drifted off to sleep. When I woke up, it was too late. Travis had crossed the center line and hit a car, head on."

I look down at the police report. The story is consistent. No one knows what happened, why Travis crossed the double line and struck a car head-on driven by sixty-eight-year-old William Stotler. The impact killed William's only passenger, Hazel, his wife of fifty years. The police charged Travis as a juvenile with involuntary manslaughter.

Lorraine and I listen as Travis speaks. He's remorseful. Travis apologizes over and over. He struggles to explain what happened and suggests that he also drifted off to sleep. Both Lorraine and I are skeptical. We don't know what happened, but it's hard to believe Travis fell asleep driving in the middle of the day. But I'm not sure it matters.

David continues to share his viewpoint. He accepts responsibility for failing to supervise Travis and wants to do anything to make this as right as possible. Travis' mother, Maria, tears up, describing her impulse when she learned about Hazel: she wanted to take their family flowers or bake them a cake. Maria's heart was broken, thinking about this family who had lost their mother and grandmother.

As the meeting ends, Lorraine and I explain the process for a victim-offender dialogue and the family does not hesitate. They want the meeting, even if it doesn't impact the legal charges against Travis. They believe participating in a dialogue could heal both families' pain.

Later that afternoon, my conference room feels empty as William walks in alone. William struggles but expresses his feelings simply. We can see that he feels distraught from losing his wife. We also see that he feels responsible, sure that he could have done something to save Hazel. He blames David. "Travis is young, but David shouldn't have let him drive. He should not have fallen asleep."

We end the meeting proposing a victim-offender dialogue. William appears interested. He wants to talk to the boy, to give him a chance to apologize. But then, he pauses. William explains that he retained a civil lawyer to represent him. He will defer to her advice on whether to participate in the conference. As he leaves, he thanks us for listening and repeats that he wants to meet the boy and see David accept responsibility for allowing Travis to drive.

William's lawyer, Beverly, has a reputation for being a "good lawyer." She takes my call. I explain that restorative justice provides an alternative way to look at harm. In this case, the state and the offender have agreed to the process. I describe the preparation for the victim-offender dialogue and explain the training and experience that both Lorraine and I have. She listens. She asks questions. She's thinking like a lawyer — the facts, the issues, the outcomes.

Could she create a theory of the case to find both the father and son liable? How would the victim-offender dialogue impact the potential resolution? How would Travis' apology affect William and his willingness to prosecute the civil case? She explains that she's concerned that William might develop sympathies towards Travis, but she will think about it.

Three days later I call William. In a three-sentence conversation, he apologizes and explains his attorney advised him not to participate. He asks me not to involve him further. I call David, who cannot conceal his disappointment. How could Travis recover? Would the family ever find peace?

When I call Kate, the district attorney, she tells me that given the facts, she'll have to put Travis on an improvement period. She'll dismiss the petition once he complies. The law will never provide these two families with any healing, justice, or ability to reconstruct their lives with this tragedy integrated into their stories.

~

BEVERLY ENJOYS A REPUTATION AS A "GOOD LAWYER" in our community. She probably settled William's case for policy limits, maybe more. But was it a great resolution? What value did she put on William's ability to move forward and make peace with Hazel's death? How does he reconcile not swerving to avoid Travis and save Hazel? Did he need a chance to tell his story to Travis? Did he need a chance to forgive him? Did he need the opportunity to confront David and perhaps pardon him? How did Beverly consider the relationships between William and Hazel, his community, and a sixteen-year-old Eagle Scout who did not intend to hurt anyone? What value did she place on William's healing?

I often hear my colleagues describe one another as "good lawyers." They typically mean lawyers, like Beverly, who demonstrate impeccable trial skills and legal analysis. Our legal educations mold our minds into being able to think differently, to "think like a lawyer." We become proficient at applying the facts to the law to create a believable narrative supported by admissible evidence and established precedent. But does "thinking like a lawyer" change our approach to harm and relationships? Does "thinking like a lawyer" change William from being a person suffering from loss into a client with a valuable claim? William was a pained grandfather and husband, not a commodity. Can we do more? Can we "think like a lawyer" while thinking like a human? Can we be healers? Can we help William recover from the loss of his wife and help Travis grow into a good man? Can we create healing in our community to grow from this tragedy rather than solely focusing on maximizing potential individual monetary gains?

2.

What is a "good lawyer"? How does a "good lawyer" find opportunities to build relationships and create healing? One of my teachers is a trial lawyer, Deb Parsons, who was a public defender for twenty-one years. While in graduate school, I worked with filmmaker Paulette Moore and interviewed Deb for a project. Our film, *Pillars of Justice*, examined how courthouse design might facilitate (or restrict) opportunities for justice.[1] We discussed the importance of privacy at the courthouse and how the bathroom often provides the most private, comfortable, safe space. Deb shared her broad vision of justice and the lawyer's unique role in working for it. During our interview, when asked to describe justice, she looked right at the camera, "... Sometimes justice is a hug in the bathroom." Deb is a "good lawyer."

How did we get here? How did we come to envision a "good lawyer?" Through the late nineteenth century in the United States, lawyers played a small role in judicial proceedings. Courtrooms were often chaotic places where elected officials sorted out community problems. According to historian James Willard Hurst, lawyers in the nineteenth century created and maintained social order primarily by facilitating parties' agreements.[2]

The education 19th century lawyers received was also different. Most lawyers learned their trade through apprenticeships. Law schools were modeled on trade schools. In 1870, everything changed. Christopher Columbus Langdell, the dean of Harvard Law School, introduced the case method, accompanied by Socratic questioning. The case method requires students to become skilled at understanding and analyzing appellate decisions, providing a primary guide to assessing rights and duties.[3]

As statutes, rules, regulations, and reported case decisions increased the body of law, the lawyer's education expanded to mastering complex statutory schemes and procedural rules. As experts in mastering written statutes, regulations, and appellate decisions as well as procedures, lawyers gained superior status over litigants in accessing legal processes.

The ability to master substantive and procedural rules now grants the lawyers an exclusive position to tell the story. Disseminating a narrative focusing on statutes and binding appellate decisions, the conflict takes the form of an insular event capable of reduction to a measurable outcome — be it dollars and cents or days of a prison sentence. Without placing value in creating, maintaining, and rebuilding relationships, the "good lawyer" has become the one who masters the analysis and creates a dominating narrative by manipulating the rules. If all goes well, the "good lawyer" secures the client the largest measurable award.

Is this concept of the "good lawyer" dated?

While legal institutions retain exclusive control of the processes for resolving legal conflicts, participation in adversarial trials has waned. The lack of trials may be due to the expenses borne by litigants or the structural demands on the institution. (Imagine if every case went to verdict!) Today, as little as one or two percent of civil cases filed go to trial.[4] Most settle through negotiation and alternative dispute resolution methods. The "good lawyer" may no longer rely on understanding procedural rules and having excellent trial skills in this legal landscape. New frameworks for decision-making have emerged, such as Collaborative Practice, Strategic Negotiation, therapeutic courts, restorative justice, and mediation. Yet, the artifacts of the adversarial system continue to permeate the new informal processes, often inaccurately framing the talents, skills, and qualifications of a "good lawyer."

We need to expand our options and reconsider the qualities of the "good lawyer." Restorative justice provides a framework for lawyers to concurrently work within the adversarial system while providing the holistic representation that clients deserve. A restorative framework expands the lawyers' tools beyond the skills and methods that excel within the narrow theater of adversarial proceedings.[5] We don't start from the assumption that two parties in conflict are polar opposites and that the best way to resolve the legal problem is to find two gladiators/lawyers to fight it out and determine the winner. The restorative "good lawyer" recreates our work — we move from being gladiators or navigators — to healers. And this requires a new way of "thinking like a lawyer" more wide-ranging than what most lawyers master in contemporary law schools.

3.

Recall when my friend Ann gave me her copy of *One L* before I started law school. She wasn't kidding about the unwitting transformation I was about to undergo. I entered an institution that promised to change my "skull full of mush" into "thinking like a lawyer." Scott Turow, the author of *One L*, describes the first year of law school in the introduction. "It is during this first year, according to a saying, that you learn to think like a lawyer, to develop the habits of mind and world perspective that will stay with you throughout your career. And thus, it is during the first year that many law students come to feel, sometimes with deep regret, that they are becoming strangely different people from the ones who arrived at law school in the fall."[6]

Scholar William Sullivan describes the training in the first year of law school as encouraging a "temporary moral lobotomy" in students. In his report prepared for the Carnegie Foundation for the Advancement of Teaching, he identifies that practical skills and reflecting on professional responsibility are missing from the training to "think like a lawyer."[7]

"Thinking like a lawyer" has historically meant looking at the facts, identifying legal issues, and creating a strategy to resolve the legal problem. This approach divorces the law from the intricate, independent client's narrative in favor of one potentially dominant version of a shared, storied life experience. It ignores complex relationships. As legal experts, lawyers and judges assume the exclusive positions of problem solvers, armed only with tools to interpret and adjudicate competing rights.

"Thinking like a lawyer" necessitates deciphering the facts and applying the law to them, creating a singular, believable story, without identifying the overriding hopes, dreams, and goals of the client. The lawyer becomes something of a headless horseman, riding with expert skill, but lacking direction or intention.

Good lawyers do "think like a lawyer." But it's not enough!

To illustrate — I sometimes volunteer to answer a legal hotline, administered by the state bar. Callers dial a toll-free number, and we answer their general legal questions. I remember one concerning call.

∾

AN OLDER WOMAN introduces herself as Janice. She explains that she retained a "good lawyer" to represent her in a legal action involving injuries she sustained in a car wreck. She describes how her attorney represented her, doing what most attorneys might do. He conducted an initial interview with the client, obtained medical records, made a demand to the insurance company, and negotiated a settlement within the typical range for this type of case. The client tells me that she felt okay with the $9000.00 settlement.

Satisfied. Janice explains that Rita had worked part-time in her home for several years prior to the settlement. Medicaid covers the costs of Rita's services: planning meals, providing transportation to medical appointments, and general housework. The two women enjoy a good relationship that provides the client with happiness, continuity, and the ability to stay in her home. A few weeks after Janice received her share of the settlement, she filled out her Medicaid eligibility reports.

A few weeks later, she received a notice from Medicaid that she was over income. Rita was no longer authorized to come to her house. Janice was on her own. The Department of Health and Human Services explained to Janice that she might be eligible after she spent the settlement money. She could reapply then. If accepted, she would be placed on a waitlist for another caregiver, but that could be up to a year. Janice explains, "I wish I'd never received the money. What am I supposed to do with that much money? Buy a baby grand piano?" Without Rita, she feared that she would be moved to a nursing home.

"I can't lose Rita."

∾

HOW COULD THIS HAPPEN? The attorney looked no further than the legal analysis as to liability and damages. More time, more understanding, and more practical and creative thinking may have saved Janice from losing Rita. In restorative lawyering, we listen to clients' articulated objectives, decipher needs, and develop long and short-term goals. We explore how a potential resolution might impact them and work to prevent potential unintended consequences.

To be a restorative lawyer, we still "think like a lawyer." But we *think like a restorative lawyer*. One way to envision our client's legal problems is to recognize that clients have complex lives, interrupted by an experience that the law will define. In other words, a legal problem is a life story impacted by an event that intersects with the law. As restorative lawyers, we work with clients to decide how to incorporate this event into the wholeness of their lives and use the legal response to meet the unmet needs created by that event. Thinking this way requires a far more comprehensive view than simply applying the law to the facts.

"Thinking like a lawyer" requires focusing on applying the law to the facts of the event. Everything moves in that direction. *Thinking like a restorative lawyer* stretches to affirm the full, complex life story. This thinking embraces the narrative of the client's life, not in isolation but in relationship with the client's community. We do not isolate the life-changing event from the broad context as we engage in legal analysis to discover opportunities for healing.

"Thinking like a lawyer," demands looking at the facts, identifying the legal issue, and creating a strategy to resolve the legal question. It often requires a divorce from the complex narrative in which the event occurs and fails to identify and repair relationships. "Thinking like a lawyer" positions the legal experts as being superior in locating a solution to a legal conflict by narrowly interpreting rights. The experts determine the suitable balance between two adversaries with competing rights. The restorative lawyer invites the stakeholders to be equally situated with one another and the legal "experts" as they collaboratively create a resolution to meet the unmet needs.

TABLE 2

"Thinking Like a Lawyer" vs. *"Thinking Like a Restorative Lawyer":*
A Comparison of Legal Goals and Tasks

GOALS/TASKS	"THINKING LIKE A LAWYER"	ADDITIONAL GOALS AND TASKS FOR "THINKING LIKE A RESTORATIVE LAWYER"
Facts	Decipher convincing account of facts.	Elicit multiple narratives without judgment.
Analysis	Apply the law to the facts.	Identify the needs and obligations of those impacted by the event.
Action	Create the most believable story.	Develop approaches to meet needs and repair harm.
Purpose of Action	Enforce a right.	Aim to meet needs to repair harm, as much as possible.
Role of Rules	Focus on rules, including procedural rules.	Focus on how rules help to meet needs and enhance trust in processes.
Value to Relationships Impacted by Conflict	Impact on relationships is often overlooked.	Focus on strengthening and repair of relationships.
Objective of Lawyer	Return to pre-event state or provide compensation or punishment.	Establish and reach goals, including financial needs. Support healing and recovery from harm.

We can contrast "thinking like a lawyer" to *thinking like a restorative lawyer* by examining the tasks we often associate with our work. This chart compares two divergent visions.

Restorative lawyering applies the principles and values articulated by the early adopters of restorative justice, such as Zehr and Van Ness, to our everyday legal practices, including the importance of relationships, healing, inclusivity, and equality. We frame our requests for the legal response not with the experts but with the stakeholders most affected. We must always find the "Ritas" in our clients' lives, appreciate their value, and not inadvertently sacrifice relationships by overlooking their full, rich impact on people's experiences.

4.

Restorative lawyering fosters expansive deliberation. The restorative lawyer contemplates deeply, broadly, and patiently. The restorative lawyer expands the potential for resolution of legal conflicts by listening to clients, their sorrows, goals, and dreams. While listening, the restorative lawyer seeks out the healing potential within the story and requests understanding from the institution charged with resolving the legal problem. Van Ness describes the flexibility and potential within this approach. "When evaluating the handling of a particular case or program, the question will be whether the response was as restorative as possible *under the circumstances*."[8]

Lawyers learn to think analytically when creating the theory of the case. But analytical thinking may not create opportunities for healing. Robert Sternberg divides intelligence into three areas: analytical, creative, and practical.[9] As lawyers, we think intelligently. We use detailed reasoning and develop wise solutions. Sometimes, blinded by analytical thinking, our creative and practical thoughts become obscured. However, the restorative lawyer brings awareness of that potential obstacle when considering the legal problem. Thinking with contemplation requires steadiness and intention. We work to maintain a well-developed and extraordinary analytical approach to problem-solving. However, we do not lose sight of our clients' humanity and potential for suffering and healing.

My lessons in restorative lawyering have come from my teachers: professors, educators, colleagues, and, more often than not, clients. Angus Hayward challenged me months after I was admitted to the bar. Judge Stalnaker's secretary, Lonnie, mailed the order appointing me as counsel. It was straightforward — Angus was charged with a third offense DUI. A few days after the letter arrived, I drove downtown to meet him at the county jail.

~

ANGUS MEETS me in the hall, escorted by two deputies. He is handsome, unpolished, with a sweet kindness and vulnerability that was immediately discernible. There was no private place to meet at the old jail, so we met in the basement cafeteria. I start by interviewing Angus with the questions on my intake sheet. I learn that he pleaded guilty to two prior DUIs. No other convictions. Uncounseled pleas.

I make a note, "uncounseled guilty pleas." Good. A legal argument! With this challenge to the charge, I might get this case pleaded down to a first or second offense with time served.

I explain my legal argument to Angus. I pull the written guilty pleas he'd signed long before I met him from the manila folder labeled "Pleas" stuffed in my brown accordion file labeled "Hayward 87-F-14." I hand the legal documents to Angus and ask him to read them back to me. I figure that after he reads them, I'll see what he understands by asking him to explain them.

He picks up the short stack of papers and stares at them briefly before turning to me, "I can't read. I don't know how to." He looks down at the floor and away from me. I've never met anyone who couldn't read. I want to show kind compassion, but I'm unsure how to do that without seeming patronizing. I try to continue my interview.

"I'll read it aloud, if that's okay." He nods. "It says: I understand if I plead 'GUILTY,' I waive these rights and lose the privilege to operate a motor vehicle." I realize I'm speaking loud in what my daughter calls "my presentation voice," and I'm reading too fast. I slow down and soften my voice. "I further understand that should I be convicted of other DUI offenses or operating on suspended license offenses, penalties will be increased with each conviction."

I stop. "Do you understand what that means?" He didn't stare at the floor. He looks right at me. I sense he has no clue what I read. I have no idea what to do next.

I ask him, "Do you know what 'waive these rights' means?"

With his beautiful, wide-eyed, and unsophisticated face, Angus sits there, politely half-smiling at me. He's across the wooden table in the cafeteria of the old county jail. He looks at me with his kind eyes and naïve smile. He raises his hand to wave, "Hello."

"Is that what you mean?"

"Let's talk." I realize that I need to slow down. I need to learn more about Angus. Who is he, and what happened in his life to bring us together? "Are you from here, Monroe County?"

"No ma'am. I'm from over in Patterson County. I didn't move here until I was grown."

We talk for over an hour about his parents, his girlfriend, and his daughter, whom he nicknamed "Peaches" because she was so sweet. We talk about his drinking and how much he wishes he had a job. Angus shows me that his prior convictions resulted from his inability to read and understand what he had signed. Being unable to read made life challenging. We talk a little longer and decide that our defense strategy will prioritize Angus learning how to read.

About a year later, we return to court to review Angus' charges. I stand to speak. I try to describe Angus. I don't argue about the police stop or field sobriety testing. Instead, I outline the circumstances surrounding the prior uncounseled convictions. I detail what Angus has accomplished in the last year by walking two miles three times every week to attend a literacy course. He would no longer be signing forms he could not read.

His dedication impresses the judge and the district attorney, who dismisses the charges.

After the hearing, a probation officer approaches me. "I've never seen a defense attorney do that before ... I mean have that type of strategy." I smile, thinking about all the "good lawyers" that regularly appear before Judge Stalnaker. Lawyers — who are well trained to "think like a lawyer." Lawyers — who abandoned the mush in their brains during the first weeks of law school. I walk out feeling successful as a lawyer and as my client's student.

≈

UNBEKNOWNST TO ME, restorative justice was developing in Kitchener, Ontario, and Elkhart, Indiana, as an alternative way to address harm and wrongdoing. Angus taught me that the way I had learned to "think like a lawyer" might not be enough to address wrongdoing. This innocent and kind man brings home an early lesson on a whole-person approach to practicing law. Beyond the inciting event, what factors brought this client to my office? What part of their life was not working even before the offense occurred? Can we, as restorative lawyers, do anything about it?

Chapter 4

Thinking Like a (Restorative) Lawyer

ACTUALIZING VALUES

The first year... aims, in the old phrase, to get you to 'thinking like a lawyer'.

— K.N. Llewellyn, *The Bramble Bush: On Our Law and Its Study*

In the last chapter, I suggest that "thinking like a lawyer" requires employing the conventional process of extracting the facts, matching them with the law, and creating a persuasive theory of the case. I also suggest that this way of thinking cannot frame a restorative practice of law since it fails to allow for the subjective satisfaction of needs. This chapter explores the potential for client satisfaction, community building, and peacebuilding by "thinking like a restorative lawyer."[1] We will determine how the values of restorative justice provide a foundation to address legal conflicts. Zehr identifies three values as central to restorative approaches to conflict: respect, responsibility, and relationship. These values may replace those such as belief in the adversarial process, competition, and objectivity in the everyday work of attorneys. We also recognize that values are implicitly integrated into our practices, whether we recognize them or not.[2] By gaining awareness of our personal and professional values and integrating them with those Zehr identified as central to restorative justice, the practice of law may increase the potential for outcomes that benefit clients, repair harm, and mend relationships.

TABLE 3

"Thinking Like a Lawyer" vs. "Thinking Like a Restorative Lawyer":
A Comparison of Guiding Values

"THINKING LIKE A LAWYER"	"THINKING LIKE A RESTORATIVE LAWYER"
Relationship: People have a bundle of competing rights best balanced by third parties (e.g., judges, arbitrators).	**Relationship:** People thrive in meaningful relationships that are best cared for by those involved.
Respect: Hierarchical and formal respect is generally preserved in formal proceedings. Participants demonstrate respect for substantive law.	**Respect:** All participants in the process are afforded equal respect. Lawyer ensures parties and families are respected.
Responsibility: Defined by laws that assign duties. Lawyers often overestimate their control over the outcome.	**Responsibility:** The lawyer takes responsibility for addressing harm, meeting needs, and upholding shared values—within a process guided by mutually accepted rules.

RELATIONSHIP

THINKING like a restorative lawyer demands that we adopt "relationship" as a value that defines how we approach our work. In doing so, we strive to identify relationships intertwined within legal disputes. To think like a restorative lawyer means we do not dismiss Travis' need to apologize. We do not inadvertently exploit William's loss of his life partner to further our financial gains. We do not ignore Travis' parents, William's children, or the other important people in the lives of the victims and offenders.

I wonder if Beverly Walters, the "good lawyer" representing William Stotler, considered that his grandchildren became intertwined with Travis in a moment. Relationship, as a value, embodies trust, empathy, harmony, and understanding with our connections, known and unknown. Seen and unseen. Living and inanimate. Inherent in adopting relationship as a fundamental value is accepting the duty to nurture defined relationships, even when they may appear to be between strangers. Travis and William needed the healing that could only be found within their relationship. Travis needed to ask for forgiveness, to recognize the harm he caused, even if unintentional. William needed an opportunity to give it.

Our judicial system evaluates a legal conflict as an event between two individuals holding bags of competing rights. The system charges the lawyers with convincing the judges to unbundle the rights and balance them in their client's favor. The conflict often involves established relationships, sometimes on the same "side." By focusing on creating the resolution around defining the competing rights, even pre-existing identified relationships are neglected. In the process, imperiled relationships become lost in the shuffle and may never be restored.

I want to introduce you to Lena, Donna, and Eliza, who taught me not to be distracted by competing rights. They taught me to first attend to the possibility that healing through the power of relationship could sufficiently address unmet needs, obliterating the necessity to compete at all. Early in my practice, Donna came through the front door of my office. I was sitting in the reception area, reading.

~

As Donna walks in, I evaluate her as a potential client. I don't think she's one of those aggressive grandmothers who fight for custody. She seems like a nice woman who lives on a farm with her husband. She tells me her story about her daughter, Crystal. After high school, Crystal became addicted to drugs and had a rocky road moving into adulthood. The Department of Social Services took custody of Crystal's daughter, Eliza, a few days ago and placed her in a foster home. Donna tells me she is sickened and does not understand why Eliza, her granddaughter, isn't with her.

Suspicious, I ask her about the father. He had been murdered a few years ago. His family? Donna describes Shawn's mother, Lena, in very fond terms. I start asking directive questions, unsure I want to get in between these two grandmothers. "Lena is a wonderful person. She is going to help me as much as she can with Eliza. We are going to share weekends and some evenings so that we will both be able to manage."

I struggle to trust Donna's answers. This level of cooperation seems unusual. Nevertheless, she seems credible. I accept the case, file the pleadings, and attend the emergency hearing. The judge temporarily places the child with her grandmothers. Over the next two years, Lena, Donna, and I return to routine court review hearings, watching Crystal fail one improvement period after another. We arrive together, and the three of us sit in a private, separate waiting area. Donna and Lena teach me about a relationship created within their shared interest in the love of their granddaughter. This love takes precedence over their differences.

～

A DOZEN YEARS LATER, misfortune again brought Lena and Eliza to my office after they were injured in a car accident. Many things had happened in the intervening years. Eliza's mother, Crystal, was unable to stay sober and had minimal contact with her daughter. With Donna and Lena's love, Eliza coped. When Eliza became a teenager, Donna found her too challenging and Eliza moved in with Lena. She continued to be close to both grandmothers and had grown into a thriving, beautiful, talented young woman. Both women fully recovered from their injuries. We settled their insurance claim consistent with their goals and needs.

Eliza sent me a note after she graduated from high school. She thanked me for being part of her life for most of her life. I wanted to thank her grandmothers for being part of my restorative growth.

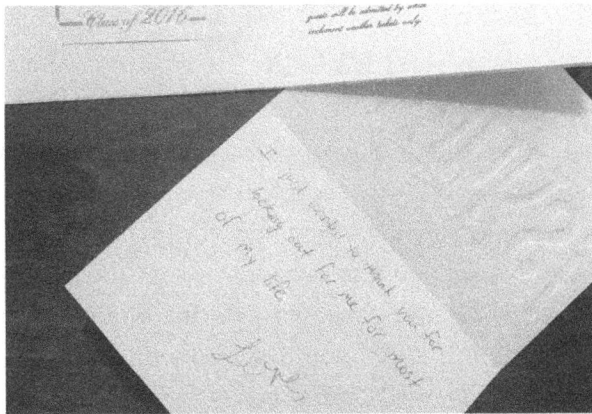

When Donna and Lena first walked into my office with Eliza in the state's custody, I did not trust them. They demonstrated that their relationship was superior to their rights. Beyond that, they taught me the potential in accepting rewarding relationships with clients. Restorative lawyers appreciate the value of the client's position in the attorney-client relationship, never fearing the formation of an equal and reciprocal relationship as they become embedded parts of each other's lives. When we allow a close, genuine, respect-ful, and collaborative relationship with clients to develop, many good things happen.

Monica Braxton taught me early in my law practice about the importance of relationship-building with clients. She was a midwife who did not carry malpractice insurance. She told me that midwives rarely get sued for malpractice because they build connected and supportive relationships with their clients. Taking a lesson from Monica, lawyers can reduce bar ethics complaints and malpractice claims by fostering a trusting and mutual partnership with clients. These relationships, operating alongside those with colleagues and coworkers, become fundamental to the restorative practice of law.

Let's turn now to another value: respect.

3.

RESPECT

Formal respect frames lawyers' activities in the courtroom, whether we are arriving at the courtroom, beginning a hearing, calling a witness, making an argument, or leaving the courtroom. You hear it, you see it. "All rise ... Your honor ... Ms. Waugh ... With all due respect ... Counsel, please speak one a time ... Please note counsel's objection ... May I approach the witness ... Mr. Miles ... The court will be in recess ... All rise."

In the restorative practice of law, respect is situated much deeper and bound with love, care, compassion, equity, and justice. Maya Angelou says, "If we lose love and self-respect for each other, this is how we die."[3] Love and self-respect for each other exceeds politeness. This respect is harbored in the heart, the gut, the soul. An internalized respect may guide our conflict resolution processes even as we struggle to heal.

Respect can be described as an "unassuming resounding force, the stuff that equity and justice are made of."[4] William Ury, in his book *The Third Side*, writes, "Human beings have a host of emotional needs — for love and recognition, for belonging and identity, purpose and meaning to lives. If all these needs had to be subsumed in one word, it might be respect."[5]

One afternoon in my restorative classroom, I witnessed a simple demonstration of deep, integrated respect far beyond usual courtroom formalities. This expression of respect engaged love, presence, and seeing oneself in another. A young man's brother revealed to me, by his example, how a simple gesture reflects deep, integrated respect.

～

It is late winter, in early 1998. One morning, I pack my files and walk to Courtroom B. The court schedules motions one morning per week, and the assistant district attorneys lug ten or fifteen accordion-style paper files across the walkway between courthouses to the courtroom. We sit behind one counsel table as the clerk calls the cases, one at a time.

I skim the docket.

One case stands out: Stephen Harwick.

On November 2, 1997, at the age of seventeen, Stephen put a ski mask over his head, seized an elderly customer at a convenience store, holding a knife to her throat, and demanded that the employees hand over money. The court transferred him to *adult status*, the crime having occurred the day before his eighteenth birthday.

This morning of open motions, I am watching the courtroom. Groups of defense counsel huddle behind the other table. The bailiff says, "All rise ... Present for the state, your honor ..." From the bench, the judge calls each case. "State versus ..." He announces the offenders' full names, including their middle names. Attorneys rotate in and out of the chairs at each table facing the judge, the bench. Each assigned district attorney moves to a chair at counsel table on the right side of the courtroom, and a defense attorney on the left. At the same time, each defendant stands and moves out of the jury box into the chair next to his counsel.

The judge reads, "State versus Stephen Blake Harwick." I rotate to an observer chair, behind counsel table. The elected district attorney moves to the seat at the table for this high-profile case. Last spring, the defendant attended a local high school, earned average grades, and looked forward to a bright future. Today he hears his name, stands up, and walks down the steps from the jury box toward counsel table.

Like the other defendants incarcerated in the regional jail, Stephen wears orange scrubs and tan plastic flip-flops. His ankles and wrists are hand-cuffed together. The short chain on the ankle restraints causes him to shuffle his feet rather than take normal-sized steps. As he shuffles, the elastic around his waist gives way, and his pants slip slowly around his hips. The elastic is not strong enough to hold the pants up. It rarely is on these orange scrubs. This view of Stephen's buttocks, as he attempts to participate in this critical moment of his life, is not uncommon. With hands shackled, he cannot pull his pants up when the waistband slides onto the hips as he shuffles across the room — further humiliation.

Stephen's older brother stands behind the bar, outside the well of the court. He is sitting in a pew, along with the press, family members of the victims, and family members of the defendants. He walks up to the rail that separates these observers from the partici-pants. Stephen walks towards his brother, and for reasons I don't know, the bailiffs don't stop him. His brother pulls his pants up, and Stephen stands at the counsel table facing the court to participate in the hearing. In other words, Stephen was no longer required to stand before the judicial bench with his ass hanging out for the full courtroom to see.

～

I WANT to be the restorative lawyer who notices when a client, a colleague, or a witness stands vulnerable and exposed. I want to provide that respect that allows them to stand before the court and speak without shame. I want to find ways for my arrogant lawyer's mind to fold into that of the humblest client.

"Thinking like a restorative lawyer" requires respect for the conflict and all persons engaged in the conflict. Sure, I often find it hard to respect judges; they make many rulings that I find unreasonable. It can be difficult to respect opposing counsel. Some don't understand the case. Some neglect to return phone calls, meet deadlines, or exercise common courtesies. Many cannot manage their anger. It can be tough to respect clients. Sometimes, they make poor decisions. Clients often say things that lawyers wish they hadn't said. It can even be challenging to respect colleagues. Lawyers may be disappointed when they are let down by their co-counsel who fail to pull their share of the weight. However, beyond these disappointments for the lawyer are bigger, more complex stories, often filled with hardships and fears. Within the stories are places for understanding and respect.

To "think like a restorative lawyer" creates respect that extends beyond the parties to the story. Respect that goes beyond the experience of the crisis that brought them to seek legal counsel. Respect that permeates into the details of the narrative that the client lives daily. When we look deeper, even those undeserving may earn respect. We can respect humanity in the overworked, deceitful lawyer when we hear the backstory, but we don't accept deception as an excuse for wrongdoing. We might find a way to respect the judge so fanatically consumed with deadlines and case resolution statistics to make an unsound or unsupported decision.

One summer, a young lawyer, Kelly, asked to shadow me on a typical day at the office to see how I run my solo practice. As she launched her career, she wanted to learn how to put restorative practices to work.

⌇

It's an ordinary day, scheduled with several client meetings, a mediation session, and a meeting with opposing counsel. As we cross the street, Wendy Wilson, a client I represented in a car accident case a few years ago, passes by. She sees me and stops her car at the busy intersection next to my office.

"Wendy. How are you?"

"Brenda! Good. So good to see you!"

She smiles and enthusiastically waves her hands. A car pulls up behind her and sounds the horn lightly.

"Oops, gotta go ..." Wendy drives away.

Kelly looks at me. "I want to be that kind of attorney — one who has a former client stop in traffic to smile at me." After the full day, we walk into the parking lot, talking. Kelly says, "The one thing I noticed about what goes on in your office is respect." I begin to think I am finding my path as a restorative lawyer.

4.

RESPONSIBILITY

What is the responsibility of the restorative lawyer? It begins with accepting responsibility only for those things that are truly within our control. We should avoid blaming ourselves for failures that result from other people's poor decisions or the failures of behemoth institutions. Lawyers often have a tough time identifying what is within their power to change. We may accept a broader responsibility than we can fulfill while failing to accept responsibility when we should.

As a value, responsibility requires one to accept accountability for wrongdoing. In criminal wrongdoing an offender may, in the course of a victim-offender dialogue, accept responsibility for their actions that caused the harm. The community might accept responsibility for the offender's unmet needs contributing to the wrongdoing. Offenders and the community accept responsibility to create and fulfill obligations created by the wrongdoing to make right the wrongs. What about the responsibility of the lawyer?

I once heard, "Reign in your lawyer instincts to protect somebody." That's good advice for the lawyer. I've often suffered from the delusion that I could fix whatever is necessary for a client. When listening to them describe a problem, it seems natural to imagine the arsenal of solutions I might deliver. This instinct may be widespread among lawyers. One morning, I was discussing this issue with a colleague from Brazil. Luis Bravo suggested that law school trains lawyers to take over the case. We learn to take responsibility for outcomes. Luis and I work in different languages, continents, and judicial systems, yet we share this experience. We jump in and direct our clients' cases. And then, we carry a burden for the outcome.

We struggle to forgive our failures when we accept this broad responsibility. If we so readily accept fault for poor consequences, something else happens. We situate ourselves at the center of the case, displacing the stakeholders who preceded our involvement, and will live with the aftermath of the resolution. Exaggerating our power in the conflict may impair the client's opportunity to create their own healing.

I felt like a failure the day that Judge Casey announced that Ella's grandchildren would be raised six hours away, and she had no guarantees of any visits, phone calls, or relationships. In sitting with that failure, I did not yet understand that lawyers don't have responsibility for the underlying circumstances or the primary responsibility for the outcome. But it took another tragedy and that hideous sense of powerlessness for me to accept that we lawyers can only accept responsibility for the process, not the outcome.

∼

I WALK INTO THE DARK, quiet office on the third floor and punch my code into the door of the district attorney's office in the judicial annex. I am here because I do not want to be inundated on Monday morning after being on vacation for a week. I am the only assistant district attorney assigned to child neglect and dependency cases. Piles of papers, unopened envelopes, and disheveled manila files cover my desk. I pick up a stack of petitions that another assistant district attorney filed while I was away. One involves a single mother with four children who was involuntarily committed to the hospital for mental health treatment. The second involves a baby born to a mother suffering from substance use disorder placed in a foster home after birth. Everything seems to be in order until I open one file involving Bethany, an infant. The petition asserts that she was found dead by a relative in her crib a couple of months after birth. There is no evidence as to why she stopped breathing.

Bethany lived in Dayton with her mother, grandmother, aunt, and three-year-old sister, Tiffany Paxton. I immediately recognize the name. Tiffany was the subject of a case I prosecuted when she was a baby. She suffered a spiral fracture to her arm and a head injury at the age of six months. We speculated that the injury occurred when the infant's crying disturbed the child's aunt, who lived with her mother and grandmother and had a limited mental capacity. We developed a sound theory of the case based on the facts and forensic evidence. The aunt picked the baby up by the arm and threw her against the wall.

After working on the case for a couple of years, the state, through the Department of Social Services, decided to return the child to the mother permanently. I opposed that motion to return the child, and the case eventually wound up in the appellate court. I lost. Without any long-term support services, Tiffany went to live with her mother, grandmother, and her aunt.

Yes, I feel confident that this is Tiffany Paxton's family — the same family that Social Service had returned the child to her mother, grandmother, and aunt over my objection. I feel faint and nauseous. This morning, I was on the beach with my children. Now, I am sitting alone in the dark, reading a report of suspected child abuse resulting in an infant's death.

I read the report. The examiner cannot determine the cause of death other than sudden infant death syndrome (SIDS). I know this meant that we have no explanation for the baby's death. I know that trying to prove the difference between SIDS and suffocation would be nearly impossible. Intentional suffocation often leaves no physical findings and can be mistaken for SIDS. I also know that this baby's aunt did not like newborns in the house.

I close the door and leave my office a bigger disaster than when I snuck in to catch up. I don't sleep that night, replaying everything in Tiffany's case and working to determine what I did wrong. Why didn't I stop the state from returning her to that home? Why didn't I save this baby? And what do I do now? The following day, I call Social Services, the police, and the medical examiner, desperately wanting to find a way to re-open Tiffany's case. We have insufficient evidence. I must let it go. And it makes me sick. It still makes me sick, but if I am to become a restorative lawyer, I must create restorative opportunities for clients, victims, offenders, community members, and even myself. It is a daily struggle to relinquish responsibility for events or outcomes I can't control.

～

WHAT ABOUT THE responsibility attached to what a lawyer can control? We do not control the legal outcome of the case, the client's personality, and the events that occurred before meeting the client. However, we control our ability to offer to heal their pain and create the optimal environment for the client to find a way to resolve, transform, or at least live with their conflict. Accepting powerlessness over the outcome may leave the lawyer feeling untethered and useless. But we become grounded and then fill our potential only when we let go of the things we cannot take responsibility for and embrace those we can: our role, and in some ways, the process. Accepting responsibility for things out of their control dooms lawyers to frustration and disappointment. Restorative lawyers surrender control over those things which they do not control, and so power is relocated to the stakeholders. The lawyer then creates the best process that is within her capacity to influence. The lawyer creates her role within that process, not only as a navigator or gladiator, but as a healer.

5.

When lawyers surrender responsibility for the outcome, they are not relieved of their commitment to address injustices embedded in the broader legal system. Every lawyer has a responsibility to protect the integrity of the processes we work in for justice. The American Bar Association describes this duty very broadly. "As a public citizen, a lawyer should seek improvement of the law, access to the legal system, the administration of justice and the quality of service rendered by the legal profession."[6]

Long before I embraced restorative lawyering, my obligation to the integrity of legal processes took form on a Thursday afternoon in August in the late 1990s, shortly after the Grand Jury handed down the term's indictments. One victim met me in the small conference room between our office and the judge's office in the old courthouse for me to explain how the case would proceed through the next few months. I had control over that meeting and elements of the process. And I intended to exercise that control consistent with individual and institutionally shared values.

THIS VICTIM IS A THIN, middle-aged man from the county's southern end. He sits around the corner of the large table from me and goes through the facts of his story. His worn flannel shirt hangs loose on his wiry frame that I imagine comes from years of poor nutrition and smoking cigarettes. I suspect this is not his first visit to the courthouse as a victim or offender. He begins to outline the story that brings him here today. Someone stole the checkbook from his car's glove box, wrote a check on it, and cashed it at the local bank. Understanding his version of the story, I move on to try to educate the victim about the law. I outline the elements of the case. The facts meet the statutory requirements: the defendant took the checks without permission. He wrote a check and cashed it, intending to steal money from the victim. I detail his financial losses. We discuss the potential for a plea and restitution, and I describe how the plea operates when he interrupts me.

"Ma'am the only reason I'm pressing charges is that the man who stole my check was Black."

I'm not sure I heard him right. "So, you are saying that if this defendant were white, you wouldn't want me to prosecute him?" I try not to use my presentation voice or be accusatory; I just try to be confirmatory.

He nods affirmatively and without shame. "Yes." I struggle to continue the meeting, but I finish the interview, tidy a few things in the office, and drive home. In every passing moment, I grow angrier.

The next morning, I walk to the courtroom with my brown accordion folders stuffed with manila files and dog-eared yellow legal pads. I stack them on our side's table — the district attorney's side, on the right side of the courtroom. The rotation of district attorneys and defense attorneys begins. I take my seat at the table. This morning, the jury box is full, with defendants brought over from the jail for status hearings for the cases scheduled for trial. One by one, they shuffle down from the box to their seat to stand before the court, with their pants falling below their waists.

"State versus James Redmond." I rotate in and take my seat.

Judge Stewart is the most formal of the judges and the smartest. "What says the State, Ms. Waugh?"

"Your honor." I stand. I'm unsure how the lawyers lined up

behind me, the public behind them, the guys in the jury box, or the judge will receive my message. I fear that I'm launching a tirade, and my rage may be misunderstood. I reconcile that potential and continue. "I met with the putative victim in this matter yesterday. I reviewed our case with him. He described his sole basis for requesting prosecution of the case is the race of the defendant. I repeated his statement back to him to confirm that I had heard him correctly, and he agreed. My job as a district attorney is to work for justice and preserve the integrity of the process. Working for justice does not include selectively prosecuting a person based on their race, and our justice system should not support this action. Our courts have a long history of the disparate and hateful treatment of African Americans, and today I refuse to intentionally contribute to that history."

My voice quivers, and my knees shake. The rage that has grown in me overnight bubbles over. Unaccustomed to such extemporaneous frankness when I address the court, I'm scared about what will happen next. I look at my audience: the defendants with motions on the docket lined up in the jury box. They listen attentively. I keep talking. "For these reasons and solely for the reason that the victim would not have the State to pursue this matter had the defendant been white, the State moves this court to dismiss this matter with prejudice." "With prejudice" is a legal term that means the case can never be brought again. It's final.

Judge Stewart often acts surprised at my creative arguments, but today, he seems alarmed. I wonder if he is outraged. He shifts papers and sits straight up in his black robe, moving with certainty and speed. "Motion granted. The matter is dismissed. I'll sign the order now and the defendant shall be released from custody. Counsel, have you prepared an order?" I hand my order to the bailiff, who takes it to the judge, who signs it. The bailiff transports Mr. Redmond back to the jail, where he is released.

∾

RESPONSIBILITY. That day we exercised our responsibility in the process to a blatant injustice. Demonstrating accountability for the process, including the client's experience, cannot be an isolated event.

Our shared values of accepting responsibility for what we can and letting it go when we cannot become part of the work of the restorative lawyer. Restorative values associated with restorative justice dovetail with many of the values we historically identify as central to our conventional judicial system: neutrality, equality, fairness, procedural consistency, and open discourse. Restorative justice principles also create a way to think like a restorative lawyer, along with the values of relationship, respect, and responsibility.

TABLE 4

Some Examples of Boundaries for Accepting Responsibility as a Lawyer

LAWYERS SHOULD NOT ACCEPT RESPONSIBILITY FOR...	LAWYERS SHOULD ACCEPT RESPONSIBILITY FOR...
Events that predate their involvement.	Listening and setting goals with clients.
Obsessing with process, deadlines, and details to the extent that it obscures the relationship with the client and their needs.	Avoiding filing motions or pursuing arguments that may harm clients or undermine long-term goals.
Overburdened or dysfunctional legal systems.	The role accepted by the attorney within the legal system.
Unqualified judges or poor legal decisions.	Showing kindness to clients, colleagues, and community members.
The outcome.	The clients' opportunities to participate in the process that produces the outcome, the compliance of the process to fairness.

Chapter 5

Thinking Like a Restorative Lawyer

BUILDING ON PRINCIPLES

Thinking like a lawyer means one can take almost any social situation and convert it into legal categories ... poignant, glaring, pitiful stories of human drama and misery begin to sail easily past you, as you take them expertly and dissect them for the 'relevant' facts.

— Elizabeth Mertz, *The Language of Law School: Learning to Think Like a Lawyer*

1.

THE PREVIOUS CHAPTER explored how thinking like a restorative lawyer requires the integration of three crucial values Zehr links to restorative justice. This chapter will dive into Zehr's five principles for creating a framework for the restorative practice of law. The conventional way to think like a lawyer requires that we match the laws to the facts to locate an enforceable right and ancillary duty. We work in our role as a navigator/gladiator, perhaps even a sooth-sayer. (Justice Holmes described the lawyer as a neutral predictor of the output of courts, policy analysts, and urban social engi-neers.)[1] In that role, lawyers move cases — off our caseloads, off the court's dockets — maximizing the gain for the client and our firms.

Historical bastions of Western jurisprudence have framed our "thinking like a lawyer" for centuries. By imagining a practice that substitutes restorative justice for assumptions of a rights-based competition approach to justice (what I called my "lost saints" in Chapter Two) we may invent a new way to practice law. How? How can lawyers expect to practice without the pilings of Hobbes' laws of nature, Bentham's understanding of the law as a command, or Habermas' lifeworld? A restorative-justice-based practice demands that we appreciate Bentham and Austin in a new way, less as authorities and more as collaborators, creating a refreshed space for a broader (and more inclusive) vision.[2]

Applying the principles Zehr outlines in his book, *Changing Lenses*, to everyday legal work, changes what it means to "think like a lawyer."[3] Those principles include:

1. Focuses on the harms and needs (Of the victims, communities, and offenders)
2. Addresses obligations resulting from those harms. (Offenders, but also communities' and society's.)
3. Uses inclusive, collaborative processes.

4. Involves those with a stake in the situation. (Victims, offenders, community members, society.)
5. Seeks to make right the wrongs.

Applying these principles to the practice of law expands further how to think like a lawyer. Thinking like a restorative lawyer requires examining a rule's underpinnings to determine how it supports meeting unmet needs. Why was the rule created? How does the rule further the development of a peaceful, prosperous community? What is the relationship between breach of the rule and consequential harm? What obligations arise out of the violation and those harms? Looking beyond the bare bones of the rule requires a deliberate change in lenses.

TABLE 5

Guiding Principles in Conventional Law vs. Restorative Justice: A Comparison

CONVENTIONAL LEGAL PRACTICE	LEGAL PRACTICE INTEGRATING RESTORATIVE JUSTICE
Focus on whether a rule is broken.	Focus on harms.
Focus on the remedy to the rule being broken.	Focus on needs resulting from harms.
Limit focus to parties designated by statute or rule.	Focus on harms and needs of victim, offender, and community.
Address harm through punitive or compensatory remedies allowed by law.	Address obligations resulting from harms.
Remedial action enforced by agents of the state.	Offender and community members accept their responsibility for actions to meet needs and make things right.
Process is exclusive, participation limited to state and offender (criminal) those with standing (civil).	Process is inclusive, participation afforded to all those impacted by wrongdoing.
Hierarchal process with narrowly defined roles performed in accordance with specific rules.	Collaborative process with value placed on equal and broad participation of stakeholders.
Judge or jury defines wrong by applying the facts to the law.	Participants seek to identify the wrong.
The remedy is imposed through rules-based procedures.	Participants seek to make right the wrongs, as much as possible.

Table 5 examines these principles and contrasts the principles of restorative justice with the conventional practice of law.

Examples of looking at a legal problem through a new lens are abundant. One afternoon, I went for a walk with a colleague who practices in employment cases. During these walks, we would often brainstorm ways to address challenging cases. She struggled with a case involving a teacher after her employer fired her. My colleague was working to get the client to get her job back. But as we walked, we questioned whether the reinstatement would right the wrong. After some reflection, she met with the client and reevaluated her objectives. They decided that finding a way to keep the teacher's career on track would come closer to making things right than returning to her old job. The lawyer admitted she had been stuck on a single remedy — focusing on reinstatement. Moving to what would make the wrong most right gave the lawyer something to negotiate for that would offer the client better options for her future. Righting wrongs requires the inclusive collabora- tion, identification of needs, and broad acceptance of respon- sibility.

2.

Sam Front limps into my office wearing a boot-type cast. He follows me down the long hall to the small conference room. His mother and father, Ellen and Ed, stream behind him. We sit down around a little round table. It's intimate — well, kind of crammed — but we sit there, looking at each other.

I can't help but notice that Ellen has a face that reminds me of another Ellen, Ellen Corby, the actress who portrayed Grandma Walton on a television series I watched in high school. But this Ellen wears a faux leopard print hat as she greets me. She has a peaceful smile that never fades, regardless of how difficult our conversation becomes. She describes her son as having done well in school until tenth grade. Sam pipes in and explains that he dropped out in eleventh grade to become a stonemason. But that was hard on his body, and Sam quit after sustaining painful injuries. When Sam's physicians decided that his pain had become unbearable, they referred him to a pain management clinic. During the early part of the opioid epidemic, little thought was given to the significant risk for addiction with the limited treatments available in those programs.[4] Within a few months, Sam developed a substance use disorder. His work was limited--piecing together odd jobs that provided no income, no purpose, and no confidence.

Sam's most recent injury came when he fell off the roof at a construction site about three months earlier. After successful foot and ankle surgery, he planned to return to work. One evening, he was riding in a car with a close friend. The driver missed a turn and tried to make a U-turn on the highway. Another vehicle hit them. The resulting wreck caused complications, pain, and a nasty infection at Sam's surgical site.

Ellen pulls out a stack of medical bills. "Sammy has no way to pay these." I begin by flushing out the facts that the courts (and insurance companies) would find relevant to resolving Sam's case. I try to assess all the injuries from the wreck, sorting out those that pre-date the U-Turn. Getting the bills paid seems impossible. Sam's work on the roof was one of his odd jobs that did not include health insurance or workers' compensation. Sam seems resigned to having these limits placed in life: physical, job-related, financial, and personal.

Yet, he is willing to strategize some potential outcomes. These include paying bills, getting job training, and addressing long-term substance use and misuse. With clear goals and a team of family members willing to invest in Sam, we get to work.

～

WE DECIDED to meet every few months during his recovery from the ankle and foot injuries to determine if we are meeting goals and meeting new challenges. First, we resolved concerns about medical bills by focusing efforts on getting Sam qualified for Medicaid. A few weeks later, an unforeseen challenge presented itself at a meeting. Sam's eleven-year-old daughter came to live with him when his ex-wife became incarcerated in a neighboring state. Ellen brought these issues to the table. She asked questions. "Is Sam ready to be a father? To find a career? To stay off drugs?" During the meetings, I learned that Sam wanted to maintain sobriety, get additional education, and have his driver's license reinstated. With Ellen's help, Sam had clearly articulated his unmet needs, and we got to work creating a plan to meet them.

Sam, Ellen, Ed, and I created an estimated budget to pay Sam's DMV fines in order to reinstate his license. The budget included the purchase of a new car with insurance and the training Sam needed to get a job. While I worked on locating vehicle infractions, Sam worked with the college to secure financial aid for a new vocational program and developed a plan to enroll.

Sam's collaborative team developed a resolution far beyond getting a cash settlement and spending it. The team helped him identify his needs and created roles with defined responsibilities to meet them. Ellen was a vital member of this team and central to finding the best resolution to meet Sam's needs.

Expanding the number of people participating in my representation beyond Sam, changed the process. While the courts restrict participation in conflict resolution processes to people who demonstrate a sufficient nexus to the harm or those with "legal standing," we worked much broader. We engaged the family in an inclusive, collaborative process. The goal was to decipher Sam's needs and find the resources to meet them, creating a more restorative response within a conventional lawyer-client relationship and conflict resolution legal framework. Restorative lawyers may find that the clients will be better sustained as they grow out of the legal problem when they, along with important people in their lives, have actively participated in the resolution. Family members who experience feeling heard and appreciated for their participation in the decision-making help the lawyer meet the client's needs. The value of creating a deep pool of resources extends beyond civil to other types of legal cases.

Another family turned out to be a key participant in resolving a legal problem encountered by a young high school football player.

3.

Finn Hammond, a talented defensive lineman on the high school football team, was in class one afternoon, supervised by a substitute teacher. Another student began hurling racial epithets at Finn, escalating into "Hit me, n*****r. You are too afraid, aren't you? Hit me!" Finn tried to ignore her, but his sixteen-year-old, still-developing pre-frontal cortex couldn't restrain him. She kept hurling the epithets, and he hit her several times. The school system expelled both students.

Cedric, Finn's father, called me the next day. I had known Cedric for almost twenty years, having represented him when he was injured in a car accident just after Finn was born. We kept up through the years. As he talked with his soft voice and heavy Jamaican accent, I feared the failures of our educational and criminal judicial systems would never address the wrongdoing of either student. The consequences to Finn could be serious, potentially shoving him into the school-to-prison pipeline.

Had this occurred in a school with a sound restorative justice program, the administration would have options beyond school expulsion. They may have created an opportunity for a victim-offender conference. They may have developed a series of talking circles with classmates to address the harm. Restorative practices may have prevented the environment that allowed this event to occur by creating forums to discuss social justice, discrimination, and hate speech. A more restorative educational program may have identified the conflict when it first arose and created a suitable process before it escalated. At a minimum, restorative justice could have created an opportunity for re-entry of both students. However, this school had not integrated any restorative practices into its discipline. They expelled both students without any opportunity to return to school during this school year.

Had this occurred in a jurisdiction in the United States (or any other country) where restorative practices exist for juvenile offenders in the court system, Finn would have been a candidate. Restorative justice is often adopted by courts for juvenile offenders more readily than adults. One lawyer who brought restorative justice to this area was Fred Van Liew. Several times in the last decade, I've met with a group of lawyers dedicated to a restorative approach to our work for mini-conferences or "Palavers."[5] During our meetings, we share our work and explore ways to make it more restorative.

In 1985, Fred worked as an assistant district attorney and attended an educational program that included mediation for a criminal case. He watched a film about a young mother with daughters who lived in a house burgled by a teenager. Fred had been a district attorney for a couple of years and never considered that a victim would be allowed to tell their story to an offender. In the film, the victims discussed how their lives had changed since their home was burglarized. The young mother's daughters could no longer sleep in their bedrooms. Upon hearing the story, the offender wept. For the first time, he understood the harm he caused victims. With this new awareness, Fred studied restorative justice and set up a program in his office, including adult and juvenile cases.

Most juvenile cases adopting restorative practices include a meeting, or series of meetings, called a Family Group Conference. During the meetings, the offender and the offender's family convene with a law enforcement person, advocates, and professional service providers. The victim, the victim's family and a victim advocate may be involved.

In most Family Group Conferences, the participants are first referred to a program where they prepare privately with a facilitator before engaging the full group. During the conference, contributors address the harm. The family, counseled by professionals, determines what further action might address unmet needs. The plan is implemented, and the group reconvenes periodically to determine how well the needs and objectives are met.

But Finn's county had no restorative justice program: no Family Group Conference, no victim-offender dialogue, no re-entry program. We expected Finn to be charged as a juvenile delinquent and placed with his parents, with minimal services, as part of an "improvement period." We also recognized that the state may attempt to place him in a juvenile detention center as the legal case worked its way through the system. Two days after Cedric called me, I met with him, Finn, and Finn's mother, Denise. A colleague who practices education law joined us in my office.

～

WE SIT around a small round table. Finn stares at the floor a lot. Here he sits, expelled from school and likely facing criminal charges. We've investigated the options and have found nothing we can do to get him back into school. We are powerless in moving to resolve the outstanding criminal charges quickly and fairly. So, we talk.

We talk for hours about the situation, trying to understand the conflict, identifying the harm, and figuring out how to best address it, with no resources but ourselves. What got Finn into this situation? How could he get out? With his expulsion, he was placed in an alternative school. Could we help him succeed there so he could return to "regular" school? Finn loves sports; what can we do to help him with that?

We decide not to initiate any action with the court, and to wait for criminal charges to be filed through a juvenile petition. We create an informal, family-based "improvement period" as a strategy. If charges were brought, I could argue that Finn was addressing underlying issues about his physical response to outrage. Perhaps the state would then postpone formal action or dismiss the petition outright if Finn addressed any underlying issues behind the visceral reaction. Finn agrees to a plan with many levels of participation. He will attend weekly sessions with a program to work on controlling his anger when triggered. He designs an online program with additional schoolwork to help him reintegrate into public school upon readmission. He sets up community service volunteer work with his church and another community group. In other words, this Family Group Conference created a plan and was ready for implementation.

❧

I'LL NEVER KNOW why the state did not file criminal charges. We assembled our team a few months later and visited two schools Finn could attend in the fall. Both schools were eager to have such a good player and were impressed by his hard work in school and his community service over the last semester. Finn started in the summer session, returning to football. That August, he came to see me alone, carrying a thank you card and the full payment for the invoice for our professional services.

A couple of years later, I received an invitation to his graduation party, with a photo of him with the football team, in his cap and gown, and at the prom. I stopped at the American Legion Hall a little before the celebration began. I walked in and received a warm welcome from friends and family members. Denise was setting up rows of disposable chafing dishes full of delicious-smelling food. The D.J. played softly, testing his equipment. It was a great afternoon to celebrate. Finn did not go down that school-to-prison pipeline.

Our meetings with Finn and his family didn't meet the format of many Family Group Conferences. I remain disappointed that we could not seek any resolution to the horrible incident that led to Finn's expulsion. I regret that Finn had to bear any burden of institutional and personal racism that created the conflict. Our legal and educational system failed him, and we could not remedy it. Our ragtag process missed the healing that might have come with a restorative dialogue. But we brought together the professionals, the family, and the student to work towards healing harm and disappointment. Finn proved that we can look for justice even without a government-instituted or controlled program. A homegrown family group conference can bring the family and the community resources to the table to create healing, even in this imperfect and incomplete world.

4.

Restorative justice calls for collaboration.[6] Collaborative processes involve stakeholders. In civil cases, that usually includes two parties and in criminal cases it may engage the victim, the offender, and their families. With civil and criminal cases, collaboration necessarily involves at least two attorneys — opposing counsel. Many attorneys do not easily adapt from being competitive to being collaborative. It may take a paradigm shift to allow for the vulnerability that a more team-oriented approach demands. That is not easy! I witnessed firsthand how hard that would be for attorneys.

After graduate school, I completed a forty-hour course to qualify as a member of the IACP, the International Academy of Collaborative Professionals. Excited to engage in Collaborative Practice, I unsuccessfully begged other attorneys in our local bar to attend the collaborative training.

One dedicated client, Kimberly Malone, approached me, having read about the collaborative divorce process. With no other collaboratively trained lawyers, Kimberly convinced me to attempt the approach with an attorney who I found easy to work with. Kimberly's husband, Trevor, hired Mark. He assured me that he would negotiate and work in an informal process. I did not realize how tightly he clung to his security blanket: "thinking like a lawyer." We held our first four-way meeting, the hallmark of the collaborative divorce process, in my office.

~

IN COLLABORATIVE CASES, lawyers begin working with clients by reviewing a standard document, the "agreement to participate." We emphasize the requirements that the parties be transparent and must obtain new counsel if they elect to leave the process and pursue litigation. We introduce the option of including other professionals, including a financial neutral, a conflict coach or coaches, and a child specialist. At that point, the parties cite reasons that they chose a non-adversarial process and elicit their hopes and fears in working with the collaborative team.

In this case, without both attorneys understanding the collaborative framework, we don't have a full team or agreements regarding other professionals. We do not review the collaborative process or the requirement that the parties secure new attorneys if we cannot reach an agreement. We nonetheless elicit their hopes and fears and generate options for addressing substantive issues, such as custody and retirement accounts. The fundamental disagreements between the parties emerge, and with that, the differences between collaborative and conventional representation in the process become apparent. We would remain at the table, talking in the collaborative process. We would examine what's happening and look beyond articulated positions to find those underlying interests we can all work to meet. We would avoid posturing, threatening, and intimidation. But for Mark, those three tools were indispensable.

When Kimberly's husband, Trevor, says he wants custody and

Kimberly suggests, that with the combination of school and work schedules, that is not going to work, the husband becomes distressed. He shifts in his chair, turns red, and taps his pen against the table. Mark, without the collaborative training, shifts into a default lawyer mode. He becomes aggressive, posturing to gain superiority. He positions himself as the authority in the room with all the control. "MY client *this*" and "MY client *that*." I've heard this familiar emphasis inflection on "my" at the beginning of the sentence. It often ends with an unreasonable demand. "Well then, MY client is not settling for less than full custody."

At this point, we are far from collaborating. My default lawyer mode wants to meet him where he's at and tell him that his client's temper and his drinking have rendered him unfit for extended custodial time, and I have the evidence to prove it. However, I know that Kimberly will not benefit from escalating this discussion to the next level. I suggest that Trevor and Mark step into the next room. I then pull Mark into the hall and try to talk him down. Of course, without Trevor present, it doesn't take long. However, Trevor is angry and unwilling to discuss anything but full custody. Kimberly asks if we can give up and try to meet again in a few weeks.

❧

KIMBERLY'S STORY does not have a happy ending. We quit meeting in one room, around one table. Instead, we keep the parties separated. They never heard their lawyers talk to the other party. Like caucus-based mediation, the two lawyers ushered offers and responses up and down the hall. We reached an agreement, adopted by the court. But the underlying conflicts never ended, and the relationship remained strained.

Kimberly wound up in and out of court with Trevor intermittently after the divorce. Unfulfilled needs left Trevor seeking ways to meet them by returning to court and attempting to control everything. Collaboration takes more than sitting in the same room, negotiating, or trying to reach an agreement. Instead, collaboration requires all participants to be willing to uncover the problem at the root of the legal conflict and to reveal their vulnerabilities and talents to work to meet the needs created by the conflict. It requires checking the lawyer's ego at the door and being willing to share everything at their disposal to meet the parties' needs.

Even without specific training, collaboration with an attorney is not always doomed to fail. In contrast to Mark, my opposing counsel in Kimberly's case, I once had a top assistant U.S. Attorney, Elizabeth Johnson, as my opposing counsel. Liz was also someone I'd known for a long time. She was my trial advocacy judge in law school. We'd formed an immediate bond since we had both been pregnant during the mock trial. Liz had raised four children and could see beyond her proscribed role as the U.S. Attorney. She didn't have special collaborative training, but she had remarkable intuition.

The case involved Kevin Henderson. At age two, while his parents lived on a federal airbase, a ceiling light fixture came loose, fell, and struck his head. He experienced increasing difficulties from a brain injury. After eight years of unsuccessful treatment, his mother, Elaine, retained us to file suit under the Federal Tort Claims Act. We had a good case for damages but recognized that we'd be challenged to demonstrate causation.

≈

SOON AFTER COMPLETING DISCOVERY, Liz, Elaine, and I attend our court-referred mediation. In this jurisdiction, mediation is always evaluative and rarely includes joint sessions. Since the mediator had an unexpected scheduling conflict, we sit in his conference room to wait for him before moving into our separate rooms where we will spend the day. Periodically, the mediator's assistant apologizes for the delay, offers us coffee, and returns to work. We chat for a while about our children and summer plans. When our attention turns to Kevin, we talk about his long-term and short-term needs. Liz shares the concerns Elaine and I have about wanting to be sure Kevin gets the best shot he can at life. We all want him to get the specialized services he needs to thrive.

As we dig deeper and generate more options, we agree that Kevin would benefit more from a structured settlement reached through agreement than from a jury verdict. The settlement proceeds could be deposited into a special needs trust to supplement the programs he was already enrolled in. This structure would expand the ability to meet Kevin's needs. With common goals and shared strategies, we outline a detailed agreement.

The mediator joins us after having resolved the emergency. He begins his opening statement, and all three of us smile. We explain that we don't need the mediation—we have an agreement. He types it up, we sign it, and we leave with the satisfaction of knowing that by putting our efforts together and collaborating, we created a superior outcome for Kevin.

∾

KEVIN CAME by my office to see me soon after he turned eighteen. He was engaged and working a full-time job. We could never have dreamed that he would have been able to grow into this successful young man as we sat in the mediation that morning, waiting for the mediator. I will always be grateful for the emergency that caused the mediator's delay and Liz's natural proclivity to understand how to be a restorative lawyer.

5.

My experiences with Sam, Finn, and Liz show us the potential of inclusive collaboration. This inclusivity contrasts with the limit imposed by legal standing. Courts limit who participates in processes by deciding who has a legal stake in the outcome. The U.S. Supreme Court has established a three-part test for legal standing. The "irreducible constitutional minimum of standing" requires the plaintiff to establish:

> First ... an "injury in fact"—an invasion of a legally protected interest which is (a) concrete and particularized, and (b) "actual or imminent," not "conjectural" or "hypothetical." Second, there must be a causal connection between the injury and the conduct complained of—the injury has to be "fairly ... trace[able] to the challenged action of the defendant, and not ... th[e] result [of] the independent action of some third party not before the court." Third, it must be "likely," as opposed to merely "speculative," that the injury will be "redressed by a favorable decision." Summers v. Earth Island Institute, 555 U.S. 488, 492-93 (2009); Daimler Chrysler Corporation v. Cuno, 547 U.S. 332, 340-41 (2006).[7]

A restorative-justice-based practice does not limit participation to those who can demonstrate meeting these standards. The underlying goal is to address the wrongdoing, heal the harm, and repair relationships. Sometimes, the wrongdoing (or conflict) has a large impact, a ripple effect. Those impacted are far more than those meeting the requirements for legal standing to participate in court proceedings. However, by increasing the conglomerate of potential resource contributors, we increase the opportunities to address the harm.

Many attorneys avoid including more people in the process. Limiting who participates in a client meeting seems efficient. Faster. We might find it easier to convince a client to agree with a recommendation, take a particular course of action, and resolve the case. We can move right along when we don't have all those busybodies offering their two cents' worth.

Limiting participation does not always result in sound decision-making, outcomes, or agreements. Excluding third parties might expedite the process, but it limits the potential to create a deep and durable agreement. The client may make a decision that moves the case along, but is it the type of decision that the client will be satisfied with within three months, six months, or three years? Stakeholders without standing can require a deeper examination of an option that will support a resolution that withstands the tests of time and inevitable challenges.

I've heard lawyers describe friends and family members as the *Greek Chorus*. These folks offer up their opinion from time to time and perhaps misdirect the client. The metaphor portrays friends and family members as less than helpful — even sometimes screwing up a carefully orchestrated strategy with their ill-informed know-it-all comments. As a theater major, I learned that the Greek Chorus wasn't a liability or an intruder. In most tragedies, the Chorus describes the terrible events unfolding while remaining uninvolved.

Maybe we should respect (and listen to) the Greek Chorus.

The *peanut gallery* is another term lawyers use to describe third parties offering their opinions. But those in the gallery are often stakeholders. They suffer alongside clients. They are the very folks impacted by a client's decisions. For restorative lawyers, understanding harm and meeting unmet needs requires us to listen to all who feel impacted by a decision. Ignoring these folks can be as damaging as ignoring a fact witness at trial. Family and community are not bystanders. Stakeholders relegated to the sidelines cannot provide sufficient participation to meet the restorative lawyer's ambitious goals.

Another client/teacher, Mandy, reminded me of the importance of including stakeholders. Mandy was a farrier who injured her back in a car wreck. After she fully recovered and wanted to resolve her case, she refused a reasonable offer from the insurance company. After some probing, I discovered that her hesitation flowed from concerns articulated by her mother, who had never met with me or participated in any discussions. We scheduled a conference call with Mandy, her mother, and the insurance adjuster.

∽

ON THE DAY of the meeting, we sit at the conference table. I call the adjustor from the phone in the middle of the table. We introduce ourselves. I briefly summarize the case and ask Mom if she wants to talk. She has a lot to say. She explains, in detail, how she'd cared for Mandy since she was injured and why she fears that this would eventually sidetrack her forever. Mom is scared for her daughter's condition in the future. Mandy's mother has a lot of concerns, and she needs me and the adjuster to understand them.

The adjuster listens. He acknowledges her concerns and validates her worries. Then we talk about resolutions, and everyone pipes in. Soon, we have a way to resolve the legal case that's acceptable for everyone, even Mom. With Mom off the sidelines, we benefit from the free flow of ideas that collaboration demands. When Mandy sees that her mother's concerns are heard and addressed, she is clearly comfortable moving to a resolution.

∽

THIS NEGOTIATION RAISES a question about the role of the insurance adjuster. Are lawyers, probation officers, and insurance adjusters professional stakeholders? Of course, the outcome won't impact these stakeholders as profoundly as the client. But they have a stake in the outcome. Will the claims rep get a superior evaluation and the raise she needs to buy a house spacious enough for the new baby? Will opposing counsel prevail sufficiently to save face with their client to secure future referrals? Will the probation officer be called out late at night when the probationer fails to comply with the terms and is outside the jurisdiction?

When, in 2008, I saw a reference to professional stakeholders in an essay on restorative justice, I felt uncomfortable.[8] I disagreed with the status of stakeholder being placed on victim service providers, or any other professionals. Now I understand. It is dishonest to ignore that professionals have a stake in the outcome. In practical terms, the professional stakeholder creates a potential conflict of interest in every negotiation. While the wrongdoing may not impact them or the outcome in the same way as those directly involved, they are community stakeholders who may be significantly affected by the outcome. A judge who sentences an offender to probation fears that the offender may re-offend, and the judge won't be reappointed. A mediator who fails to settle a dispute doesn't get future referrals. Lawyers who appear too compromising or weak in a resolution lose their reputation.

Stephen Levy, a developer of Legal Project Management, provides great insight into the restorative practice of law. He recognizes the breadth of stakeholders in a legal process:

> Litigation includes a complex group of both real and imagined stakeholders. There are attorneys, of course. For corporate clients, the senior executive, the CO for larger trials -- is a stakeholder as are the leaders of the business division suing or being sued. There are professionals who put their careers at stake at each trial, such as jury consultants and expert witnesses, who may want to tell you how to do your job. Each witness, each deponent also behaves like a type of stakeholder, with credibility at stake, and with both story and backstory coloring statements.[9]

The bottom line? Most lawyers can quickly identify the stakeholders to participate in a collaborative process by identifying those harmed most by the wrongdoing. However, the inclusivity required by the restorative practice requires that participation be extended more broadly, if desired. Family, friends, and community members impacted by the conflict and those bringing resources to the table should be included in the hard work to address the legal problem. Even though professionals may not be intimately engaged in the conflict, they may also be impacted by the resolution and should remain honest and transparent, as the impact of any resolution makes it impossible for them to be entirely objective. Once assembled, the expanded group of participants may work as equals to identify and meet needs and to work to right identified wrongs. A criminal case involving two neighbors demonstrates how accepting responsibility extends the capacity to make right the wrongs beyond legal remedies.

6.

One evening, Phyllis Findley asked her neighbor, Anita Graves, to drive her to Food Lion. When they arrived, Anita parked, and Phyllis, an eighty-three-year-old grandmother who did not drive, said she'd go in the store and be right back. Unbeknownst to Phyllis, Anita darted into the liquor store, picked up a fifth of vodka, and slugged it down while Phyllis was shopping.

On the way home, Anita wrecked. She totaled Phyllis' van. Phyllis remained hospitalized for over a week, suffering from a fracture and further damage to her knees and legs. I met Phyllis after her daughter Theresa called. Their biggest concern was how the medical bills would be paid. I explained insurance, medical payments coverage and liability, the crime victim's fund, and restitution. Our relationship began.

The situation necessitated three legal cases involving the civil suit, the criminal action, and the crime victim's fund application. As they progressed, I often met with Theresa and Phyllis, revisiting their needs and goals. Phyllis continued to harbor bitterness towards Anita, having been friends since childhood and feeling her trust was violated. She needed the wrongdoing to be identified and for us to try to make it right.

Their jurisdiction does not have a restorative justice program, but they were interested when I mentioned the potential for a victim-offender dialogue to Theresa and Phyllis. I contacted Anita's lawyer and explained restorative justice, describing the Victim Offender Dialogue.

People sometimes equate restorative justice with the Victim-Offender Dialogue. In this form of a dialogue, also referred to as a Victim-Offender Conference, the victim and the offender voluntarily participate in a meeting arranged and facilitated by trained facilitators. The meetings may occur at any stage of a criminal case, from before charging as part of a pre-trial diversion to years after sentencing. The purpose may be to resolve a legal issue, such as a criminal charge or potential charge, or to create an opportunity for a discussion without a focus on producing an outcome.

The public defender, Troy, approached Anita and explained this option. Since no restorative justice program was funded in the region, I recruited a trained volunteer facilitator. The court accepted Anita's guilty plea and included the Victim-Offender Dialogue as a term of her probation. Filing the civil case involving the insurance company and negotiating the Medicare lien became additional steps to create resources to fill Phyllis' unmet needs.

Following the Victim-Offender Dialogue, the volunteer facilitator, David, created a report. "Overall, the parties were direct, at times very emotional, but at all times respectful. The offender acknowledged that the accident was her fault. It was the result of her driving. She offered a straightforward apology. She said she could understand if Phyllis and Theresa would never forgive her. Phyllis said she was disappointed in Anita and could not foresee forgiving her; Theresa said she hoped she could forgive her. Victims explained how seriously the accident hurt them, putting Phyllis in constant pain. Phyllis and Theresa emphasized that the misbehavior complicated the relationship between the two families, and they made it clear that they remained fond of Anita's mother."

Phyllis needed to hug Anita's mother. That was never part of any conventional case. And all of this happened without any program, grants, or direct oversight by the court. The results extended far beyond the meeting.

Putting things right didn't end when the clerk closed the case. A few years later, the victim advocate called from the district attorney's office after receiving a check from Anita for a balance due on her restitution. The payment exceeded the amount ordered by the court, and the victim advocate needed Phyllis' current address. In restorative lawyering, restitution is no longer a box to check for the court. It becomes a way for the offender to recognize the harm and do what they can to make amends.

TABLE 6

"Thinking Like a Lawyer" vs. "Thinking Like a Restorative Lawyer":
A Comparison of Approaches

"THINKING LIKE A LAWYER"	"THINKING LIKE A RESTORATIVE LAWYER"
The lawyer extracts the facts from the client, and other sources, focusing on relevant facts.	The lawyer extracts the client's story by listening without judgment and analysis, allowing for a broad revelation of facts.
Once the facts are elicited, the lawyer applies them to the law to determine legal rights.	Once the story is told, the lawyer and client identify the needs and obligations.
Objective is to create the most believable story, the best theory of the case.	Objective is eliciting multiple narratives from client (and others) and explore how multiple narratives coexist.
Objective is to enforce a set of rights.	Objective is to meet needs and fulfill obligations.
Relationships are defined as competing rights held by participants in conflict to be managed by a third party.	Relationships are defined as a critical part of both process and outcome.
Participants in processes restricted to parties with standing and professionals.	Participants in the processes include anyone who demonstrates a stake in the outcome.

The stories from my teachers, Sam, Kevin, Finn, Mandy, and Phyllis, illustrate how Professor Zehr's five principles guide the restorative lawyer working with stakeholders, defined very broadly, to identify unmet needs and resulting obligations to make things as right as possible. In other words, these principles demonstrate how to think differently and move our work in an entirely different direction. In the succeeding chapters, we'll leave this world of theory and learning to think like a restorative lawyer and enter a world of practicing and becoming a restorative lawyer.

Chapter 6

Rules of Engagement

10 WAYS TO BEGIN IN THE RESTORATIVE PRACTICE OF LAW

Rules are not necessarily sacred, principles are.

— Franklin D. Roosevelt

I.

RULE #1: THERE ARE NO RULES FOR RESTORATIVE LAWYERING, ONLY GUIDEPOSTS THAT GIVE FORM TO PRINCIPLES.

LAWYERS LOVE RULES. Lawyers love identifying rules, informal and formal, figuring out the purpose of the rule and cultivating the nuances, and strategizing a way around them. Rules frame our expectations, serve as reminders, and provide a ceiling and a floor for our behaviors. While restorative justice looks less at consequences for breaking the rules than the harm sustained when wrongdoing occurs, I've drafted these rules to provide guidance to those seeking a more restorative legal practice.

These Rules of Engagement for the Restorative Lawyer remind me of the types of rules that direct our professional actions, such as the Rules of Civil Procedure, as well as the unwritten rules we often voluntarily follow. These rules include no sanctions and few exceptions. They articulate a way of being — a way to engage professionally with clients, counsel, courts, colleagues, and ourselves. I borrow the term: *Rules of Engagement* from the military, who use this term to describe the internal directives that define the limits of and authorization for the use of force — a fitting metaphor for guidelines to restrict lawyers from unnecessary use of adversarial processes.

These Rules of Engagement for the Restorative Lawyer may serve as a guide, as statements of consensus, and as articulated common understandings, without sanctions and coercion. In launching into a new practice guided by restorative principles, these parameters, guidelines, and informal policies provide a measure, a structure, and a framework for a new practice of law.

2.

RULE #2: LEARN TO SAY "NO" TO "NO."

"They," say lawyers, don't like change. Just look at how long we held onto Word Perfect! We are risk averse. We don't want to lose control. We don't like to be afraid. We are the first to list a myriad of reasons why "it will never work!"

During my first year of graduate school at Eastern Mennonite University's Center for Justice and Peacebuilding, Dr. Cheryl P. Talley introduced me to neuroscience in a guest lecture that provided insight into our approach to working with conflict. She introduced me to the evolutionary value of "no." As humans evolved, the presumption when deciding to do something new was to say "no" — food may be poisonous, a water source could be polluted, and a new animal may be vicious. Once safety can be determined, the "no" gives way to "yes." This impulse helped us to evolve, but it also created fear.

I am not the first observer to recognize that lawyers share a tendency to say "no" and to avoid the unknown. In *Structured Negotiations,* Lainey Feingold describes how negotiation may be hampered by lawyers who fear outcomes and are quick to say "no." Feingold claims that lawyers are trained to fear the worst and worry about the "what ifs?"[1] John Lande, in *Lawyering with Planned Early Negotiation: How You Can Get Good Results for Clients and Make Money,* describes the paralyzing fear that many lawyers feel when engaging in negotiation, observing that the prison of fear prevents lawyers from wanting to negotiate in the first place. He says the keys to the prison door involve ways to deal with the fears.[2] An anonymous law professor cited by Michele Leering in *Conceptualizing Reflective Practice for Legal Professionals* observes how detrimental fear is to the lawyer, noting that "fear and adrenaline hamper the ability of the inexperienced lawyer to practice effectively."[3]

After Dr. Talley's lecture at C.J.P., I wondered how many times I sat back in my chair during a continuing education program or a class and crossed my arms, refusing to hear anything a speaker offered about a new idea that did not fit into my paradigm. I'd listen but shake my head, cherishing what I considered a healthy dose of skepticism. Was I afraid of something new? Would an unfamiliar, original idea make me feel like I had failed a client in the past? Maybe.

But I'm finding that giving up my fears creates endless opportunities. Relying on "no" as the "go-to" response stymies growth and steals away our professional chances to find new ways to work on legal problems. I am trying to embrace a measured but fearless approach that exchanges the "it'll never work" for healthy curiosity to explore innovative ideas.

As a drama major, I took an acting course that involved a lot of improvisation. One game, "Yes, And!" requires that the improv partner accept whatever is offered and incorporate it into the improv. For example, you come onto a scene. One character sits in a chair. You say, "Hello, what's up?" as you try to gauge what is happening. The character says, "I'm here waiting for a bus." You accept the statement and build on it, "Yes, and ... I heard drivers went on strike this morning, and we'd better get an Uber." You've accepted the statement but then redirected the action.

When opposing counsel claims, "I've seen no proof that your client's neck pain was not caused by the injuries sustained 10 years ago." I don't get fearful. I don't disagree, yell, or argue. I try to find a way to address their question. "Yes, and ... did I forget to send you the M.R.I. she had a year ago?"

It's a bit of a plot twist that when we become fearless, we become capable of approaching creative and non-adversarial ways to resolve legal conflicts. I work with a friend, Paul, as co-counsel in some cases. One of our clients fell on the ice and fractured her arm at a commercial property. When the two carriers refused to negotiate, we filed the lawsuit. We slogged through formal discovery for almost two years after filing. The attorney for the insurer of the corporation that owned the building refused to negotiate. They needed more depositions, they needed more documents, and they needed more, more, more.

Fearless. Some lawyers would not have continued to try to engage opposing counsel in negotiation, early neutral case evaluation, or early mediation. They may have feared that the opposing counsel would think the plaintiff's case was weak. But we were confident in our case. During negotiations, we would show them our valuation. We may say, "yes, and ..."

Two months before the trial, after exchanging hundreds of pages of documents and having a half-dozen depositions, the defense counsel still refused to schedule mediation. Our client was sick of it and did not want to incur expenses on experts. We had a scheduling order that required mediation. I aggressively pursued getting a date on the calendar, but my opposing counsel avoided us. I emailed. I called. And then I called and called and called again. I finally reached him one night, sitting in my car in Costco's parking lot the day before Thanksgiving. Still, he refused to set the date for mediation. I drafted a "Motion to Compel Mediation" to file with the court that outlined my efforts to schedule mediation. I sent it to the opposing counsel.

Mediation occurred three weeks later. We settled for twice the amount my client had authorized me to settle for before we filed. As a restorative lawyer, when I hear about a new approach, I try to be like Paul. I avoid rushing to negatively critique the new idea and shut it down. I try to keep the brainstorming going. "Yes, and..." creates new strategies for individual cases and creates new philosophical foundations to approach our work.

Imagine the advantages if we work to be open-minded as we consider new ways of advocating for clients. Even those lawyers who excel in making adversarial, rights-based arguments may benefit from expanding their skills and the way they approach their efforts. We can avoid shutting down a new idea with "that's not right. It can't happen that way. Our clients aren't like that. Our opposing counsel isn't like that." We can give "Yes, and ..." a chance.

3.

RULE #3: IMAGINE WORKING "OUTCOME BLIND."

Driving home from a rough day filled with back-to-back mediations, I turned on the radio to hear an interview with Annie Duke. A champion-winning poker player, she described the secret to winning — making decisions "outcome-blind." To win, she focuses on the behaviors, the variables, and her choices. She claimed that otherwise, she would not win. Focusing on the process leads to a good outcome.

When I got home, I found an article interviewing Duke. In her two decades on the World Series of Poker Circuit, she met many players who "scaled the learning curve, then flattened out at mediocre." She says, "You'd see people making the same bad decisions for twenty years over and over." Duke describes the trap they fall into by judging their performance on outcomes. "If they win, it's because they made good decisions. If they lose, it's because they were unlucky."[4] Is that mentality the kiss of death for any high-stakes decision-maker in poker, business, and all areas of our lives?

The alternative she describes is an "outcome-blind" approach to decision-making as a poker player. Duke insists that all great poker players think this way. In fact, she says she had a small peer group of elite players who regularly got together and talked shop. "When we told each other 'the story of a hand,' we wouldn't mention whether we won or lost. It was all about the behaviors, the variables, the decisions — not the outcome."[5] We can learn something from these poker players. Being outcome-blind doesn't require abandoning goals or outcomes when representing clients. It demands attention to the process as we elicit a client's objectives and create a process to maximize the client's benefit. In *Legal*

Project Management, Stephen Levy brings a similar viewpoint to working on legal problems. Being process-driven, including excellent communication with clients and determining interests, creates a superior approach that increases client satisfaction.

Crime victims often come to my office when formal processes have not provided them with any resolution. The offender may have died, or the prosecuting authority refuses to file charges. We work to find a process that is healing, independent of outcome — in other words, outcome-blind. Cathleen Piper was one of those crime victims.

Between her intake notes, several interviews and the police report, I was able to piece together the tragedy that changed her life. One evening, Cathleen's ex-husband, Jamie, brought their daughter, Hanna, home after his custodial time and left Hanna, buckled in the back seat of his full-sized F-450 truck. Jamie went inside the house to find Cathleen and argued about daycare. Cathleen went outside to get Hanna. As Cathleen went to open the door to the truck, Jamie jumped into the driver's seat and peeled off quickly, dragging Cathleen fifteen feet before she fell off the sideboard onto the pavement, unconscious. She woke up in the I.C.U. a week later. She remained hospitalized for four weeks.

My strategy involved work in three spheres: filing an application with the Crime Victim's Fund to seek payment of her medical expenses, pursuing insurance claims, and determining the basis for the failure of the district attorney's office to file charges against Jamie. Much of my work occurred behind the scenes and involved paperwork. Eventually, insurance paid a significant portion of Cathleen's outstanding bills and provided compensation designed to ease her pain and suffering.

However, the Crime Victim's Fund denied the claim, and we requested a hearing. At the hearing, some of the officers who responded to the initial scene testified. Three local male police officers responded to the scene that night when Jamie dragged Cathleen down the road. One reported that the offender was "cradling"

Cathleen's head when he arrived. Another police captain decided not to charge Jamie with a crime but charged Cathleen with joyriding. Eventually, they dismissed the charges against Cathleen but never filed charges against Jamie.

Since the Crime Victim's Fund denied her claim, our appeal included a hearing, which provided me with an opportunity to cross-examine the police officers, who had a very difficult time justifying their actions. Cathleen testified about the events, her injuries, and her bills. We needed the Fund to pay future medical bills related to the incident since she was an "innocent victim of crime." The judge believed her, and she was awarded the payments.

Only one part of the case remained — Cathleen wanted to understand why Jamie was never prosecuted. We arranged a meeting with Mattie Sams, an assistant district attorney with whom I had a solid professional relationship.

~

ON THE DAY of our appointment, we meet outside and ride up the elevator to Mattie's office. She sits behind her desk, piled high with brown accordion files, listening carefully to Cathleen's story. I am relieved to hear Cathleen articulate a much more fully developed narrative, more direct, more linear, more nuanced, and more capable of locating healing within the story than the confused rambling she shared with me at our first meeting.

Mattie listens attentively. She outlines the legal basis of why the case could not be prosecuted. She recognizes that the flawed investigation contributes significantly to her decision. She apologizes and suggests that if we find new evidence, she will review it. After our hour-long visit, Cathleen and I get back into the elevator. She sighs, "I feel relieved."

~

As I PREPARED to close out Cathleen's case, I invited her into my office to discuss this long and challenging journey and mark the closure of her legal case. Cathleen spoke clearly as the articulate master's-degree-candidate that she had become. She explained how she felt from the first day we met. She no longer felt helpless. Before, she felt like no one had heard her describe this life-changing event. She says that my listening gave her hope. The resources helped her realize she could recover and that she has something to contribute to the world. Cathleen explained that the fact that the police hadn't handled her legal case properly became something she could live with after meeting with Mattie. She explained that my representation meant that she could focus on her recovery and "not worry about advocating for myself because ... recovery was hard."

Cathleen did not get a substantial personal injury award (due to policy limits). She did not get the moment when Jamie would have been handcuffed in the courtroom after a jury announced he was "guilty." She did not get the outcome she initially sought. But we focused on the behaviors and variables and made good decisions within them. Cathleen was able to find processes to help her heal.

4.

RULE #4: LISTENING IS PARAMOUNT.

Imagine this: You and your co-counsel meet with a client going through a rough time. Co-counsel repeatedly interrupts your client as he explains what matters to him most. Co-counsel tries to be helpful by explaining the law, what is "relevant," and outlining strategies. Bored and slightly irritated, you decide to conduct on-the-spot field research and tally up the talk time: the client speaks less than twenty percent of the time and the lawyer eighty percent. This is a true story.

Is healing possible when the lawyer does all the talking *about the client's problem?* Rachel Naomi Remen says, "Listening is the oldest and perhaps the most powerful tool of healing."[6] I agree. What changes does the client go through while talking, while we listen? Can those changes occur when they aren't given the opportunity to speak? To feel heard? We may know the law, but we don't know much else.

We don't know the facts that are essential to the client. We don't know what our client is feeling or thinking. We don't see how our client imagines their life in five or ten years and how this "legal problem" fits into their life story. If we don't figure out how to be silent and listen, we may never hear the client communicate their objectives in resolving the conflict.

In restorative lawyering, we listen deeply and without an agenda. We allow clients to structure their thoughts, even when they are challenging to follow. We work to discover the importance of what our clients say and how they compose their stories. We are not interrupting to get to the relevant facts quickly! One of my teachers, Judge John Michaels, claims there is no such thing as an irrelevant fact when the client talks. If the client decides that it's important enough to communicate with the lawyer, it is relevant. Listening exposes the world of possibilities for resolution — resolutions developed to give clients what they need.

A colleague, attorney Mandy Burr, understands listening. Along with her law partner and husband, Dick Burr, she has represented clients on death row in Texas for many years. Mandy describes her process as "listening to listen," not listening to "fix" someone. One afternoon, she spoke with me about this kind of listening — a listening that happens by being open and listening to gain insight — not just to hear words being spoken. Mandy experiences her need to engage in intense listening most acutely after clients on death row decide to abandon their appeals. Mandy listens to the client, re-engaging the client's connection with life. This connection develops as the client tells the story and as they are listened to without judgment.

Mandy values the impact of deep listening to clients, even when it does not impact the legal outcome of the case. She remembers one client who received a death sentence. The client did not have a lawyer before Mandy's post-conviction appointment, and her job was to develop the case to mitigate the circumstances, if possible, for the state not to execute the client.

Mandy met with the client to uncover his motives for his crime, personal history, or any means to mitigate the punishment. The client continued to insist that he had not committed the crime, the murder of his close friend. After a long series of legal proceedings, the court granted the client a new trial, and he continued to insist that he was innocent. As they were preparing for the new trial, Mandy played his recorded confession to him. The client broke down and realized he'd blocked out the entire evening. As he came to terms with what he had done, Mandy realized that her client could not bring himself to acknowledge it before that moment. She decided not to engage in a confrontational situation with him.

After the client began to accept what he had done, he wrote a letter to the victim's family to apologize. Mandy describes her experience as an attorney working with a client to provide the best representation she could. She found his revelation to be "(I)ntuitive and accidental, but it taught me you can't make assumptions about why someone denies an event. We have to listen and develop trust for those types of things to happen, but they won't happen if you don't approach people that way." Mandy describes this experience as being open as she listens to gain insight rather than for the purpose of "fixing" them.

Listening is the core of healing. One client emailed me after our first meeting. "Thank you for listening. That was the most important thing anyone has done in a long time. I took a risk (in talking) because I trust you." The next chapter will examine techniques and methods to improve our listening. We'll look at how to listen and expand the ways that lawyers listen. Listening is paramount. Listen.

5.

RULE #5: RIGHTS ARE A MEANS, NOT AN END.

"Thinking like a lawyer" often obliges lawyers to zealously enforce every identifiable right a client may have without pausing to understand how enforcing the right helps meet the client's objectives. Sara, an attorney in my community, represented a father of four young children in a divorce, taking the case over from his first attorney. The situation demonstrates a potential tension as to what rights to enforce versus what rights to leave alone to meet the client's stated interest. The mother was waiting for an organ transplant and was often too sick to care for the children during her custodial time. She'd call the father to come and care for the children until she felt better. As the mother's illness became worse, the father grew concerned about the children's long-term well-being. He hired his first lawyer to provide him with an assurance that the children would always be adequately cared for during the mother's hospitalization.

But the attorney went the usual route and filed and served pleadings. Borrowing a common term that relies on a war metaphor--the "custody battle" ensued. The mother quit calling the father for help. Everyone kept copious notes and detailed calendars. The court appointed a *Guardian Ad Litem* to interview the children, visit the homes, and submit a report to the judge. The father retained Sara, but it was too late. The court held several hearings, each one escalating the level of the conflict.

How did this strategy, this "custody battle", benefit anyone in this case? What interest did asserting every legal argument serve? Did the parties not share many interests and needs? Did the attorneys promote meeting those needs or enforcing abstract rights?

How does this tension look in other practices? As I have launched into my work as a restorative lawyer, I have learned to work within needs-based inquiries to map out criteria and strategies for resolving the client's legal problem, or what we call "the case," in all situations. After understanding the client's subjective and individual needs, legal analysis helps locate enforceable rights to fulfill those needs.

Lauren and Rose Ringer helped me to understand this tension and the potential resolution through a personal injury case. When I met with the two women in a pre-mediation meeting, they articulated that they wanted to move on from the hurt and trauma of the car accident they'd experienced. Lauren, the daughter, wanted a down payment for a house to buy with her new husband. Her mother, Rose, wanted to return to school for a career change in the next six months.

We provided bills and records to the insurance adjuster, who continued to value the case much lower than we did. Their offer to resolve the case was too low to meet Lauren and Rose's articulated financial needs.

After filing suit, the carrier's lawyer agreed to informal discovery and early mediation. This agreement was important to me since both women had personal deadlines to meet in the next six months, which increased the subjective value of an early resolution. Counsel for the carrier also agreed to early mediation and that both the party and the insurance adjustor would attend the full meeting.

∽

Lauren, Rose, and I show up for mediation at about the same time and are seated in the conference room. Defense counsel, his clients, and the claims rep arrive and sit across from us at the oversized wooden conference table. The mediator is a former judge who exclusively employs evaluative style mediation. He comes into the conference room, sits down, and does his introduction — describing the process, the location of the restroom, and confidentiality requirements. After twenty minutes, he turns to me to make our opening statement. I defer to Lauren, who has asked me for the opportunity to tell her story.

"I'm sorry. I'm nervous. But on the day of the wreck, I was driving my Toyota. It's old and not worth much, but it's all I could afford. Mom and I had been to Target to pick up some things for a birthday party. I was pulling out onto the highway and was going to turn left. I was waiting for a chance to pull out, and then the other car rear-ended me and pushed me into the road. We got hit by another vehicle. It was terrible ..."

"You know what made me really mad? The lady who hit me didn't do anything. Nothing. She didn't even get out of the car to see if my mom and I were okay. She just sat there. And that was just the beginning."

Lauren does not pause. "She didn't even call the insurance company. They didn't do anything. My car was so messed up, and I was terrified to drive it. The back end was entirely smashed up, and it had no bumper. But it was the only way to get back and forth to work, so I kept driving. And their insurance company did nothing to help me."

Rose pipes in. "It wasn't safe for my daughter to drive that way. We both were hurt pretty bad. We had to go to physical therapy and the chiropractor for months. I missed a lot of work, and really, I can't even go back to my job now." The defendants listen politely. When Rose finishes, I summarize and make a few legal points about negligence and causation that no one pays much attention to.

The mediator asks the defense counsel if he has a response. He responds to legal arguments. Ron, the defendant's husband, asks if he can speak. He looks right at Lauren and Rose. "I am so sorry you went through all of this. It is a terrible mistake, and I am sad that you had to go through it. I got to the wreck about ten minutes after it happened. And you are right; my wife was sitting in the car. She had not moved a muscle. She just sat there, staring straight ahead. I don't know if she was in shock or if she just didn't know what to do, but I had to talk her calmly out of the car and take her home. If she were right in her mind, she would have gotten out to check on you. It's not like her not to care about somebody in this kind of situation."

Lauren looks at him. "Thank you."

Ron speaks with compassion. "I'm sorry."

The defendant, Margaret Woods, looks at both women. "Really. That's true. I'm sorry."

Ron continues. "And this is the first time I ever heard about the insurance company not helping you out. We called the insurance company and reported the claim as soon as we got home that day. They did not tell us to do anything else. I'm glad you were not hurt driving your car around. That must have been scary after having just had the wreck."

Lauren still has something to say. "They didn't even offer to fix my car or get me a new one for weeks. It was too long."

"I will have to talk to my agent because that is not right. I'm sorry."

The mediator asks if anyone has anything further. I think he's slightly off his game since nothing happening today has anything to do with establishing rights based on negligence. He gets back into his stride. He escorts the defendants, the claims adjuster, and their counsel down the hall. He leaves us in the conference room, where we will remain for the balance of the mediation. The mediator will usher offers and responses back and forth to reach a resolution.

After about an hour, we reach an agreement.

〜

REFLECTING ON THIS EXPERIENCE, I recognize that we didn't base the settlement amount on probabilities or statistics, anecdotes, or guesses stemming from the clients' legal analysis of their rights. We found our settlement on what the clients needed. The plaintiffs received the amount that they sought to move on with their lives immediately. Both the plaintiffs and the defendants left the table transformed, enjoying better relationships as members of the same community and more at peace with this traumatic event that changed everyone's life. We argued Rose and Lauren's legal rights to get to the negotiation table. Once there, we could work on meeting their needs.

Does this mean that we should ignore clients' rights? No! Rights are considered, evaluated, and re-evaluated throughout the development of the case. Rights constitute part of the information we provide to the clients from the beginning as we engage them in their decision–making process.

Rights form the backbone of our laws. Rights are the means by which our government cannot become tyrannical. Rights are constructed and provide a framework for us to strive to be equals among each other. As a restorative lawyer, I am not recommending abandoning rights. Instead, I want to ensure that the level of enforcement of the right is integral to meeting the client's needs and that rights are not elevated to be superior to the people they protect.

What are the client's needs? If meeting needs is integral to enforcing legal rights, how do we identify them? Many lawyers tell me that the case's resolution is all about numbers: dollar amounts or prison sentences. Yet, these same lawyers tell me when they get the client the dollar amount or jail term, the client is not satisfied. Even when a right is identified, the needs must be identified and met while attending to the right.

A few years ago, a young woman came to see me, wanting me to enforce her right to privacy in the most fundamental way.

∽

"I TAN every week at Quick Tan Salon in Mason. A few months ago, I answered the door, and the Sheriff was standing there. He tells me that a guy who works in the same strip mall has been video-taping me in the tanning bed. We have a hearing next week." I spend about an hour with Amelia, trying to figure out how she feels and what she wants. I come away understanding that her biggest fear is that the videotape will not remain private. Her goal is that no one ever sees the tape. She feels exploited and does not want it exhibited.

On the morning of a status hearing in the case, Amelia and I ride the elevator to the third floor of the courthouse and walk down the hall lined with benches full of litigants towards the swinging double doors that lead to the courtroom. Amelia was not the only woman he photographed. Just outside the door, Heather sits on a bench, waiting for the hearing. The hearing is postponed, but Amelia, Heather, and a third victim, Brittany, hire my firm within a few weeks. Other victims also hire counsel.

This case goes on for months, and then years, and extends into many hours of meetings with our clients, the district attorney, and defense counsel. We file a civil suit against the tanning salon. We spend hours with the other victims, the insurance carrier and their attorneys, and the offender in meetings, negotiations, and mediation.

Amelia, Heather, and Brittany learn to clearly articulate their big and small goals in resolving their legal dispute. For criminal penalties, they are less interested in a lengthy incarceration period and more interested in the offender accepting responsibility, a public conviction, publication of that conviction, and sufficient conditions established to prevent him from doing this again. They also want to avoid a criminal trial since they do not want the video-tape shared with attorneys, the jury, or the public. They want everyone to agree that the videotapes be destroyed.

Their goals in the civil case are related. They do not want to have a trial, and they want the tapes destroyed. They want the offender to pay damages out of his pocket for a period of years as a reminder of the harm he caused. They welcome damages that insurance may pay, but getting the largest settlement possible is not as high a priority for these victims as their other goals.

We continue to work to meet those well-developed goals, interests, and needs. Orders are issued to destroy the videotape, and we oversee their destruction. The offender pleads guilty and is placed on probation with restrictions. The civil case is resolved with a settlement from the insurance carrier and periodic payments directly from the offender. The three women are not "made whole." However, we have worked to make things as right as possible.

〜

As IN LAUREN and Rose's case, this situation describes how an effort to enforce rights may help the restorative lawyer seek to make things as right as possible. A more extended period of incarceration or a higher sum from the insurance company may have been within their legal rights. Having identified an essential need, the destruction of the tapes, the three women resolved the legal case and the lawyers met our obligation to satisfy the clients in identifying and meeting that need.

6.

RULE #6: LET GO OF THE SEARCH FOR THE TRUTH — WORK TO CREATE OPPORTUNITIES FOR MULTIPLE COEXISTING NARRATIVES.

The established legal process allows a "finder of fact" to determine the truth after being presented with two independent theories of the case by advocates. However, most lawyers understand that our clients' narratives are complex, each containing details that coexist with discrepancies created by multiple viewpoints of the events. I remember one time when a young colleague articulated feeling frustrated upon first hearing that an adjudicatory process may not establish an objective "truth." As an assistant district attorney, I filed a petition to remove Cassidy Guttenberg, a two-year-old, from her mother, Brianna, after the child suffered second-degree burns. The Department of Social Services worker identified the pattern of the burns as consistent with abusive behaviors sometimes observed incident to toilet training. In the mid-1990s, the experts would have had no trouble establishing this fact. Brianna persisted through the initial hearing, sticking to her story that this must have been an accident. The child was temporarily placed in a foster home. After a few months, we returned to court for the adjudicatory hearing to begin the process of terminating Brianna's rights. Both sides called witnesses sufficient for the judge to adjudicate the facts necessary to determine if Cassidy was an abused child, consistent with state law.

~

THE MORNING OF THE HEARING, Brianna sits alone at a table in the courtroom, joined only by her attorney. After listening to the testimony of several social workers, a nurse, and a doctor, it's her turn. She moves to the witness stand, next to the judge's bench, and takes a seat. She raises her hand and swears to tell the truth. On direct examination from her attorney, she testifies that her father routinely provided Cassidy's care since birth. While he had physically abused Brianna throughout her life, she had no reason to believe he would harm her two-year-old daughter.

I begin my cross-examination. Brianna articulates a new story, accusing her father of scalding Cassidy when she peed her pants. She continues, and her answers are inconsistent with her prior account, creating a story of the young mother as an innocent victim, placing too much trust in her abusive parent. But I wonder if her bravery is genuine and sustainable. What has happened, as the months passed, for Brianna to distance herself from her father? Could Brianna be strong enough to keep the child away from her grandfather?

Brianna's lawyer calls another social worker, Mary Griffith, to testify. She doesn't know much, having been assigned to the case for about six weeks. She has been in Brianna's home and describes it favorably. She also testifies that Brianna bonded with Cassidy before the state placed the child in the foster home.

Jane Chattam, the child's *Guardian Ad Litem*, calls Dr. John Cavanaugh, the psychiatrist who evaluated Brianna's mental health. He testifies about her abusive upbringing, level of cooperation, limited intellectual capacity, and the lack of any other firm mental health diagnosis. As he concludes, the court looks at the clock hanging prominently on the long wall to my left.

We adjourn for lunch.

Dr. Cavanaugh joins Jane, Mary, and me for lunch at a small café near the courthouse. We sit outside and wait for our meal. We speak casually about this family, the subject of the case, and complex relationships. The young social worker, Mary, stirs her iced tea and stares at us with wide, innocent eyes. "What is the truth?"

Dr. Cavanaugh smiles and shakes his head, "the truth." Jane and I smile, but then Jane turns profoundly serious. "This is not about uncovering a truth — I don't think that's possible. We can only figure out what should happen to this child now."

Mary persists. "But I want to know the truth — did Brianna know this would happen? What happened? Who else was there?"

Dr. Cavanaugh responds, "We don't know."

❧

WE DID NOT SPEAK from an academic viewpoint. We have observed and participated in decades of litigation. Most people testify about what they see, feel, and remember. However, the evidence does not create truth. The stories about the events cannot be unified and singular. Even an omniscient viewer arrives at a story with their viewpoint, personal history, and unique interpretation of events, creating a diverse and nuanced story.

Does anyone believe that the adversarial process discovers the one narrative that comprises the "truth"? Is it possible that two or more advocates, applying trained, logical reasoning, selecting bits of pieces of a story (limited and sequenced by the rules of evidence and procedure), reveal the "truth" to a neutral finder of fact?

No. There is no absolute truth, much less one that is discoverable through an adversarial argument.

As lawyers and judges, we can listen to and respect each participant's stories in the legal process.

We can understand that narratives create a way to order, describe, and give meaning to the moments of our lives. For example, when faced with an occurrence that becomes part of a legal conflict, we can observe the participants working to integrate the parts of the event, the people, the locations, and the activities into a broader context of a vast life story. The narratives built around situations giving rise to conflict often help organize our life experiences, creating context and providing structure for analysis and decision-making. The stories become integrated into identities.

In a TED Talk recorded in 2009, author Chimamanda Ngozi Adichie introduces the idea of the "single story." She described the single story as something like a stereotype. A person living outside a community narrowly defines the people and places they inhabit through their limited, narrow observations of the community. This single story creates stereotypes that lack multiple dimensions, perspectives, and experiences. In acknowledging the danger of the single story, Adichie provides clues on where to find hope. "Stories matter. Many stories matter. Stories have been used to dispossess and malign, but they can also empower and humanize. Stories can break the dignity of a people, but they can also repair it. When we reject the single story, we regain a kind of paradise."[7] I have discovered that the danger of the single story lies not only in using the story to describe a people, but also an experience.

During my career, I have observed that the law has not created opportunities for complex narratives to be developed, respected, bridged, and integrated. Instead, each side in the adversarial process looks at the multiple narratives and creates the most believable one, consistent with the client's objectives. In other words, each advocate posits a *single story*. The challenge is to develop a theory of the case that the factfinder adopts. The theory of the case is our effort to weave the client's story into the law and create a believable story, the dominating narrative. Law professor Binny Miller describes it, "Once a case theory is selected, it serves as the centerpiece for all strategic and tactical decisions in the case."[8]

Developing the theory of the case was the centerpiece of my Trial Advocacy class in my last year of law school. We spent a semester working the case up and presenting our theory of the case to a mock jury. My partner, Mary Lee Blackman, and I drew the case of Trudy Doyle, the waitress who died from a shooting in the vestibule of a restaurant where she worked.[9]

Suicide? Murder? Our task was to convince the jury that her boyfriend, police officer Johnny Diamond, murdered her. Witnesses observed what happened before and after the shooting, but no one saw the event. In our mock trial, the jury acquitted Diamond.

The mock jury, the factfinder, believed that Trudy shot herself. The story ended. In 1986, our theory of the case about a depressed, abusive police officer shooting his girlfriend at work was not believable. We lost. His narrative became dominant, and the story of Trudy Doyle disappeared.

During this time, my third year in law school, I was already skeptical of any idea of two lawyer-gladiators battling opposing theories of the case to arrive at "the truth." I already guessed that the party with the power would create the dominant narrative, and any other part of the story would disappear. However, my understanding of the relationship between respecting multiple life experiences, stories, and becoming a restorative lawyer developed further when I had the opportunity to study with Professor Sara Cobb at the Jimmy and Roselyn Carter School for Peace and

Conflict Resolution. Professor Cobb posits that conflict narratives have weak, undeveloped plots without interaction. They wind up producing good and bad characters who are polarized. They tend to focus on the past and future, not so much on the present. In mediation, Professor Cobb tries to "rehydrate" the story — put some water on it to give it depth.

The restorative lawyer recognizes the existence of multiple stories and works to understand how they may survive alongside one another without one story being privileged. The lawyer no longer works to locate the most believable theory of the case and elevate it to be the dominant narrative. Instead, the lawyer collaborates with other lawyers, mediators, and parties to find ways for multiple narratives to define parties' identities and stories.

In my mediation training, we learned, "You can't mediate facts." In Collaborative Practice, we try to be future-focused and not dwell on differing accounts of an event that cannot be reconciled. Those lessons help the restorative lawyer look at complex stories about events in a larger context, with opportunities to bridge or weave stories together. More profound stories provide more significant opportunities for healing through the subjective reconstruction of stories that permit the integration of new information as it is discovered.

Bridging narratives joins stories together through their common ground. Even a litigator cross-examining a witness recognizes that stories have common points and elicits those during testimony. As restorative lawyers, we can find those spots early in the conflict and give those common points attention. When the stories divide, we avoid pushing them into opposite corners of the arena. Stories are not ranked. Instead, multiple narratives are developed. As restorative lawyers, we work to find methods, such as transformative mediation, to permit organic and energetic storytelling, allowing the stories to find their natural bridges and points of intersection.

In addition to creating bridges that join complex narratives, we also find opportunities for those working through legal conflicts to change their stories. As more information is learned, participants may find new ways of describing their experiences. As time passes, identities often undergo changes that are described through new, emerging narratives. Lode Walgrave, in *Restorative Justice and the Law,* discusses re-story and how "re-biographing changes the conception of the self."[10] Revising how the actor sees their experiences changes for the offender, the victim, and often everyone involved in a conflict resolution process.

Rather than single-mindedly creating a theory of the case and diligently supporting it, the restorative lawyer embraces the potential for healing and repair in relationships by encouraging the development of multiple, complex stories. The restorative lawyer recognizes four important aspects of the parties' narratives while exploring options for addressing disputes. (1) There is no single story; it is an act of power (and violence) to deconstruct multiple accounts into a singular narrative.[11] (2) Legal language can be adapted to avoid the single story or the dominant narrative. (3) We avoid creating a dominant narrative by encouraging expansive, nuanced, and integrative storytelling. (4) We become skilled in encouraging remodeling, re-storying, and repositioning, creating opportunities for bridging and weaving narratives.

7.

RULE #7: LOOK INSIDE YOUR BAGGAGE AND MAKE YOUR LEGAL PRACTICE A REFLECTIVE PRACTICE.

After I lost Ella's case, I picked my litigation strategy apart — trying to discern what I did wrong and discover what I could have done differently. For starters, when filing an action after a father killed a mother, I would ensure the mother's family had the child in their physical custody before initiating the legal proceeding. As I have endeavored to become a restorative lawyer, I've worked to expand my capacity to reflect on my work beyond trial strategy and into the essence of the work. In other words, as a restorative lawyer, I work to develop a "reflective practice." In *Zen and the Art of Motorcycle Maintenance,* Robert Persig describes the reflective life. "You look at where you're going and where you are, and it never makes sense, but then you look back at where you've been, and a pattern seems to emerge."[12]

D.A. Schon, a writer in the field of professional education, created the term "reflective practice" to describe how professionals gain awareness of their implicit knowledge and learn from their experience. Theory becomes integrated into practice so that the professional may continue to grow and learn.[13] My early lessons from Ella's case included improving my trial skills. I wanted to create better researched and articulated arguments. In other words, I wanted to master my skills within the adversarial process. Most of the lawyers I've worked with Monday-morning-quarterback cases, sometimes for years.

I propose a reflective practice for the lawyer that extends beyond individual cases and litigation strategies. I am challenging the restorative lawyer to adopt a practice encouraged by Michele Leering in *Integrated Reflective Practice: A Critical Imperative for Enhancing Legal Education and Professionalism.*"[14] A reflective practice creates room for personal and professional growth. We move beyond asking ourselves, "Okay, I did this thing or that thing today ... did it go where I wanted it to ... Did I pick the right arguments? Could someone else have been a better witness?"

Instead of focusing on how to be a better adversarial advocate, the restorative lawyer identifies their values and determines how the work promotes those values. The restorative lawyer reflects on their thoughts and feelings about their work. We consider the emotions and concerns of our clients, their families, and their communities. Leering describes reflective practice by using a metaphor that describes the hand as representing the practical/technical reflection (skills), the head, for the critical reflection (knowledge), and the heart, for the self-reflection (values.)[15] This metaphor helps to appreciate the broad reflective practice of the restorative lawyer — moving beyond evaluating our skills and knowledge into considering our values.

About twenty years after Ella's case, I represented Evan and Louise Warren, another family whose daughter was murdered by her husband. We filed the petition for them to retain custody of their granddaughter, Emma. I learned that reflecting on my work in an adversarial process requires me to examine my arguments, my values, and my attention to my relationships during the legal proceeding.

~

THIS COURTHOUSE WAS BUILT in 1836 and reconstructed in 1871. Producers selected it for a set in the Civil War movie, "Gods and Generals." The courtroom is huge, the bench high, the well of the court spacious. Spectators sit on long pews at graduated elevations behind the well of the court. You could easily fit 200 or 300 spectators in those pews.

But this is a child neglect proceeding, and the only spectators are family members. We arrive and take our assigned seats. Like Ella's case, I'm still outnumbered. But this time, the children's court-appointed attorney sits at my table. Norman, the defendant, his family, his criminal lawyer, the custody lawyer, and an intern sit at the other table. The bailiff comes in, "All rise." The lawyers all do a half squat as the judge comes in for a motions hearing.

I doodle on the top of my legal pad and watch to see how Louise is doing. We have agreed that the expert may testify by telephone. The judge dials from the speaker telephone on the bench. It doesn't work. Judge McDougal asks us to move to his chambers for the call. We stand up and walk to a carved wooden door behind the bench. I am preoccupied, focusing on the questions to ask this potential expert witness. I look up as Louise and Norman come through the doorway side by side. Louise looks pale and faint. She stands inches away from the man who had, months earlier, murdered her daughter.

I miss it, too focused on my legal strategy and anticipating my questions. I fail as Louise's advocate, too busy being her lawyer. Afterward, I reflect on this experience and learn from it: hand, head, and heart. While my reflective practice was young that day, it was engaged. And this reflective practice propelled me to create this book. My reflection revealed the shortcomings I experienced in the "law as lived." These reflections build the course of study for me to become a restorative lawyer.

~

When I first read about reflective practice, I had to "say no to no." I wanted nothing to do with it. It seemed full of pitfalls. I had concerns. Fears. Would it be easy to fall into a trap and become self-absorbed in our practices, in ourselves? Would this self-absorbed approach benefit clients? Would my "critical thinking" background as an attorney cause me to be too harsh on myself? But, as a restorative lawyer, we find room for a small part of the day to include positive, healthy reflection on the work and find that reflective contemplation creates a vital building block of the restorative practice.

My reflective practice has become habitual, intentional, and has extended my awareness of what's happening within and around me, as well as inside the institutions. The restorative lawyer will accept those "disorienting dilemmas" (concrete and theoretical things that challenge our experiences and assumptions.)[16] The reflective practice requires diligence and focus and may be tethered to something concrete and routine. Some journal, others meditate, exercise, or find ways to think broadly about their work. The reflective practice for us, as restorative lawyers, demands that we examine where we are in our practices and where we might be able to go with our clients, our colleagues, and our communities.

8.

RULE #8: YOU CAN'T IGNORE TRAUMA.

As restorative lawyers striving to meet clients' needs, we should understand a few things about trauma. We should be able to consider our client's experiences of trauma when we are working with them. Most clients have experienced trauma, sometimes in the events that bring them to us.[17] We provide legal services in a way that is accessible and appropriate to the person who has experienced trauma. We learn about trauma-informed care to decrease the potential of triggering or exacerbating trauma symptoms or retraumatizing our clients. Trauma-informed practices change our thinking from "what is wrong with this individual" to "what happened to this individual." When I began my legal career working with legal services, no one was talking about trauma awareness. One evening I was working late, alone in the same office where I first met Ella.

≈

SITTING at my desk in deep concentration, I sense someone coming in. I look up. Zuri stands in the middle of the room. She is a skinny woman with thick blond hair, wearing tight jeans and high-top Reebok sneakers.

"Can I help you?"

"Thank you." Still standing, she hands me a petition filed by her mother. She stares at me with a wide-eyed, scared expression as I read. I skim the petition; she still stares. The paragraphs allege that Zuri's boyfriend abused her son. I read a few paragraphs of the petition aloud.

"Petitioner asserts that the Respondent has failed to protect said child, to-wit: she has exposed him to a live-in boyfriend, Larry

Martin, who has recently been released after serving a period of incarceration for a series of violent attacks."

"What's going on? Do you know anything about this?"

Zuri's eyes gloss over. She disengages from our conversation and then, nearly catatonic, speaks. Softly, she describes in detail how Larry Martin lives in her house. She tells me that he stripped the boy naked, abused him, then held him into the air and dropped him, ritualistically, on his head. As she ends the story, she stares off into space.

I listen. My mind actively engaged, thinking about my legal strategy to regain custody. I know how to do that. But I do not know what to do with this catatonic woman. Intuitively, I ask her, "Has anyone ever hurt you?" She continues staring but grows more intense and looks off in the distance. Her full body begins to tremble. Through her whispers, she tells her story of being physically and sexually abused throughout her childhood. I have no idea how to help her continue to describe her traumatic upbringing in a safe, protected way.

I ask Zuri if it's okay for me to call my friend, a counselor, and she nods her head. I call Becca who coaches me through the interview. Zuri moves through the past and into the details of her current situation. She shares sufficient facts for me to draft a responsive legal pleading.

∼

I FILED THE RESPONSE, and Zuri began working with a counselor. A few weeks later, she moved into a new apartment without her boyfriend. A few months later, her son came to live with her.

It would be another twenty years before I would begin to understand that listening to Zuri's story challenged me to understand her trauma and how to begin her recovery. Eventually, I would find additional training and education on how to approach legal representation while being mindful of a client's experience of trauma.

It would also be twenty years before I would begin to understand that listening to Zuri's story and being engaged in her recovery exposed me to tertiary trauma. Dr. Cheryl Talley, the professor who introduced me to our neurological response to say "no" also explained tertiary trauma. Many professionals, such as lawyers, experience secondary trauma when working with clients to address legal problems, often related to the client's experiences of trauma. Dr. Tally described a study involving rats where scientists followed biological measures of two rats in a physical fight alongside those of a rat witnessing the event. The chemical changes of the witness rat indicated the witness suffered a more substantial neurological response to observing the trauma than the rats engaged in the physical fight. Additional research and programs with Pauline Tesler and Laura van Dernoot Lipsky provided me with insight into how to respond in a restorative way to our client's trauma and our experience of secondary trauma.[18]

Restorative practices, by focusing on building relationships, collaboration, and working to meet needs, potentially create a proactive and healthy response to secondary trauma experiences. The practices provide ways to hear the traumatic experiences of clients and incorporate our understanding within our strategies to resolve the legal problem. Counselors-at-law never substitute for mental health therapy, but the trauma-informed practice of law positively impacts our lives, including our work.

9.

RULE #9: MAKE SURE YOUR LIGHT IS FULL BEFORE YOU DECIDE TO SHINE IT.

On an afternoon in late summer 2020, watching a webinar produced by the American Shakespeare Theater, "Perhaps My

Protest Looks Different," I discovered another teacher. Addressing the challenges of being an outspoken dissident and organizer, speaker Bria Samoné Henderson reminded me of the importance of caring for ourselves. She said she makes "sure my light is full before I decide to shine it."[19] The term *restorative lawyer* expands beyond using restorative processes and practices in our legal work to heal the client, the victim, the offender, and the community. It also stands for using restorative measures to sustain us, making sure our light is full.

Since I graduated from law school in 1987, I've read the reports published in many state bar magazines about colleagues being sanctioned and disbarred for missing deadlines, court hearings, and other derelictions that could be attributed to being overextended, experiencing depression, or abusing alcohol. One autumn after I had been out of law school for over thirty years, the toll our work can take hit home. Three lawyers whom I've had close relationships with during my career died. Two of them were barely fifty years of age. One was just under sixty. None of them had heart disease or cancer or were in accidents. The three drank too much, and they died too soon.[20]

During the past few years, I have worked with Elliot Hicks, a colleague who shares both my experience of grief in losing colleagues and a desire to create systemic reform to help prevent further losses. We conduct workshops on the "Art and Science of Lawyer Well-being."[21] We explore opportunities for incremental changes, consistent with restorative principles and values, to improve lawyer wellness. They involve four easily identifiable areas that are particularly relevant to the restorative lawyer: (1) Using collaborative, problem-solving approaches to reduce the fight-flight-freeze response, (2) Appreciating natural empathic responses, (3) Valuing relationships, and (4) Creating work that feels rewarding and is consistent with personal values.

A collaborative, problem-solving focus helps eliminate fight-flight-freeze responses at work. During a typical day at the office, it is not unusual for a lawyer to face multiple situations that trigger the response. A client blames you for failing to inform them of an outcome properly. Opposing counsel sends a threatening email because you did not return a call. A quick telephone hearing triggers stress when an argument for sanctions is made, and you can't be sure that you provided requisite notice.

Fear triggers a primitive fight-flight-freeze response in animals. The reaction is necessary for self-preservation when animals are threatened by predators or other dangers. People have the same neurological primitive reaction when triggered. Fear creates an anxious state, ready to defend or retreat from our position. In this state, the amygdala part of the brain guides the quick decision to create safety. The full cognitive abilities of the prefrontal cortex are not engaged. In the practice of law, stress often artificially triggers the response, and many lawyers enter a cycle that may be difficult to escape. Overeating, drinking, and other negative responses result from prolonged engagement in the fight-flight-freeze response.

When we work collaboratively with multiple stakeholders to jointly seek resolutions to legal problems and conflicts, the fight-flight-freeze response is less likely to be triggered. Staying in the calm, rational prefrontal cortex of our brains increases our ability for creative and rational responses.[22] Lawyers who commit to using a less adversarial approach to resolve legal problems may make better decisions as well as enjoy an improved sense of well-being.

Working collaboratively also creates opportunities for better by honoring our natural empathic responses towards compassion and empathy. Contrary to some economic theories, substantial contemporary evidence suggests that people are inherently compassionate.[23] Like some mental health professionals, lawyers are impacted by empathically engaging with clients experiencing pain and trauma. Failing to recognize that takes a toll on mental health and may create further stress, anxiety, and discord for lawyers. Additionally, lawyers may naturally experience empathy for other parties or witnesses. The adversarial approach then demands that attorneys act contrary to those natural empathic responses, creating additional stressful biological reactions impacting emotional and physical health. The restorative lawyer recognizes and respects the empathic responses to clients, opposing parties, and witnesses and creates opportunities to reduce harm resulting from that response by working compassionately and cooperatively.

In contrast to restorative justice, the adversarial approach to conflict tends to minimize the importance of creating and maintaining good relationships. We often develop a destructive way of interacting with opposing parties and opposing counsel. This pattern impedes relationships with our colleagues, family, and friends. Lawyers Pauline Tesler and Louise Phipps Senft have written extensively about the importance of relationships to lawyer wellness. Millions of years of evolution have required that people rely upon one another, facilitating reliance by building alliances and creating interpersonal bonds. Without deep, constructive relationships, people often fail to thrive in almost any community. Lawyers who cultivate transactional successes over developing positive connections inevitably damage healthy, valuable relationships at work and at home.

The restorative approach provides opportunities to increase the lawyers' health and well-being by providing a means for work to be rewarding. In the restorative practice, lawyers may feel less anxiety when they bring the same values to their lives at home and work. Work becomes satisfying and enjoyable when the lawyer switches from the adversarial, competitive approach to a broader relationship-building and problem-solving style to resolve conflict and promote healing.

10.

RULE #10: LEGAL PROBLEMS ARE NOT COMMODITIES, AND NEITHER ARE THE LAWYERS WHO WORK TO RESOLVE THEM.

The restorative lawyer collaborates with clients to identify harm, objectives, and needs. The work often involves finding the best process to heal the harm and repair relationships. People and their experiences are not commodities. The restorative lawyer does not approach a legal problem as something holding financial value to be maximized. What does a practice look like when a client is not a commodity? What happens when suffering is not analyzed as an entity for which we must maximize economic value, but instead as a harm to heal? Sandy Carter and her son Russ came to see me after a neighborhood dog bit Russ' son, Ashton.

∽

ON THIS RAINY, gloomy day, we meet in a small, cramped, conference room. Russ sits across from me. He seems detached. Sandy stands behind him while we talk. I wonder if Sandy is an overbearing mother/grandmother. I study their dynamic, trying to figure out the parties' interests. This may take time. Sandy talks a lot and describes her relationship with her grandson. His mother died several years ago, and Russ relies on Sandy to take care of Ashton.

As we talk, we delineate immediate needs. I'll start by verifying that the dog has vaccines. We'll contact county animal control officers to protect future victims. Next, we will locate the insurance carrier and identify sources for payment for medical bills. We outline Ashton's medical treatment with Russ and Sandy and detail options for payment. We decide to wait until the child is emotionally and physically healed before filing a lawsuit.

~

SINCE THIS JURISDICTION permits a child to reach eighteen before the statute of limitations begins to run, our timeline extends for a few years. I worked to build a relationship with Sandy, Russ, and Ashton. The needs shifted and changed when Russ died unexpectedly. Sandy decided to adopt Ashton, who continued his life-long healing journey after losing both parents and suffering the trauma of the dog-bite as a child.

We gathered supplemental medical information and made a demand to the insurance company and the parties. Everyone ignored us. We persisted. As Ashton's 18th birthday approached, I scheduled a meeting to create a strategy to finish his "dog-bite case." We created a budget, projecting how he might best allocate the proceeds from a potential settlement, concentrating on maximizing his educational opportunities.

A few months after we settled for the amount available under the insurance policy in the case, I saw Sandy, and she let me know that Ashton was doing well, going to community college and preparing to transfer to finish an engineering degree at a university. For me, Sandy, Russ, and Ashton were never "the dog-bite case." Their case was never treated as a potential policy-limit product for me to cash in on. Like all families, this family had needs that I worked to meet, using the skills of the restorative lawyer.

Clients (and their legal conflicts) are NOT commodities. They are people, not objects or injuries, that can be defined, boxed, valued, and traded. We cannot negotiate the value of our clients' suffering. Instead, they engage us as individuals with unmet needs. Although our system establishes criteria to place dollar amounts on clients' injuries, that process does not convert the clients, or their hardships, into a commodity. The restorative lawyer does not trade in pain.

Lawyers and the minutes and hours of our days are also not commodities. The afternoon in my first year of law school when my husband returned from the bookstore with Duncan Kennedy's book *Legal Education: Reproduction of a Hierarchy* raised so many questions. Could a company consider employees commodities? Could a law firm describe the attorneys as assets or inventory?

Law school creates lawyers who too often become machines, tools for the law firm to exploit for profit. The billable hour turns lawyers into things of economic value. A senior partner at a large law firm, Jana Cohen Barbe, published an open letter saying:

> Billable hours and revenue generation are the two key metrics in how law firms compensate attorneys. ... Partners, including the most senior, ... have billable-hour targets, and their compensation may rise or fall with the achievement or missing of those targets.... The pressure — to work seven days a week, to miss family events, to forgo vacations, to miss needed doctor's appointments — cannot be overstated. We feel guilty taking a Saturday or Sunday off, and it takes several days to let go of the guilt and begin to feel the relaxing effects of a vacation.[24]

In the modern practice of law, lawyers, clients and the conflicts that become cases can be assessed by the amount of money they generate. The restorative lawyer may work to develop financial resources sufficient to maintain a healthy law practice, while concurrently never losing sight of the fact that people are people. Not commodities. Not products.

These Ten Rules of Engagement describe a few ways to bring restorative principles and values to our work. They can be a convenient way to remind ourselves of how we can strive daily to create a better way to advocate for our clients. While they begin to describe some of the hands-on ways we are changing the practice of law, the next section of this book will describe concrete skills, methods, and techniques that any lawyer may include within their practice to make it more restorative.

10 Rules of Engagement for the Restorative Lawyer

RULE #1:
There Are No Rules for Restorative Lawyering.
Only Guideposts That Give Form to Principles.

RULE #2:
Learn to Say "No" to "No."

RULE #3:
Imagine Working "Outcome Blind."

RULE #4:
Listening Is Paramount.

RULE #5:
Rights Are a Means, Not an End.

RULE #6:
Let Go of the Search for the Truth.
Work to Create Opportunities for Multiple Coexisting Narratives.

RULE #7:
Look Inside Your Baggage and Make Your Legal Practice a Reflective Practice.

RULE #8:
You Can't Ignore Trauma.

RULE #9:
Make Sure Your Light Is Full Before You Decide to Shine It.

RULE #10:
Legal Problems Are Not Commodities, and Neither Are the Lawyers Who Work to Resolve Them.

Chapter 7

Approaches and Methods for the Restorative Lawyer

MATERIALIZING A NEW WORLDVIEW

Healing is an art. It takes time, it takes practice, it takes love.

— Pavana Reddy, *Rangoli*

I.

WHAT IS GETTING in the way of creating a new, healing practice of law? Lawyers might be stuck in old habits, perfecting the skills gained in formal education. We approach legal problems "thinking like a lawyer." We use the settled procedures we know to move our cases through a system. We approach resolving legal problems with the mindset we learn early in our career, in law school, or from our mentors. This theoretical approach emphasizes rules, rights, and punishments. In this chapter, we will explore changing the approach to legal conflicts by exploring methods developed by several innovative conflict resolution scholars and practitioners that align with restorative justice principles and values. Law school indoctrinates students to prioritize methods based on the assumption that adversarial argument produces truth and that rights are allocated based on the dominating narrative. Those methods include legal analysis, trial, and appellate advocacy. The restorative lawyer expands those methods to embrace the potential for proven approaches, such as Nonviolent Communication and Legal Project Management, to help frame the practice.

2.

Chapters Two and Three detailed how principles and values create a theoretical framework to approach wrongdoing and conflict with healing. This chapter explores the approaches and methods a restorative lawyer may engage when collaborating with a client to resolve a legal problem.

Several modern approaches to conflict resolution and the practice of law provide specific methods for the restorative lawyer. Legal Project Management, Nonviolent Communication, interest-based negotiation, narrative theory of conflict, Collaborative Practice, and Strategic Negotiation create specific approaches that allow for integrating restorative justice principles and values into the practice of law.

LEGAL PROJECT MANAGEMENT

Legal Project Management by Steven B. Levy goes beyond a "we'll do whatever it takes" approach to working on a legal problem to a more strategic process that maximizes communication to identify and meet the client's goals. The approach that underpins project management emphasizes the necessity of effective communication while the lawyer focuses on a client's needs and goals.

NONVIOLENT COMMUNICATION

The restorative law practice regards communication broadly, beyond oral and written advocacy. Restorative lawyers speak and write from a communication base consistent with that identified by Marshall B. Rosenberg as Nonviolent Communication (NVC). NVC is a way to communicate in "both speaking and listening — that leads us to give from the heart, connect us with ourselves and with each other in a way that allows our natural compassion to flourish (referring)... to our natural state of compassion when violence has subsided from the heart."[1] NVC creates opportunities for lawyers to communicate in ways that promote compassion for clients, opposing parties, and those in our working community. Rosenberg emphasizes that the carefully considered language in NVC promotes the opportunities to communicate in a way that demonstrates our shared values. "It allows space to abandon blame, judgment, and domination and creates dialogue that promotes healing and reconciliation ... Nonviolent Communication provides guidance for lawyers who are trying to learn how to communicate not just for advocacy, but for relationship, empathy and compassion."[2] Adjusting from adversarial and analytical communication to values-based communication provides the restorative lawyer with a foundation for the collaborative relationships central to the restorative practice.

INTEREST-BASED NEGOTIATION

Another key method of the restorative lawyer borrows from an approach to negotiation that moves away from an adversarial, "winner take all" viewpoint in conflict. Interest-based negotiation, also referred to as integrated bargaining or win-win bargaining, requires that parties collaborate to find solutions by creating mutually beneficial agreements to meet their underlying interests rather than their positions. This approach, first articulated by Roger Fisher and William Ury in *Getting to Yes*, creates one way for the restorative lawyer to approach the conflict with an agenda not focused on identifying rights and opposing parties, rather, working first to identify the stakeholder's interests that are often tied to needs. Identifying these interests and the unmet needs is at the heart of restorative lawyering.

NARRATIVE THEORY OF CONFLICT

Narrative Theory of Conflict is a way to approach legal conflicts that explores thinking of a legal problem as one of multiple stories that need to be integrated rather than the one story that needs to be elevated. This approach accepts that multiple stories exist in every conflict. Professor Sara Cobb posits that within the "narrative" framework, conflicts take shape as competing stories, each trying to delegitimize the other. In a restorative practice, providing a respectful and collaborative process elicits multiple narratives to allow potentially divergent stories to develop concurrently, creating opportunities to find common ground within the stories.

COLLABORATIVE PRACTICE

In the restorative practice, we may adopt elements of Collaborative Practice. This method, developed in 1990 by family law attorney Stuart Webb, approaches the legal problem by creating a team of specially trained counsel, mental health professionals, and financial experts to work with the parties to resolve the legal problem without court involvement. This approach brings those most impacted by the conflict to the table. It provides them with sufficient resources to define the conflict, broadly explore options, and develop an acceptable and durable agreement. Critics of Collaborative Practice cite qualities of the process that are inconsistent with restorative justice values and principles. Those include extensive involvement of professionals, processes that exclude stakeholders, and the high cost of the process. While Collaborative Practice may create situational power imbalances and structural inequality between stakeholders and experts, we may borrow the collaborative nature and needs-based viewpoint that Collaborative Practice provides.

STRATEGIC NEGOTIATIONS

Strategic negotiation approaches legal conflicts by bringing the stakeholders and their advocates, often in civil litigation, together to maximize creativity and generate mutually advantageous options to resolve the conflict. Created by attorney Lainey Feingold in her litigation practice, Strategic Negotiation invites all parties and their counsel to the negotiation table in a structured process framed by specific procedural steps and agreements. Strategic Negotiation employs some of the same tools as the collaborative approach. Full disclosure, open communication, and mutual problem solving are integral to creating mutually acceptable resolutions.

These six concrete approaches can bring restorative processes into the practice of law. The restorative lawyer approaches the practice ready to address "cases" as problems or conflicts that have created needs and interests to be met. We replace rigid exclusionary processes with ones that expand the participants to include stakeholders and resources in a respectful and collaborative process. These approaches, both independently and collectively, support specific methods that guide the restorative lawyer in the everyday practice of law.

TABLE 7

Some Alternative Approaches to Conflict Resolution and Their Role in Restorative Lawyering

CONVENTIONAL LEGAL APPROACH	ALTERNATIVE APPROACH	RESTORATIVE LAWYER'S APPROACH
"Working a case up" often requires exploring theories without defining a specific outcome (goal) with the client.	Levy (LPM): Practice of working with a team to define success criteria and attain specific goals.	The lawyer identifies unmet needs of clients, family, community, and impacted parties and helps to frame them as goals. Strategizes how to meet them.
Communication is a tool for persuasion.	Rosenberg (NVC): Communication (nonviolent) promotes connection, relationship, and equitable sharing of resources.	Communication can be part of the process. It provides means to improve relationships and create healing.
Negotiation is about convincing the other party that you are right and getting "more" in the process.	Fisher & Ury (interest-based negotiation): Negotiation requires determining all underlying interests and exploring options to meet them.	In any negotiation, a lawyer should understand all parties' needs and interests. They should try to meet them--creating opportunities for healing.
The job of the lawyer is to determine the most viable story and convince the fact finder, creating a dominant narrative.	Cobb (narrative theory): Conflicts can be addressed through allowing fully developed stories to be bridged or braided together.	The lawyer should allow for the development of multiple stories and work within them to find ways to create healing and meet needs.
The adversarial system requires that each lawyer create the best argument and convince a third party to prevail.	Webb (collaborative): People with a legal problem can be cognizant of their rights and work with an advocate to create an optimal resolution for all impacted.	The lawyer collaborates with those impacted by a conflict or legal problem to produce an optimal outcome and process while maintaining loyalty to the client. The lawyer shares knowledge about how legal rights are implicated.
Civil cases are best resolved through litigation (even if they do not go to trial) where multiple procedural options create safeguards and increase opportunities for the client's advantage.	Feingold: Negotiation is possible without litigation. Negotiation can involve expansive informal discovery and collaboration that may produce superior outcomes than litigation.	The lawyer should (with clients) broadly examine before choosing a process to resolve a legal conflict. They should consider all factors important to the client, the financial cost, and the damage to relationships with each process.

3.

The six approaches described in this chapter are not incorporated into the typical methods lawyers learn in law school. Law schools teach legal methods such as "methods of persuasion," "methods of statutory drafting and interpretation," "legal theory," and "problem-solving for lawyers." For example, Lewis and Clark Law School offers a Legal Methods Course as a two-week class to introduce the American Legal System. The program includes these objectives:

> [L]earn how to read, analyze, and apply case law and statutes; explore the development of American legal institutions, investigate the changing styles of legal analysis of American jurists, assess the role of judges and legislatures in the legal system, discuss the role of ethics and professionalism in the legal community and acquire the skills essential to their work in other law school classes.[3]

These methods include some essential to the restorative practice of law, such as understanding institutions, judges, and legislatures and reflecting on ethics and professionalism. "Yes, and ..." We broaden these conventional legal methods to expand our ability to meet the client's interests and needs, to make right the wrongs, and to heal.

This chapter delineates implementing the new practice by sketching out how these six approaches support four critical methods to create a restorative way to resolve legal problems. The methods include (1) Comprehensive, respectful, and strategic communications that expand relationships, (2) Identification of interests, needs, and goals, (3) Negotiation to meet the interests of all stakeholders, and (4) Creation of opportunities to develop complex narratives capable of reconciliation.

4.

The primary method for the restorative practice requires taking steps to ensure "quality and quantity" in all communication. What does this method look like? I've relied on both Levy and Rosenberg to inform the legal methods for communications within our new practice. Levy reminds us, "Clients aren't mushrooms. You can't expect a good outcome by keeping them in the dark and occasionally shoveling some you know what over them."[4] The restorative lawyer intentionally and mindfully approaches communication to create an environment and relationship to meet the client's needs. Many lawyers are too tied up in legal questions and institutions to honor this foundation's importance, which is central to restorative lawyering. Mr. and Mrs. Gordon were two court-referred mediation clients who reminded me of who drives the car in legal proceedings.

∼

ON AN ORDINARY AFTERNOON, Calisa and David Gordon walk in together, interacting pleasantly. I find it odd that the court ordered them to mediation. In this jurisdiction, judges only order mediation in contested custody cases and require that the mediation occur at the courthouse. This couple seems amicable. They sit down and we talk. I like to start custody mediations with a casual conversation to become acquainted rather than a "he said" or "she said" account of positions.

"Tell me about your son. What kind of child is he? What does he like to do? Does he have a schedule?" They respond together, excitedly describing their nine-month-old, who just started sleeping through the night and can say "mama" and "dada." Calisa changes the subject. "We don't disagree about the baby. We just want a divorce. We had pretty much reached an agreement, and the lawyers wrote up our papers. We drove to our court hearing together, went inside, got through security, and signed in with a deputy outside the courtroom."

David jumps in. "Then, our attorneys came out of a room, and her attorney took Calisa off. I wasn't sure where they went. My attorney took me to a room. She went over everything about my pension and selling the house and told me we couldn't get an agreement today because we had too many issues. She told me we'd have to get some documents and records and ..."

"My attorney was saying a lot of the same thing," Calisa continues, nodding. "I just wanted to get this over with. She told me I couldn't agree with anything and that I shouldn't give up full custody. When I told her what we wanted to do, she told me this was just a temporary hearing, and I couldn't talk in court. It went on until someone knocked on the door and told us the judge was ready. When I walked into the courtroom, David sat next to his lawyer, looking at the floor."

"The judge came out and asked the attorneys a lot of questions. Calisa's lawyer said she was fighting me for full custody. This was the first time I'd heard of this. I thought we had an agreement before we got there. I felt like Calisa seriously blindsided me. My attorney kept arguing with Calisa's lawyer. The judge said he referred the case to mediation."

"I was as surprised as you, David. I couldn't believe you backed out of our agreement. I trusted you! I just want to do what we agreed to — but it sounded like you changed your mind. I tried to whisper to my lawyer to tell her about the agreement, but she wouldn't listen to me." Calisa looks at me sincerely," What can we do to get our attorneys to listen to us?"

∽

I FELT ashamed of my profession. Both attorneys had good reputations as advocates, but what are they advocating for? Mr. and Ms. Gordon met with their lawyers once before their hearing and then briefly in the attorney conference room before the hearing. The lawyers did not listen, understand their client's needs, or hear their goals. The lawyers saw no need to answer the parties' questions or conduct the investigations necessary to advise the clients during their first meetings. The parties did not feel like they were moving in any way to resolve the conflict at this stage. They simply skipped to the next stage of the proceedings. They created an alternative narrative. The argument created skepticism and distrust in Calisa and David. Levy says, "In the absence of a story people will make up their own — inaccurately and unfavorably."[5]

The Gordons' lawyers failed to advocate for their clients' needs because they had never discussed them. Unmet needs and client goals can only be deciphered with excellent communication — both in quality and quantity. The restorative lawyer should develop a method of communication that relies on the groundwork laid by Levy in *Legal Project Management* and Rosenberg in *Nonviolent Communication*. Quantity requires more than sporadic short meetings or monthly emails. Levy observes that many lawyers provide clients with paper copies of everything, monthly summaries, and a bill. It's not enough. "Good communication, however, means more than status reports delivered with monthly bills or chargeback statements."[6] To avoid that situation, Levy recommends we circulate weekly or bi-weekly progress reports that include goals for the representation. I regularly schedule telephone, video, and office appointments to update clients about their cases. If we have no events to report, the time can be used to build our relationship.

The Gordons' lawyers also failed in the quality of communication. They didn't listen. They failed to employ a comprehensive communication method that places value on openness and understanding and rejects judgment-focused communication. Marshall Rosenberg's Nonviolent Communication provides specific guidance for the lawyer who wants to do more. NVC creates the opportunity to allow for observation, identification of feelings and needs, integration, and articulation of requests. Rosenberg also emphasizes the importance of non-verbal communication. The method of communication promoted by NVC, and central to restorative lawyering, rests on the assumption that we work to restrict our speaking to thoughtful, intentional, and necessary speech. The communication methods embraced by Levy and Rosenberg blend seamlessly with one value adopted by the restorative lawyer: respect.

One lawyer in our community, Tony Britland, provides an excellent example of communication methods to avoid. Soon after I started graduate school, two clients made appointments with me after meeting with Tony involving injuries they sustained in car accidents. Peggy and Mandy didn't know one another, but they both reported that he cussed at them, called them names, didn't listen to them, and tried to bully them into doing something with their cases they didn't want to do. The pattern described by Peggy and Mandy reminds me of what it feels like for a client to be on the other end of disrespect.

Tony provides an extreme example of how not to approach work as a restorative lawyer. However, I have heard reports of comparable behaviors, including feeling pressured to settle a case by my colleagues. Unlike Tony, the restorative lawyer creates comprehensive communication methods within the practice to optimize relationship opportunities, discover unmet needs and interests, and find ways to heal through communication. For the restorative lawyer, communication becomes a cornerstone that holds up our practice, not an afterthought. We can expand upon the methods articulated by Levy and created by Rosenberg as they easily integrate with restorative values and principles.

5.

Another critical method in the restorative approach to a legal problem aims to focus on the harm and resulting needs in an effort to put things right by identifying and reaching client goals. Levy in *Legal Project Management* recommends that rather than saying, "I'll do whatever it takes," when we accept a matter for representation, we say, "I ask what they and we need to be successful, and what they would spend to achieve that goal. I will ensure that all work we do furthers that goal. I'll still do whatever it takes, but only on work that moves the ball toward the goal."[7]

Levy recognizes that clients may articulate that their goal is to settle the case for a lot of money or get as short of a sentence as possible. Levy advocates for lawyers to do more than focus on numbers, and to identify problem-solving goals.

> Client legal goals can be simplistic at times. You're often providing legal services, either directly or indirectly through in-house intermediaries, to a business department whose leaders have little skill in legal matters. Imagine a client who commissions a new house from an architect by saying, 'Create something nice for my family for $X and call me when it's done.' Yet attorneys hear similar requests on a regular basis.[8]

The restorative methods include locating needs and establishing goals to meet them. Without clearly identified goals, clients may drift aimlessly through their cases. How can we expect someone to be satisfied with an outcome when we never set objective criteria to evaluate a resolution? How can a parent be pleased with a negotiated parenting plan when we never agreed on the overriding objective? Chad Hammond taught me to look beyond the numbers to what might be achievable when resolving a claim involving numbers.

When I represented Chad, I had never heard of "Legal Project Management." Despite frequent visits with Chad, we never developed a "done" statement. We followed the usual course when he completed his medical treatment; we requested bills and records and sent the demand to the insurance company, setting forth our case. I anticipated that I would get as much money as I could for him. I assumed that would make Chad happy. Once the claims representative reviewed the demand, we started negotiating. His medical bills totaled about $7000.00, primarily for evaluations and chiropractic care. At that time, our best guess for our jurisdiction was that the case might settle for about $18,000.00 to $22,000.00. Chad stopped by the office one morning, slightly disheveled, suggesting he had something urgent to discuss with me. He did not sit down right away. He stopped at my doorway as he often did when he stopped by unannounced.

∾

"I REVIEWED the letter you sent to the insurance company. Thank you. It was good."

Feeling slightly proud of the demand letter I drafted, I smile, "Thank you. Would you like to sit down?" I gesture at the chair across the table, and Chad sits down.

"But one thing. How much longer is this going to take?" I feel disappointed — I thought we would have a short social visit today. But I get this question often from clients when they feel that settlement is imminent. Chad continues. "I feel fine, really. Dr. Reynolds is good, and I haven't had any issues for over a year. I want this over with. I still have some bills and want to get them paid."

Although we've gone over it before, I explain the process of making the demand on the insurance carrier and determining if a resolution can be negotiated. "At this point, we are in negotiations with the insurance company and will do everything we can to maximize their offer. If they are out of the ballpark of what your case should be worth, we need to file a complaint and proceed. It's hard to tell what they'll do, but I don't want you to sell yourself short. You've been through a lot, and you deserve to be compensated."

"Ms. Waugh, I understand. You are trying to get me as much as you can. But I want you to know something. Since the wreck, it's been terrible. I got laid off from my job — it didn't have anything to do with the case, they eliminated many positions."

I know about this. We talked about it when it happened. This is the first I've heard that he has not gotten back to work. "That sounds like it has been a big hardship."

"Yes. I'm a year behind in house payments. I'm not good with money and missed some payments even before getting laid off. I got a notice about foreclosure." He reaches into his pocket, hands me a document confirming what he told me, and sets forth the process to bring the payment current. I know that if he lost this house, he would not be able to have the credit resources to get a new house for years.

I read the document and noticed Chad rubbing his forehead, looking down. "That's not all." He sighs. My wife doesn't even know about this. And my uncle is sick." Chad looks out the window. "He needs the money ... and well ... I borrowed some money, about $2000.00, from him just after the wreck. I feel terrible that I haven't repaid him. He can't work and ..."

He trails off. I think he's about to cry. "What can I do?"

Thinking about how clients get their money and blow through it in a few weeks frustrates me. I also hate it when they don't get what they deserve because they need money immediately. I worry that some clients had to settle cases for less than their value due to economic hardship. At the same time, I see that this is neither my case nor my position to evaluate the timing or the value of the settlement to him.

"Let's do this. Let's look at what you need to get your house back on track and repay your uncle. We can create a budget. We can try to reduce the liens on your settlement and have you net enough to cover the budget." His expression changes.

"What do I do about this notice?"

"I'll call the lender. I suspect that they don't want to foreclose on you. I'll see if I can negotiate more time and make this work."

"Is that possible? Really?"

"I don't know. But we can try."

❧

CHAD TAUGHT me how to create a "done" statement without judgment and without importing my values. After this exchange, I learned to ask questions and find ways to attach value to the settlement beyond dollars and cents. What are you going to do with the settlement? How might that make your life better? How will it make it better five years from now? Where do you feel the losses from the wreck? Can anything help you regain some of what you've lost?

We worked up a budget for Chad. To pay his bills and make his mortgage current, he needed to net $8000.00. I called to negotiate reductions in outstanding liens for the insurance that paid his medical bills. I called his mortgage holder and negotiated a reduced total payment required to bring his account current. I looked outside the settlement proceeds to locate additional value.

Using the "done" statement to meet a client's subjective needs still raises my hackles. Is it fair? Will we settle for less than what I think the case is worth? Would the settlement amount differ for a client who didn't need money to meet basic needs? Could a verdict at trial be higher? However, I remind myself of Chad and consider what parts of decision-making belong to the client. Chad's life was the one most impacted by the decision, and I needed to accept that.

Was Chad satisfied with the outcome? A few months after we finished the case, I opened my email. "Thank you for all your help. You don't know the depth of gratitude I have. You are very good at what you do. :)" The restorative practice of law requires the lawyer to identify that "done" statement in collaboration with the client, and then work to meet it. Only after getting the "done" statement can the lawyer engage in the hard work to meet unmet needs and truly make right any wrongs.

6.

When we work to determine the "done" for clients, we concurrently identify needs and interests — both forming the foundation of a key negotiation method for the restorative lawyer — "win-win" negotiations. Many lawyers fancy themselves as good negotiators when they perceive themselves as bullying the other side to get their way. A good negotiator creates an engaging argument and further employs multiple strategic methods to reach identified goals. Negotiation is not an afterthought, not a raw talent that you are born with, not a quick chat in the hallway, a quick email, or a five-minute phone call. This casual, simplistic approach to negotiation often results in a tit-for-tat argument.

The value of determining interests and goals before engaging in negotiations is often apparent in disputes between parents regarding their custodial schedules. For example, I mediated a parenting plan for two parents who worked weekdays in the hospitality industry with unpredictable and demanding schedules. The father, a naive negotiator, agreed that the preschool selected by the mother would be suitable. Then, he told me he would not allow her to select the school unless she traded him another overnight. Given their unpredictable schedules, it was impossible to carve out another overnight when the father was not working.

This type of bargaining may be suitable at a flea market. Entirely transactional, the demand focuses only on a tiny aspect of the full conflict. It's a fixed pie: for one person to gain anything, the other must lose something. I don't fault the father for his simplistic view of negotiation. However, I am surprised and disappointed when fellow attorneys' skills are limited to the same shallow bargaining method the father employed with his custodial schedule.

It often looks like this: Lawyer #1 calls Lawyer #2 to make an offer, accompanied by a well-reasoned and articulated argument. Opposing counsel dismisses the offer as absurd and makes a counteroffer, articulating a good enough counterargument. Lawyer #1 moves the resolution number closer to Lawyer #2's proposal and reiterates their argument. In each round, the lawyers run their numbers closer together and articulate their arguments louder.

They sprinkle in a threat or two and eventually agree on a number. It might be the eve of a court-imposed deadline, like a trial. Everyone feels relieved the thing is finally over. This is the least sophisticated and most ineffective way to negotiate. It is a zero-sum game — in other words, for one person to move closer to their goal, the other moves away from theirs.

Since about ninety-eight percent of civil cases filed eventually settle before trial (often assisted by a mediator), negotiation is the usual pathway to resolution. Negotiations also drive the case through the process. Whether those negotiations are with a client about when to schedule an appointment, with "opposing counsel" about a discovery issue, or with the court reporter about producing a transcript, we negotiate to move the case along.[9]

The restorative practice of law approaches negotiation using the methods of integrated bargaining. The lawyer negotiates with an understanding of the harm, needs, interests, goals, and positions of clients, the other party, and impacted bystanders. We cultivate a free exchange of information (or potential evidence) between the lawyers. With that information, we deliberately create a strategy, considering the environment and process for the negotiation. In creating the blueprint, we consider outcomes and variables. When should the first negotiation be timed? Will a preliminary discussion pave the way? Can it be in person? By video? How can that discussion be most useful in understanding parties' harms, needs, interests, and goals? How do we avoid positional bargaining and look for a win-win solution?

We put the same energy and thought into negotiating as we might into any important event in the case, such as a procedural hearing or deposition. Having created a plan, we use interest-based negotiation methods to work towards the client's goals. However, the restorative lawyer's negotiation method is not limited to interest-based negotiation.

7.

Discerning the parties' interests, framing goals, and unearthing complex stories are fundamental steps in negotiation. How might the parents in the example with hospitality industry jobs negotiate if they had a more skilled approach to negotiation? What if they understood that interest-based negotiation produces better results than distributive bargaining? Developed by Robert Fisher and William Ury and described in *Getting to Yes*, "win-win" negotiation looks beyond the numbers and the interests of the parties to negotiate from shared interests.[10] Fisher and Ury suggest that negotiators need to look beyond position and determine the underlying interests that fuel the position. Once determining the interest, we may brainstorm options to meet those interests, often for mutual gain. In evaluating those options, Fisher and Ury recommend we determine the best (BATNA), worst (WATNA), and most likely (MLATNA) alternatives to reaching an agreement through negotiation.

Students are often introduced to interest-based negotiation through the Ugli orange role play, encouraging participants to ascertain interests before engaging in negotiation. In the scenario, three participants assume roles acting out a conflict over a rare produce, the Ugli orange. The owner wants to maximize profit on this limited number of oranges in this year's crop. A scientist needs an entire year's supply of oranges because the rinds contain material to neutralize nerve gas. A third participant has developed a serum from orange juice to treat a severe disease requiring the crop's entire yield for sufficient juice to make the serum. In the role play, all participants will get what they need only if they discover that one needs the pulp and the other needs the peel.

When I first participated in this role play at the Center for Justice and Peacebuilding, I thought back to another role play in my academic journey. In law school, we assume the role of attorney in several courses. The first one was during my first year. Unlike the role play with the Ugli orange that provided context for the dispute, this law school Moot Court simulation assigned us to act as opposing counsel in an appellate argument and provided no opportunity to consider the dispute other than as two competing legal arguments. (Moot Court reminds me of a galloping headless horseman. The legal argument becomes the body roaming about without guidance about the stories, interests, or goals embedded in the conflict's past and future.) Our professor assigned my friend, Janelle Jones, as my opposing counsel. We privately rehearsed our argument one evening in an empty law school classroom. We position ourselves at podiums, holding tight to carefully researched briefs and notecards. We stand on either side of an elevated platform in this classroom with stadium-style seating.

~

WE LOOK out into the imaginary audience, seated in tiers. Janelle begins, "May it please the court. Janelle Jones, counsel for the plaintiffs, Center City. Our clients contend that the lower court did not err when they ruled that (1) the taking of the plaintiffs' land was authorized under chapter 132 of the General Statutes; (2) economic development constitutes a valid public use under the takings clauses of the state and federal constitutions, and that these takings will sufficiently benefit the public and bear reasonable assurances of future public use; (3) the delegation of the eminent domain power to the development corporation was not unconstitutional; (4) the taking of the plaintiffs' land on parcel 3 was reasonably necessary to the development plan; and (5) the development corporation, by allowing a private social club, but not the plaintiffs' properties to remain on parcel 3, did not violate the plaintiffs' federal and state constitutional rights to equal protection of the laws."[11]

It's my turn, "Brenda Waugh on behalf of the property owners, Mark C. Mayhugh and Mary D. Robinson. We contend that the trial court improperly concluded that: (1) the condemnation of the plaintiffs' properties on parcel 4A was not reasonably necessary to accomplish the development plan; and (2) the city's general power to widen and alter its roadways did not justify the taking of the plaintiffs' properties on parcel 4A."

I get about halfway through my argument and suddenly feel the weight of the first year of law school and hear how absurd this jargon sounds. I've studied the role-play facts and the appellate opinions from several jurisdictions, and I am confused. It feels like the real problem in this community is obscured by the appellate decisions controlling this outcome. I pause, imagining a process creating a structured conversation between stakeholders articulating their interests in lieu of this appellate argument.

Janelle stands at her podium. Apparently, she shares my frustration with this exercise. She reaches behind her and picks up a piece of chalk sitting in the tray below a blackboard. She throws it forcefully to the cinderblock wall at the back of the classroom. The chalk shatters. She smiles.

I look behind me and see chalk piled up. I think about the two of us competing in this argument so that the judges may decide who is most persuasive. I grab a piece and throw it hard, delighting that it shatters like Janelle's chalk.

Janelle looks behind her, smiles at me, picks up another piece, and hurls it to the back of the room, aiming a bit higher. The pieces fall to the floor.

Trying to make this appellate argument feels frustrating. I've spent weeks combing through Westlaw and reading cases, but I just want to talk with the parties. However, that's not part of the assignment. We can't find a way for the city to create the park while meeting the property owners' interests. We focus only on the skill of appellate argument without context. I pick up a handful of chalk and throw it. The pieces shatter.

Janelle picks up the rest of the chalk behind her and tosses it at once.

We both laugh uncontrollably until we finally run out of chalk. We've thrown it all at the wall and watched it shatter. We suspend our practice argument, clean up the mess, turn the lights off, and leave.

～

MY MEMORIES of the actual Moot Court argument are less vivid, but my frustration at participating in this disjointed process has persisted. Law students should be aware that all role plays replicate real-life conflicts. The tasks of learning and practicing advocacy skills should reside within contexts of conflicts, even as young lawyers strengthen their ability to create oral and written arguments. The restorative practice does not divorce the context of the party's dispute from the process of resolving it. We persist in striving to identify and satisfy what matters to the parties experiencing the conflict.

Divorcing the context, as we learned in the appellate exercise problem, removes opportunities to negotiate. I suspect this context was as important in the case involving the property owners and the park development as in the case I mediated with the parents working in the hospitality industry who shared underlying interests and needs. With interest-based negotiation, the dialogue and resolutions may terminate any need to explore the appellate argument. Would the children benefit from deep relationships with both parents? How can the children maximize their time with both parents? How can they minimize the time spent in childcare?

Levy understands the critical role of identifying interests in the context of Legal Project Management. Levy says lawyers often claim to understand the client's interest but confuse those interests with positions. He explains, "... Clients have interests that are often stated as positions. It's up to you as a project manager to dig behind those positions to understand their interests. Once you understand their interests, it is a lot easier to negotiate your way to common ground, to help them see how your interests ... align with theirs – or to modify your interests to attain better alignment."[12] Levy advocates avoiding being bogged down in advocating positions and directs lawyers to "focus on solving the client's business, alongside the legal issues."[13]

Unlike interest-based negotiation, fixed pie or zero-sum negotiation assumes that each side must give up something to meet in the middle. If you agree that legal conflicts involve a fixed dollar sum to distribute, all you can do is split the compromise. At least it's fair — we all lose the same amount. I've heard judges and mediators say, "I did a good job, everyone is unhappy." But what if everyone can be happy? Can we consider what the parties value beyond what is contained within a "fixed pie?"

Recall the Ugli orange exercise. Suppose the negotiators agreed to meet in the middle and split the difference. Everyone gets one-half of the oranges. Both sides fail to secure sufficient material to accomplish their purpose. The seller receives less proceeds from the sale. Everyone loses. Interest-based negotiation, on the other hand, requires negotiators to determine what is valuable to the stakeholders — creating value. That value expands what's on the table to negotiate. When the rinds and juice are sold separately and meet the needs of both buyers, they can manufacture the product and the seller maximizes their gain.

When I work with families on custody matters in mediation or Collaborative Practice, we figure out how to celebrate holidays. With less time to uncover interests, judges often divide the children's time during the holidays between the parents by alternating holidays on even and odd years.

This is a compromise; everybody wins and everybody loses.

Instead, we approach the holiday schedule considering interests. We discover that Mom's extended family doesn't celebrate Thanksgiving, but Christmas morning is a big deal. Dad's family goes to church and opens gifts on Christmas Eve. Suddenly, no one must compromise. Dad has the children with him on Thanksgiving and Christmas Eve, and Mom every Christmas Day. Both parties' interests in having their children enjoy extended families during these important times are met.

Another critical tool for negotiation requires identifying consequences if we do not reach an agreement. I have this conversation with clients, co-counsel, and other stakeholders early and often. We locate the client's BATNA, WATNA, and MLATNA.[14] In my restorative practice, I don't limit the alternatives to those directly associated with the conflict, such as a dollar figure. We identify tangible and intangible impacts of when and how the conflict is resolved.

Incorporating interest-based negotiation methods into the restorative practice maximizes opportunities to meet clients' needs as we satisfy their interests. What is the difference between needs and interests? Are needs simply very powerful interests? Does meeting the interests and needs minimize conflict? An academic who explored this topic, New Zealand diplomat John Wear Burton, created a theory that conflicts arise when individual or group needs are threatened, such as fundamental needs like identity, security, recognition, or equal participation. The conflict may be reduced or resolved if the needs are identified and accommodated. Under Burton's theory, needs are fundamental and greater than simple interests.[15] My client, Reagan McCallister, taught me the importance of meeting fundamental needs such as security, participation, and recognition. Reagan came to see me about the same time as the now-infamous Rolling Stone exposé of a sexual assault of a young woman by fraternity members on a university campus.

∾

REAGAN SITS down across the table from me. She is a composed, confident young woman. She talks about her hometown and characterizes the years she's attended the university as a happy time. That is, until she experienced the event that changed her life.

She details an evening of partying that ended when a popular student-athlete sexually assaulted her. Reagan explains that she had been drinking heavily. Despite months in counseling, she feels responsible.

As we talk, Reagan articulates two actions that the university took that are unbearable. The university had failed to create a resolution to prevent her from running into the assailant in student housing or classroom buildings. She missed a semester of classes after the assault but continues to be responsible for student loans incurred during that period, and those she continues to require in completing her degree. She explains, however, that she doesn't want to wind up like "Julie," the young woman in the Rolling Stone exposé. We create a proposal to resolve the legal problem without exposing her to exploitation by local media. We explore options for the best atmosphere for her to finish her degree.

⁓

WHEN COUNSEL for the university failed to take our proposal seriously, I forwarded the civil complaint to the attorney before filing it. Finally, they seriously engaged in negotiations. Reagan's interests were satisfied without filing a lawsuit. She received a full report on the offender's status and the agreements reached that postponed his return to school until after her graduation. The university refunded some of her tuition from prior semesters and waived all future tuition and fees. Reagan regained control over her education and her life by doing the difficult work of examining the harm she sustained and creating the best response possible for her. The resolution addressed both her interests and needs. The situation was made right, as much as possible, and Reagan was able to finish her education and begin her career in social work.

8.

Sometimes, interest-based negotiation may not provide the best approach. Broad-based negotiation methods, such as a narrative theory of conflict, create one potential framework to evaluate options when interest-based negotiation fails. Often, we realize we must change tracks when a client indicates that their identity is at the center of the dispute. The client may say, "I'm her mother." "It's like this because I'm the supervisor." Identity cannot be negotiated. For example, one's identity as a parent, complete with cultural assumptions about that role, illustrates the necessity to explore additional approaches.

~

COLE AND JESSICA TOMPKINS come to my office one afternoon after the court ordered them to mediate their contested custody matter. After we review the agreement to mediate and talk a little about their five-year-old daughter, Emily, I start working to identify their respective underlying interests when each filed petitions to have what they referred to as "sole custody."[16] Jessica seems to want Emily to live with Cole during the school year, but she hesitates. She waffles back and forth during the conversation, saying she'll agree and then saying she won't. We decide to return to mediation a few days later.

Jessica articulates her position over and over. Emily should be with her during the school year and visit Cole on weekends. Her position is that the child will do better in school if she lives in one household. At the same time, she tells me that her interest in Emily being happy and safe would be satisfied if Emily lived with Cole and his parents. When the time comes, Jessica cannot commit to permitting Emily to live with Cole during the year. I struggle to determine how to meet the needs she articulates and suspect that something else is at play.

Basic human needs are more than having optimal childcare and include recognition and respect of identity. When Jessica articulates her position, she concurrently reconciles her identity as a mother with a young child sleeping at Cole's on weeknights. Culturally, we define mothers in a certain way in the United States. While Jessica thinks it's okay for Emily to stay overnight during the week with Cole, she cannot reconcile it with her identity, as imagined in contemporary western culture, as a good parent.

~

What does that mean for the lawyer who is trying to negotiate but is hindered by the issue of identity? We dig deeper – beyond position, beyond interest – and work to uncover identity and values. We employ a multi-faceted negotiation method that identifies and meets interests but also includes methods to reconcile divergent narratives, often manifested in stories about identity. Those stories need time to develop, to be told, and to be shared.

9.

I've found that creating opportunities to reconcile divergent narratives requires digging a client out of their (often) well-worn narrative. Usually, by the time clients come to see a lawyer, they have been living with their story for a while. They may be entrenched in it. Like an old road, they traveled the well-worn story so often that it becomes deeper, less malleable. Locating the underlying rich and nuanced narrative may create opportunities to find potential coexisting stories.

The restorative lawyer explores the potential of narrative by respecting the story. We resist our impulse to reshape it to create a single narrative – our theory of the case. We engage in legal analysis that broadens rather than restricts the story. We avoid stripping the client's narrative of detail, "irrelevant" storylines, and complex characters that may all provide opportunities to bridge conflicting narratives. The restorative lawyer respects the healing capacity of storytelling. By opening up the narratives, we maximize opportunities for parties in the conflict to experience wrongs being made right.

In Jessica and Cole's mediation, I tried to create an environment for them to tell their complex stories, full of nuances and common ground. I avoid starting mediation with a he-said-she-said structure that immediately pits two narratives against one another. That approach replicates what we see in courtrooms, immediately placing the parties on opposite sides of a "v." Finding another way to begin the storytelling can be as simple as starting the meeting with a question, "Since you've separated, can you tell me what's worked for you?" This question produces rich stories filled with experiences and details that increase opportunities for re-story and reconciling the narratives.

Bridging narratives is not limited to parties who have a long-standing relationship. Chapter Four examined the mediation that resolved the car accident case involving Lauren and Rose Ringer. Lauren told the story at mediation. After their wreck, they lived with a narrative that the defendants didn't care about them or their suffering. When Lauren told her story, she emphasized her frustration with the defendant failing to get out of her car to check on her after the wreck. She was angry that the insurance company didn't promptly repair or replace her car. When the defendant's husband told his story, I saw multiple narratives emerge. When he arrived after the wreck, the defendant was still sitting in her car, catatonic and unable to get out from the sheer shock of what had happened. The defendant's husband explained that he called the insurance company to report the wreck the same day and had no idea why it took them so long. Both apologized.

These parties were permitted to tell their full, nuanced stories. We listened without imposing an agenda and without endeavoring to manipulate the stories to fit into a theory of the case. I watched how Lauren and Rose took this new information and found ways to integrate it into their narrative. The two stories, once existing in isolation, became interwoven. Within the nuanced details, we found opportunities for the stories to coexist — the very act of talking and listening provided healing.

Clients' storytelling concurrently affords an opportunity to be heard and to explore locations for narrative integrations. Sara Cobb explains how a similar approach can be employed as a mediator during an interview with Julian Portilla for Beyond Intractability, recorded in 2003.

> My goal was the evolution of narrative such that they are different than they were when they came in. And they are less pancaked and everybody is legitimized. My goal is not agreements. My goal is not fixing anything, not helping people reach consensus. However, I do focus on the evolution of the narratives and the formulation of summaries. These then provide the platform for documenting the legitimacy of all the folks involved and people figure out what they are going to do. I have the same kind of fabulous success rate that all mediators have usually. Mine's well over 80%, which is the industry standard. In fact, I would say that I've maybe had very few instances where things haven't worked.[17]

Creating opportunities to hear a client's full story provides the restorative lawyer with the resources necessary to create a negotiation strategy that can address the client's needs and interests while going a step further to account for issues impacting identity and reconciling divergent narratives.

10.

Restorative lawyers can borrow from well-articulated methods to develop an approach to legal problems consistent with restorative justice. These include Legal Project Management, Nonviolent Communication, Collaborative Practice, narrative theory, and Strategic Negotiation. Each of these approaches also integrates procedures in a way I have found to create a methodical and structured process for legal representation. These methods overlap with restorative values in several areas:

1. Development of comprehensive, respectful, and strategic communications that expand relationships.
2. Identification of interests, needs, and goals.
3. Negotiation to meet the interests of all stakeholders.
4. Creation of opportunities for the recognition of complex narratives that may be reconciled.

I integrated aspects of each of these methods, and the strategies behind them, when I met with my client, Rebecca Downey, one afternoon.

∿

REBECCA DOWNEY DROPS into the office to discuss her case. We are negotiating with opposing counsel before starting formal discovery. Defense counsel has provided me with a formal response to our demand. Rebecca and I review the legal arguments he has raised. The questions center on the cause of Rebecca's injuries and propose that she undergo an Independent Medical Examination (IME). The defendant has asserted that some fault should be attributed to the client.

Rebecca and I worked together on a case a few years ago unrelated to this one and we have an excellent relationship. We talk about these issues and some family problems unrelated to her injuries. Then, Rebecca turns back to her case and tells me that she doesn't want an IME and would not be getting any further surgery. We talk for an hour about what the resolution of this case means to her. She talks about her husband's terminal illness, her son's special needs, and her daughter's college costs.

She tells me her dream is to own a house.

I listen and cannot help but feel that I want to help Rebecca create a life that works for her, especially after her husband passes. Her goal is not to go to trial and get as much money as possible. She wants her bills paid and a down payment for a house. She has delivered my marching orders. I will prepare for my next meeting with defense counsel to determine how to meet Rebecca's needs while concurrently fulfilling my full duties in representing a client in our legal system. I want to know, and I want Rebecca to know, that I am not looking at her tragedy as my payday. I do not view Rebecca as an isolated victim of tragedy. I see her as a complete person with dreams and hopes for her future. Can we make them come true?

～

CHAPTER EIGHT WILL PROVIDE FURTHER detailed ways to incorporate restorative justice's values and principles into any legal practice. Looking beyond the method, we'll examine the techniques and skills the restorative lawyer may use to help clients reach their goals.

Chapter 8

Techniques, Skills, and Strategies For the Restorative Lawyer

NOTES, LESSONS, AND TIPS FROM THE ROAD

We're trying to train a skill, but what we really need to be training is a state of mind.

— Steven Kotler, Jamie Wheal, *Stealing Fire*

1.

HAVING DESCRIBED the principles and values, rules, approaches, and methods of the restorative practice of law, we can now detail the required skills and specific techniques to support and implement the practice. However, I want to proceed with caution. These skills cannot be trained unless they are supported by both an understanding of the principles and values, along with the approaches and methods for the restorative practice. In other words, the skills must not only be learned but also lived.

A restorative practice of law requires expanded skills beyond those mastered in most conventional legal practices. Six are essential to implementing restorative values in the practice of law.

- Employ strategies to select the best medium for communication.
- Become a polylingual listener (both in person and in writing).
- Get the hang of story listening more than storytelling.
- Become versed in "Re" not "Di" when responding to almost anything.
- Understand how to create environments to help improve outcomes.
- Skillfully evaluate needs.

2.

EMPLOY STRATEGIES TO SELECT THE BEST MEDIUM FOR COMMUNICATION.

When we communicate, we should think about it. Plan it out. Be intentional. Be strategic. We should ask ourselves several questions. "What are the best means to communicate on this issue?

How may I best assure the speaker that they have been heard? How may I invite reframing or reweaving of the narrative?" When working to develop the client's goals at the outset of a case — would a personal meeting be best? When negotiating a resolution of a small or large issue with opposing counsel — is exchanging thirty phone messages and emails the best way to communicate? Would a scheduled in-person or video meeting be more efficient?

TABLE 8

Comparison of Some Communication Forms

METHOD	ADVANTAGES	DISADVANTAGES	BEST USE
In-person in comfortable, private location.	Keeps participants out of "Fight or flight" mode. Chance to confirm listening. Secure.	Can be logistically difficult to arrange.	Best for decision making, goal setting, and listening.
In person at a less comfortable location (courthouse or jail).	Improved listening since non-verbal communication is included. May be private.	May be a stressful environment.	Use when no better in-person alternative is available. Allows for spontaneous or urgent discussions.
Video conference-with camera and audio.	Enables participation from multiple locations. Accommodates health, safety, or logistical concerns.	May present access or privacy issues. Environment may be uncontrolled or distracting.	Good substitute for in-person communication when physical meetings are not feasible.
Telephone	Convenient and quick to arrange.	Lacks non-verbal communication and cues for conversational flow.	Arranging longer meetings. Last resort for discussing significant matters when visual communications are logistically impossible.
Email and Snail Mail	Convenient and provides a written record. Communication is available after hours.	No ability to listen. Response tends to be centered on author.	Scheduling. Confirming. Short status or updates.
Social Media (Facebook, Twitter, Instagram)	Convenient. Quick. Easily accessible.	No privacy. Lacks potential for dialogue.	Limited use for quick updates. May be faster than other means.

Restorative lawyers identify and master multiple communication methods and strategically pick the best means to relate and receive information while concurrently building relationships with clients and opposing counsel. This table summarizes ways we may communicate, identifying the advantages and disadvantages of each.

A good example of failing to select the best medium for communication is email. Shooting emails off without a target can be as damaging as shooting arrows into the wild. The sender does not know the location or condition of the recipient. Email may efficiently schedule meetings, send reminders, or provide for a routine check-in. However, email fails to create a free exchange of information, confirm that the speaker has been heard, generate mutually beneficial ideas, or create opportunities for re-story or reframing.

The body of an email I was copied on sent by my co-counsel Mark in a civil case nearing a trial date demonstrates email's shortcomings to communicate.

> Rob: I had talked with you by phone previously and then sent you messages about the mediation Judge Stevens ordered we undertake in this case. The last of those (on April 27) is attached here. As with so many other things, it has gone without response from you. Now I have your "Plaintiff's Motion to Extend Time for Depositions and Expert Disclosure," which also ignores the mediation requirement.
>
> We are still holding Monday, May 15, for the mediation we had tentatively set, and which date Bob Parsons told us earlier he had available, but I have still heard nothing from you. Now, with only 1 week to go and other unrelated matters pressing, we are going to have to release the "held" date if we are not going to proceed. Therefore, if we don't hear otherwise from you by the close of business today, I will presume that we are NOT going to mediate on May 15. —MARK

Imagine Mark's email as a telephone call (or, even better, as a lunch meeting). A conversation may permit us to understand what is underneath Rob's reluctance to schedule mediation. Why does he need more time? Is it a stall tactic, or is something happening with the parties? Counsel? By refraining from snarky comments that may make the sender feel better for a few minutes, we are more likely to understand interests, better negotiate, and strengthen the relationship.

To determine the best medium for communication, start by identifying the purpose for contacting the other person. What are the goals of the participants? Where and how can these best be accommodated? When all communication is intentional and strategic, the potential to create relationships and identify needs expands the potential for solving the legal problem. Otherwise, we communicate without a strategy, often situated in a personal, emotional discourse that rarely promotes a client's objectives. For example, Mark's email included his remark, "as with so many things, it has gone without response from you." This comment did not strategically further the professional relationship or the client's interests.

The restorative lawyer should recognize the optimal use of written communication to best create legal documents. Lawyers necessarily rely on formal written communications such as pleadings and responses to discovery requests. Written communication also effectively memorializes a conversation and provides time to select words and tone carefully. When we decide that written communication is the superior way to communicate, Nonviolent Communication techniques should be employed, focusing more on meeting needs and less on making judgments and blaming. Writing ceases to be a means to position or grandstand and is more an invitation to confirm our understandings and to communicate further.

In strategizing to select the best means of communication, the restorative lawyer is mindful of the intention of the communication and selects the means and tone in conformity with that intention. The key is to approach every communication purposefully and methodically, following well-developed steps and maintaining a focus on the long-term potential outcomes.

3.

BECOME A POLYLINGUAL LISTENER — BOTH IN PERSON AND IN WRITING.

As I described in the Rules of Engagement, listening is paramount. Just as many skilled communicators may be able to speak and understand many languages, lawyers learn to listen in different forms — or become polylingual listeners. One way to examine lawyer listening is to consider six modes of listening restorative lawyers strive to master. They include adversarial, ana-strategic, active, reflective, empathic, and universal listening. Each form requires reactions in both written and oral communications.

ADVERSARIAL LISTENING

Every lawyer reading this paragraph is probably skilled in adversarial listening. Lawyers listen to find the weakness in the story, find the deficiencies in the argument, or challenge the assumptions that underpin the theory of the case. A client's narrative, seen through the theory of the case, forms a backdrop. Advocates match the two positions, confronting the opposing viewpoint's perceived weaknesses. The restorative lawyer masters the skill of adversarial listening in the practice but recognizes the limitations. If only two percent of cases are going to trial — why should this type of listening dominate our work?

ANA-STRATEGIC LISTENING

Every lawyer reading this paragraph is also skilled in analytical and strategic listening. Lawyers analyze everything: statutes, cases, and clients' stories. At the same time, they integrate that analysis with how to strategize best to win. Ana-strategic listening dominates the first meeting with a client as we ferret out facts that may be "relevant" within the confines of the law and decide if they support a sound theory of the case. Lawyers may interrupt a speaker to get immediate clarification. "What county?" "Do you have photos?" "What did he say then?" This language of listening provides an essential base for building a legal case, but we often engage in it too early and too often. Ana-strategic listening continues to be a building block in legal analysis but works alongside deeper listening that creates opportunities for healing and relationship development, upon which the restorative lawyer depends. Ana-strategic is only one of the listening-languages for the restorative lawyer to master.

RESPONSE ORIENTED LISTENING

When listening is engaged primarily to prepare a response, the communication may not be effective for most of the work of the restorative lawyer. This is the type of listening when we listen to determine how we might relate to what the speaker is saying and then respond by comparing or contributing a story to demonstrate that the speaker has been heard. Response oriented listening moves the focus from the speaker to the listener. It may be effective in an interview or in limited circumstances to demonstrate that the listener shares an experience. The restorative lawyer should be cautious about employing listening to focus on a response, since the focus moves from the client to the lawyer, making it more difficult to ascertain the client's needs and goals.

ACTIVE LISTENING

Active listening dominates the work of many mental health professionals. The restorative practice of law broadens the lawyer's listening spectrum into this territory: open, deep, and non-judgmental listening. The listener fully engages with the speaker — avoiding looking at the phone, computer, or anywhere other than the speaker. Unlike ana-strategic listening, the speaker is not interrupted. The listener concentrates on what the speaker is saying rather than how the listener may respond. The listener may nod in agreement and should remain attentive to the speaker, sending an implicit message that the speaker is heard.[1]

REFLECTIVE LISTENING

The barista at Starbucks depends on reflective listening. Remember the last time you heard someone order a skinny dry decaf mocha cap, hold the whip, and the barista repeated, "Skinny, dry, decaf, mocha cap, no whip?" The consumer immediately knew that the barista understood what the speaker intended. This confirmation is equally effective for lawyers in communications with clients, opposing counsel, and even judges.

One way to demonstrate or reflect on what we've heard is to use something a little trite but still works for some people: "What I hear you saying is ..." I prefer something like, "I think I have this right — let me check ..." I try to recount what the speaker has articulated, using a combination of my own words and those the speaker used.

Asking for confirmation on what has been heard is not a new skill for trial lawyers. They often repeat comments made by a witness during cross-examination. But the motivation in that context is not to assure the speaker they have been heard, but instead to confirm details sufficient to prevent the narrator from changing the story. In restorative lawyering, we expand our reflective listening skills to confirm that we have it right, assure the speaker they have been heard, and allow them to correct or modify their comments.

After spending hours studying and practicing reflective listening, I find that I nonetheless easily lapse into comfortable habits, trying to expedite or direct a conversation rather than assure the speaker that they have been heard. I struggled during a mediation with Michael and Kate Roper.

∾

THE MEDIATION STARTS EARLY in the afternoon, and the parents sit at the glass conference table in my office. We talk about what is working in their custodial arrangement and what makes their children thrive. They describe their children and their needs regarding schedules and activities. They describe their jobs and work schedules. One works as a nurse, and the other is employed as an Emergency Medical Technician, creating a demanding routine that limits his opportunities to provide childcare.

I sketch out a few typical families' parenting schedules, and they seem to understand them. However, as we talk, Michael's voice becomes louder. He taps his fingers nervously on the glass table. He keeps complaining that he does not understand why he can't have more custodial time. I feel frustrated that he doesn't understand the limits of his work schedule.

Finally, I realize he does not think I've heard his factual representation of his work routine and his deep desire to spend time with the kids. I stop with the schedules and look directly at Michael. I repeat everything he said about his work schedule limitations and his concerns. He looks me in the eye and says, "Thank you." With both parties feeling understood, we get to the heart of the negotiation and find the parenting plan that works for this family. Beyond making the parties feel heard, we must confirm we've heard all stories correctly to create a common starting place to discuss the conflict.

∾

EMPATHETIC LISTENING

Pauline Tesler, from the Integrative Law Institute, suggests that lawyers often suppress their natural empathic response.[2] This empathic reaction could be towards a client, a witness, a colleague, or even an opposing party. The restorative lawyer recognizes this empathic response and does not attempt to conceal it, accepting the natural emotions that are evoked in listening. In my practice, I have witnessed lawyers being touched by an empathic response and, in an attempt to keep a professional distance, shutting it down. As a young assistant district attorney, that is precisely what I did. The empathy I felt for the child victims was heartbreaking. The empathy I sometimes felt for many parents was confusing. Either way, I suppressed that empathic response. I typically refused to listen with empathy during the trial and restricted myself to an adversarial/ana-strategic mode of listening.

~

In an average routine hearing, one mother, Amy Strickland, walks into court and sits beside her counsel. The hearing involves her motion to regain custody from the state. After reviewing the case's history, she testifies for about half an hour. She says she loves her children and wants nothing more than to take them home. She has started a new job, is attending counseling, and recently got some furniture, including new beds for the children. She seems convincing and loving. However, I know that she is not telling the whole story.

I begin the cross-examination kindly. I am trying to make the young mother feel comfortable and trusting. Once she seems relaxed, I move to a pointed, revealing question. "Who else lives in your new apartment?" She admits she now lives with the man who abused the children. She loves him. She did not think it would happen again.

At this point, I am mad. Amy got much of her life together, yet she continues to place her children at risk. I persist, "And you are aware that your daughter has reported that he sexually abused her?"

She starts to cry. "Yes."

"Do you believe your daughter?"

"Yes." She breaks down in tears.

"And your son, he has disclosed that this man caused him to suffer the injuries that led to this child's overnight hospitalization. Are you aware of that?"

"Yes." I feel no empathy. I continue drilling down on every detail until I feel confident that I've elicited every answer that would forever preclude her from regaining custody. She continues to cry.

I pause to ask my friend Jim, the children's lawyer, if I had neglected anything. He whispers, "No. Stop right now. Look at the judge."

With wide eyes and a clear frown, Judge Paul Klein's twisted face observes Amy, his empathic response fully triggered. He has a duty to protect the children, but he also feels compassion for this young mother. I've gone too far — from a strategic and humane point of view. I've lost the fact finder. And once I pause, my empathic response seems to return. I see this young mother, probably herself a victim of childhood sexual abuse. Perhaps she wants to protect her children, and at the same time, she wants to be in the relationship with her boyfriend, feeling valued and protected.

～

I LEARNED something important that afternoon. Even when I am advocating during a trial, restricting my ability to listen with empathy stifles the potential for effective cross-examination. Adversarial and ana-strategic listening are not enough. To be effective as a lawyer and feel integrated personally, we need to master another way to listen during hearings, depositions, and client meetings. I am engaged and empathetic. Whether I'm working with a client, opposing counsel, opposing parties, parties to mediation, or any potential collaborators in resolving a legal conflict, empathic listening must be integrated to maximize information gathering and healing.

UNIVERSAL LISTENING

A few years ago, at a workshop on listening skills, a group of experienced lawyers/mediators described the optimal type of listening for proper engagement with mediation clients as "universal listening." They contrasted this to the adversarial listening that most lawyers master. In universal listening, we listen to the speaker, willing to let them go off course, and just speak. We universally accept what they say. No judgment. As this group of experienced lawyers described, universal listening reminds me of Nonviolent Communication by bringing respect, kindness, and openness to listening. While expanded listening often takes more time, understanding where the speaker is coming from is usually time well spent. Universal listening creates opportunities for the speaker to create the agenda for the conversation. It establishes the potential for open, transparent communication without judgment and with respect. Since collaboration, relationship, and respect form the backbone of a restorative law practice, universal listening should be a standard part of all conversations.

POLYLINQUISTIC LISTENING — IN A NUTSHELL

Regan McCallister, the young woman who was sexually assaulted on her college campus who helped me to understand the importance of understanding goals also provided a chance for me to practice polylinguistic listening. I started our first meeting with an open-ended question. "Can you tell me what happened to bring you here?" She told her story about how she came to attend college, where she lived, and how her education had gone. She then focused on September 29 and described the sexual assault. How might different modes of listening impact the dialogue that will follow?

An adversarial listener looks for details and weaknesses in the case. "You had six beers in two hours?" A strategic listener might listen, and when Regan pauses, say, "I understand your case. It sounds like a second-degree sexual assault and that the university, or fraternity, might have some liability for permitting excessive alcohol consumption. Did the offender leave bruises? Was anyone else in the room?"

An active listener sits upright, nodding and making eye contact as the young woman speaks. If she pauses for a long time, the active listener might hand her tissues or ask questions about the victim's feelings and recollections. The reflective listener waits until the speaker finishes her story. After a period of silence, she may say, "As I understand it, you went to a party and had six beers and then went with friends to another party? Do I have that right?"

The empathic listener waits for that period of silence, reflects, and then may say, "This sounds very traumatic. Were you scared?" Without judgment, she waits to let the speaker direct the conversation.

The restorative lawyer adopts and practices multiple listening methods. The restorative lawyer continues to improve on skills as a polylinguistic listener. The lodestar is a listening that involves genuine listening. During workshops with lawyers on listening, I often hear them describe themselves as good listeners. However, when we engage in a role play, I watch them. They interrupt. They are calculating their response while the other person is talking. They are asking questions that change the pace and direction of the conversation. They summarize in a way that re-stories the narrative. In other words, they think they are listening, but they are not. They are interrupting. The restorative lawyer continues to learn to listen —genuinely.

TABLE 9

Types of Listening for the Restorative Lawyer

TYPE	DESCRIPTION	USE OR EXAMPLE
Adversarial	Listening for gaps, weaknesses, and deficiencies in stories.	Capitalize or address deficiency to promote client's position.
Ana-Strategic	Listening to provide legal analysis and strategy.	Case development in litigation.
Response Oriented Listening	Listening to prepare to respond.	During interviews or consultations when questions are expected.
Active	Listening carefully and demonstrating the speaker is heard.	Everyday communications. All clients want to feel heard.
Reflective	Listening followed by reflections sufficient to confirm the speaker has been heard.	Most communications, particularly when wanting to build trust or assure understanding.
Empathetic	Listening while engaging empathetically with speaker.	Creates genuine emotional response; may create connections.
Universal Listening	Open listening that lets the speaker set the agenda.	Discussions with clients, witnesses, or opposing counsel. Especially at intake and narrative building conversations.
Polylinguistic Listening	Flexibility in integrating of multiple forms of listening, as needed.	Used by highly skilled practitioners in complex or shifting conversations.

4.

GET THE HANG OF STORY LISTENING — AT LEAST AS MUCH AS STORY TELLING.

Lawyers are often good storytellers. Some even pen fantastic fiction, such as Scott Turow and John Grisham. We love stories and learn how to tell them. In restorative practice, we also learn to be excellent story listeners and recognize the client as the superior teller of their story.

The stories of our clients' conflicts are told several times in legal proceedings — at the opening and closing of the trial, perhaps in the opening of mediation, and perhaps during negotiations or arguments. Usually, they are told in the lawyer's legal framework — reduced to emphasize the portions that the lawyers find match the theory of the case. The problem presented when lawyers assume the role of the best storyteller in the room became apparent to me during a role-play in graduate school at the Center for Justice and Peacebuilding. I enjoyed my time with colleague Sylbert Sackie from Liberia. How could I not? He had an enthusiastic sense of humor that he readily shared, along with his delicious fried plantains. I worked with another lawyer colleague in the class, Marshall Yoder, who could not fry plantains but could sing beautiful traditional hymns. Marshall and I created a realistic role-play of a preliminary hearing for a juvenile offender charged with a misdemeanor to help our classmates understand the court proceeding and how it felt to be a participant.

~

THE CLASSROOM IS SET up to replicate a courtroom. Two tables face the back of the room, where another classmate is seated as the judge. The rest of the class is in rows behind the table. As defense counsel, Marshall is seated at one table with Sylbert, who portrays Steven Donivan as a youthful offender. I sit at the other table as the district attorney. Marshall stands to give his opening and faces the classroom. Sylbert sits in his seat as Marshall recounts the facts of the case.

"At that time, Mr. Lambert became alarmed by the action of the other young men ..." Sylbert squirms in his seat, contorting his face in anguish, demonstrating his discomfort. "He asked the other men if they would be willing to take this discussion to another location." Sybert's movements become exaggerated, and it becomes impossible to listen to Marshall.

"Since this is a role play, let's stop here for a minute." Marshall could tell that no one was listening to him. "Sylbert what's going on? If this were in court, the judge would have put you out in the hall!"

Sylbert stood up. "This is all wrong! Why are you telling this story? It happened to me! And you are not getting it right at all. I don't understand this process where I have to listen to you tell it this way."

Marshall and I again outline the proceedings and that Sylbert may (or may not) be able to tell his story. Sylbert is unsatisfied and does not understand why the lawyer would create the opening statement — why couldn't he tell his own story? We explain self-incrimination, due process, and the protections the process provides. Still, there is no explaining away that a stranger cannot dissect these dynamic parts of our life story to determine their rank and validity objectively.

~

WHEN WE TELL OUR CLIENTS' stories, a few things happen. We change the language into our learned legal language that tends to flatten the story, removing the nuanced facets that could create the potential for the client to integrate their experience of events into their life story. We change the framework, elevating facts based on their relation to the legal theory rather than the importance to the client. We change the storyteller, and the story's star often becomes the lawyer rather than the client. Finally, we create a single dominant narrative rather than an integrated one. Most legal processes, even alternative dispute resolution (ADR) processes such as evaluative mediation, demand that one version of a story be adopted as truth to elevate one narrative as dominant.[3]

The restorative practice increases the opportunities to be the story listener. Clients know the full context. They are best suited to develop the plot and respect the characters as complex people. At the same time, clients do not have the technical skills to give an opening statement in a jury trial. We can embrace other opportunities for the client to tell their full stories in our private meetings, negotiation, and mediation. It requires preparation and patience but maximizes the opportunity for resolution and healing. Lawyers can be excellent storytellers — and story listeners!

5.

BECOME VERSED IN *RE*, NOT *DI*, WHEN RESPONDING TO ALMOST ANYTHING.

What happens AFTER clients tell their stories and after the lawyer has fully listened? What happens AFTER an opposing counsel makes an argument that has limited merits? Lawyers have a few options, and — the restorative options do not include delegitimizing the speaker. The restorative lawyer doesn't disagree, diminish, diagnose, differ, disbelieve, disregard, or do anything that starts with *Di*. Instead, the restorative lawyer explores the *Re*: reflect, reframe, and respond. Other *Re*-s are implicit, such as repeat, refine, rehear, remake, rebuild ... you get the idea.

REFLECT

What has the client said? Why is opposing counsel bringing up this topic? How does the client's partner see the trial ending? The initial reflection allows the lawyer to determine if a response requires more listening, talking, or waiting. Lawyers often tell clients to count to ten before responding during cross-examination to give them time to think. The restorative lawyer takes this advice and slows it down. The restorative lawyer asks questions such as, "Did the person speaking unquestionably finish their sentence, their thought, and their idea?" "Am I assuming what they are going to say and being impatient?" "What will happen if I wait a few seconds and test it out?"

Listening and thinking provide time to process information and deliberately consider solutions. Reflection may allow for an interest-based view of the problem. In the Ugli orange exercise, all interests could be satisfied if both sides communicated their needs. Rushing into a response makes it difficult to think expansively about potential resolutions.

REFRAME

Once the restorative lawyer feels confident the speaker has completed their story, they may confirm they have heard the story through active or reflective listening and then move on to potential responses, such as reframing. Reframing involves looking at something in a new way. Imagine a picture we look at every day. Maybe it's been hanging in the office or the living room for 10 years. It will look different if we take it down, find a new matte, and change the frame. The subject appears in a new way.

The same thing happens with ideas. Reframing provides new insight. It may be with opposing counsel, our client, or a supportive family member. For example, I once litigated a case involving a considerable family conflict over an estate that involved a large and valuable farm. After years of discovery and posturing, we had a good proposal for a resolution. My co-counsel and I met with the client, who articulated his frustrations with the case over the last few years. We had heard it before but listened, reflected, and confirmed. Then, we outlined the proposal. We described the settlement to our client in terms of a dollar division. The client refused to consider the resolution, thinking it was not fair, and again articulated his well-worn narrative about his family's lack of contribution to the family estate over the years.

We listened and confirmed that the client was heard. My co-counsel, a former coal miner turned litigator, reframed the description to include a summary that the client would receive more than fifty percent of the total amount available for the entire family. The client said, "When you put it that way, yes that sounds fair. Let's accept it."

RESPOND

Sometimes, listening and pausing generate more questions. Restorative lawyers ask the questions as a response. The best response is often not an observation or exposition but a question that arises organically in a conversation. Before asking the question —we still slow things down and pause first. What's the purpose of the question? How should the question be framed? Open-ended or directive? Sometimes, lawyers become accustomed to efficiently gathering facts and nailing down stories but forget that there are many ways to ask a question. We need training and practice to be intentionally selective about when and how to ask questions.

The restorative lawyer works to accept what the speaker says and builds on it as a response. This technique may be particularly effective in an argument with opposing counsel. I was a theater major and enjoyed improv exercises. In the "Yes, and..." improv exercise, participants accept whatever situation the partner creates and find a way to incorporate that into the next action of the improv. For example, if a person comes onto an improv scene and sees a person standing on the stage, he might say, "What are you doing?" The other actor says, "Waiting for a bus." The response is not to say, "No you are not—there are no buses here—we are in the Alps!" Rather, the answer is accepted. "Yes, and I hear they are not running this morning due to a strike."

Sometimes, when negotiating, I like to play "Yes...and" to see where it takes us. Can I agree with everything the other person says? Can I repeat it and add something to make it accurate? This worked well in a negotiation with another attorney, Theresa Elmore, in an education case.

Theresa called me after receiving my invitation to negotiate, which was drafted in a way inspired by Strategic Negotiation.

Before the call, Theresa read my letter and evaluated my legal and factual arguments. During the call, she prepared and argued each point. With each one, I refrained from issuing my counterpoint. Instead, I looked for a way to integrate her argument into the client's narrative without damaging it. Answering "Yes, and ..." moved us closer to finding places where the narratives intersect. We uncover where the golden bridge can be built for both parties to cross, where responses can be generated for mutual gain, and where the harm a young student experienced can be addressed by improving the institution that created the harm.[4]

By embracing the *Re* and rejecting the *Di*, we maximize the opportunity for the speaker to feel heard while also creating the environment for both parties to consider new options. We avoid arguments and counter positions in favor of integration and respect. And most of all, we listen first. Restorative justice early adopter Lorraine Stutzman Amstutz once suggested that before responding, she thinks of the word "WAIT." It stands for "Why am I talking." Before responding, let's be sure we have a good reason!

6.

UNDERSTAND HOW TO CREATE ENVIRONMENTS TO IMPROVE OUTCOMES.

As a costume designer, I drew inspiration from Edith Head's observation that "You can do anything in life if you dress for it." For lawyers, it is not so much that we dress ourselves as we dress our offices. I strategically create opportunities to improve communication with clients after we choose our office. I avoid having important discussions at the courthouse, where onlookers see and hear fragments of our conversations. For clients, the courthouse is not a comfortable workplace but an unfamiliar, intimidating place where they have no control. In contrast, our offices may be where we can optimize the opportunity for speakers and listeners to feel comfortable and safe. However, many lawyers miss this opportunity to create the space.

When my husband and I bought a house a few years ago, the closing occurred at our lawyer's office, a beautiful, two-story, eighteenth-century limestone building. We entered the building from a walking mall into a foyer and joined the adjacent room through a large arch. I told the receptionist, seated behind a waist-high Formica counter, typing on a computer, that we'd arrived for our appointment. She invited us to sit on one of the uncomfortable settees in front of her counter. Behind her, a half dozen women typed on computer keyboards that were stationed on desks piled high with papers. Stacks of papers and books filled the shelves behind them. Banker's boxes sat piled up in the back of the room.

Our attorney emerged and escorted us up narrow steps, past several more piles of banker's boxes, past a room with a copy machine, and into a stark, dingy, beige-painted conference room. We took a seat in one of the burgundy vinyl chairs on casters that surrounded a large wooden table with a protective glass top. File cabinets lined one wall. The fluorescent light buzzed while we read over the documents.

I felt relieved that my only experience here would be to execute contracts we'd already read. This room was no place to talk or think. It did not feel like a place to build relationships and solve problems but rather a place to process papers. It reminded me of mediations I've facilitated in some courthouses, seated in cramped rooms at Formica tables lit by overhead fluorescent lights. Besides the echo of litigants and their attorneys arguing in a nearby room, the only sound was an annoying buzz produced by those lights.

My awareness of how the environment maximizes opportunities for successful conflict resolution spiked during graduate school when I attended a hearing at a newly remodeled courthouse. When I presented my argument, the judge could not hear me, raising questions about courthouse function and design. In Chapter Two, I described working with fellow student Paulette Moore to create a video interviewing Deb Parsons, the good lawyer who described justice as sometimes being a hug in the courthouse bathroom. In the video, we investigated the impact of courthouse design on justice. A few months later, I met architect Deanne Van Buren. Deanne researches how our environment shapes our thinking and has developed an approach to the design of judicial spaces that incorporates what we know about neuroscience and decision-making.[5]

We cannot create a restorative practice of law when conflict resolution spaces are arranged thoughtlessly and function to facilitate adversity, competition, and power relationships. We need to reform from creating spaces where documents are generated and cases are processed to sites where clients feel comfortable enough to linger to tell their stories at their own pace. Spaces can be created where clients may feel calm. In that space they are not intimidated. Clients, lawyers, and other participants may engage in problem-solving without fear, and without triggering the fight or flight reflex. Details matter.

Unlike the buzzing fluorescent light distracting me at the closing of my house, my office includes lots of light: ambient, task, and accent that enable reading documents and create a pleasant mood. We expanded the potential for natural light, which improves mood and productivity. We created a space for contemplation and discussion. Rather than having walls covered in diplomas, awards, and trite prints, we have installed large fabric-covered panels that look nice and provide sound dampening between rooms. When clients wait in the reception area, they enjoy lots of natural light, a floor-to-ceiling forest mural on one wall, and they may pass the time moving sand around in our tabletop Zen garden.

Henry David Thoreau knew the power of nature to ordinary humans. He calls it a tonic, "We need the tonic of wildness ...We can never have enough of Nature."[6] One conference room wall is covered with black and white nature-based photographs, framed by hanging plants. The prints bring nature into the space and sometimes are conversation starters. Clients share their memories and dreams of visiting these locations. A spontaneous conversation sometimes gives me more information than a series of questions on an intake form.

In the middle of the twentieth century, every law office had at least one typewriter, yet I have not seen one now in years. By the end of the century, they had faxes and copy machines — and they, too, are disappearing. What are our new tools? Do we cling to obsolete devices? Can we find the instruments to create a new practice of law? What do we have or need to increase the opportunity for meaningful conversation?

Redesigning our offices creates opportunities for developing optimal spaces for communication. When the copy machine, the printer, the intimidating diplomas, and the stacks of papers dominate an office, the client and the lawyer can be overwhelmed. We can choose to focus on nurturing relationships, creating hope, and developing strategies to move beyond the conflict. We can see beyond paper and into the hearts and minds of our clients.

7.

SETTLE THE CASE BACKWARD: START BY IDENTIFYING THE GOAL AND THEN WORK TO MEET IT.

For the first ten years of my personal injury practice, I felt frustrated when clients settled their cases and immediately bought a truck and satellite dish. Not anymore. I embrace *settling the case backward*. It's about goals. The restorative lawyer starts the first and final negotiation by understanding how the client wants this case to end. Working with the client, we develop goals and financial costs and create a budget to meet the goals. Sure, I continue to evaluate the case according to what an insurance company might do or with my best guess of what a jury would do. Those numbers are part of the picture. These reference points help guide us in locating an objective value.

But I try not to lose sight of what matters most to the client: their subjective values and goals. Collaborative Practice uses the law as a reference point, but the primary objective is to determine and reach client goals. I recently worked on a collaborative team to divide the assets of a couple who had been married for thirty-plus years and saved about two million dollars. Meeting their needs, we engaged a financial neutral, who ran projections with various fifty-fifty divisions of the assets. The neutral helped the couple feel more comfortable working on a resolution. Our client, Jackie, detailed her goals, including travel, spending time with grandchildren, and maintaining an investment property. We worked towards those goals.

Jackie had non-pecuniary needs. As she left the marriage, she wanted assurances that her contributions to the family, even though she never worked outside the home, mattered. Jackie's contributions at home allowed the family to acquire their assets. Part of reaching her goals required working to eliminate the husband's language about giving her "his pension" and "taking care of Jackie." Eventually, he explicitly recognized her contribution, allowing us to find an acceptable resolution.

Earlier, I introduced you to Chad Hammond, who wanted to resolve his personal injury case in a way to get him a fresh start. He needed enough money to pay a personal loan and catch up on his mortgage (which had become delinquent before the wreck) to stay in his house. Chad taught me to settle my cases backward — what does the client need? What will they do with the money? How can I help clients reach their goals?

8.

Now we have it! We have the basic concepts that support both the theory and practice requirements for the restorative lawyer.

We've talked about principles and theory, the history, rules of engagement, approaches, methods, techniques, and skills. We've plowed through how principles and values frame a restorative practice. But I promised you that this concept is real — restorative lawyering can thrive in the lawyer's ordinary, everyday practice. In the next section, we'll get down to the nuts and bolts: How these values and principles impact what you do at the office or the courthouse every day. And to do that, I'll introduce you to Max Stallard.

Chapter 9

Let Me Walk You Through a Case
TRAVELS WITH MAX

A journey is a person itself. No two are alike.

— John Steinbeck, *Travels with Charley*

1.

AFTER A FEW YEARS of finding my way in a restorative practice, I met Max. His case might not appear extraordinary to someone reviewing the pleadings, but it is phenomenal. Our story combines many pieces of my formal and informal education as a restorative lawyer. And for that reason, I'll share it with you ... along with the struggles, bumps, and detours that accompany any arduous journey to seek justice after wrongdoing and healing after harm.

By the time I met Max, I had already realized that my relationship with clients starts long before we meet for the first time. My new reflective practice pushed me to examine questions about the cultural depiction of the relationship between the attorney and the client. How do we interact with the world? What is our professional image? Do advertisements include images of warriors and wild animals? How do our websites and social media posts reflect our identity? How do we answer phones and emails? Think about the first time a prospective client contacts a law office. Do they call? Is it respectful to answer the phone, "Law office ... He doesn't do those cases?" Do they send an email, never hearing an answer? Or will they leave a voicemail and wait for days without a response? How do we demonstrate that we genuinely appreciate that initial contact with us? Restorative lawyers want to deserve to be invited into our clients' lives, and we want them to be comfortable as we invite them into ours.

My relationship with Max started with his email asking for help with a life insurance claim. After a few canceled appointments and several months, I checked back in on Max to see if he was doing okay or if he'd resolved his legal case. Eventually, he responded, "I finally started going through my email and found your correspondence the other day. Thank you so much for your time. I truly have not done anything but try to go forward with my life and have for far too long put this on the back burner. Yes, I still need your help."

2.

Max arrives in my quiet, empty reception room, and I immediately invite him into the conference room. We sit in comfortable chairs at the round, glass-topped table with the afternoon light streaming into the room.

"I never did this before. I don't know where to start." He hands me a letter from an insurance company, and I glance over it quickly. I see the case number and name at the top of the page: William Benton, 3223-434-33AJ2. "Please accept our sincere condolences for your loss. We have evaluated your claim for the above-referenced benefits. For the reasons detailed below, we must deny your claim." I skim the two pages packed with excuses for why Max is not eligible for benefits. I do not ask any questions about the letter. "Do you want to talk about Will?"

"We weren't married, but the policy didn't require that, and I don't understand why they wouldn't just pay it. Will thought we had this insurance, we talked about it." I listen. The legal problem may be a little tricky to understand. I decide to focus more on Max's loss before examining the legal issues.

"Did you live with Will?"

"Yes. For fourteen years." Max now speaks warmly and openly, pausing occasionally to look at the black and white photos of the Blue Ridge Mountains on the wall opposite him. I have an hour for this first meeting and plenty of time for listening. I don't interrupt. I don't elicit facts. I just listen — for needs and fears, as well as legal issues. Max shares a rich, nuanced story full of love and opportunity for healing. I'm quiet, making a few notes. I'm beginning the hard work of building our relationship.

Max describes a rich history with Will. They had been partners for fourteen years. They lived on a few acres in a remodeled house just outside town. Will worked long hours as the manager of a retail store in a nearby strip mall, and their home consistently provided respite and space for the life they shared. Max recounts last

Christmas when Will worked late on Christmas Eve and came home. He showed me Will's Facebook post describing it. "... Tonight was like a breath of fresh air and a night spent with my love, best friend, and soul mate. He got me some very nice presents, but the best present is just spending time with him. I love you, Max Stallard. You are truly a special person." I smile and nod. The room is quiet, and I decide to sit with that quietness.

Sitting with quietness doesn't come easy for lawyers. I think about another teacher, Monica Braxton, who was the midwife for my third child and emphasized the practical implications of relationship building I described in Chapter Four. Monica also taught me the importance of patience when waiting for a client to share their story or to create options to resolve disputes. She said that midwives "sit on their hands" during labor. It might look like they are not doing anything, but they are waiting, listening, and observing to permit the birthing mother to set the timetable.

Sometimes, I've seen the modern practice of law look more like the modern practice of obstetrics led by surgeons who never learned to sit on their hands. I've watched lawyers interrupt clients to get to what the lawyer finds to be relevant facts. They interject to defeat a client's narrative that seems inconsistent with an evolving theory of the case.

As Max speaks, I sit on my hands and watch his story emerge, with the needs and priorities tightly interwoven in his text. Max tells me that two days after Christmas, Will suffered a seizure during the night and died at age thirty-one. "We created a world together, and it ended just like that." Max summarized the next several months. Devastated and depressed, he barely carried on his day-to-day life. He became financially devastated. "I finally pulled it together enough to start the claim. I filed it online and sent Will's death certificate online. Then they sent that." He pointed to the letter. Max struggles to maintain composure and moves between outlining the computer-generated letters from the insurance company and reminiscing on the relationship he's lost.

3.

Max continues to switch between talking about the communication with the insurance company and Will. He talks about how both men struggled with a lack of acceptance from their extended families. I make notes:" Dog — London, Christmas favorite time of year, trip set for Key West." I sit on my hands, working to be patient with Max's diversions, the "irrelevant" tangents included in his narrative that are critical to my understanding of his legal problem.

∼

MY FRIEND AND COLLEAGUE, Judge John Michaels, served as a mediator in an adoption case I once worked on as co-counsel. During a private caucus, the biological mother began to tell her story, rambling into issues of abandonment and abuse in her childhood and her relationship with her other child. My co-counsel tried to redirect her, "We are focusing today on the case involving the baby. So, let's only talk about that."

Judge Michaels said, "You know, if she is telling me something that is important enough for her to tell me, it's relevant." Like my co-counsel I felt like the mother's rambling was tangential, at best. Legal training typically demands that lawyers focus narrowly, centering on the facts and laws that create the legal theory of the case. But the restorative lawyer practices patience. Disjointed fragments of a story often hold the substance of the harm that needs healing and create a strategy to meet the client's objectives.

Allowing the client to direct the conversation creates an opportunity for the lawyer to view their priorities. Another client, Katy Harvey, needed help paying medical bills after she fell at a home improvement store. During the first 30 minutes of our initial meeting, she rambled about being afraid to cross under a bridge on the way to my office. It turns out she had been raped under that bridge. At the jury trial, defense counsel projected a 5' by 5' image of her torn perineum on a screen before the jury. The jury convicted the defendant, but Katy's trauma was not over. She told me she would never go near another courtroom after her traumatic experience at trial. Her experience as a victim of a sexual assault who went to trial was not relevant to the potential civil case involving her fall at the home improvement store. However, the description of what she endured at trial was critical to understanding her goals, objectives, and developing our "done" statement.

4.

As a client's narratives flow organically, the restorative lawyer also listens for opportunities for repositioning. Clients with legal problems often view themselves as victims. The restorative lawyer considers the change in position a client may undergo, perhaps from "victim" to "survivor" during their work together. The repositioning may be part of the "done" that will guide the representation towards the client's goal.

Similarly, the restorative lawyer listens for opportunities for those harmed to rewrite the narrative of their experience into a story of healing. During my first course at the Center for Justice and Peacebuilding, Barb Toews described examining an experience and revising the narrative as a "re-story." Creating opportunities for re-story may lead to pathways for healing and, consistent with narrative theory, chances to weave diverging narratives into a multi-dimensional, complex, shared narrative.

The restorative lawyer listens openly and without an agenda, as the client relates their experience. After understanding the narrative and confirming it, questions may help to locate needs and potential for re-story and repositioning. When asking a question, the restorative lawyer allows plenty of time for the answer. Sometimes, when the question is complex, the pace of the conversation will slow. Clients may sit quietly, thinking.

It's okay to be in a room with a client without anyone talking.

They may fall silent when considering challenging questions or ordering confusing thoughts. The initial discussions often push the client to imagine their future. The questions may require the client to reflect on why they have a legal problem and how a resolution might correct the parts of their life that don't work. It is beneficial to wait for the answers without interrupting an intentional silence.

5.

Eventually, my conversation with Max turns beyond sharing his loss of Will — and he begins listing what else is missing. His dire financial situation creates anxiety and deepens his depression. He struggles with the concurrent need to move on and hold on. Max says he needs to be treated respectfully and "not like garbage or an outcast." Some building blocks emerge to help create both the objectives of the representation and a collaborative strategy.

Once I feel confident that Max feels like he's told his story, I summarize what I've heard. He confirms I understand his legal problem and his objectives. He wants to move on with his life, even without Will, while respecting what they shared. His re-story will find a way to create peace with his loss and emerge with sufficient financial resources to retain the property that represented their shared life. Max is interested in feeling like his efforts may prevent others from suffering from the carelessness he experienced by the act of the insurance company.

We create a practical foundation for our relationship. At the first meeting with Max, we agree on how to keep in touch. I try to meet with clients in person every three to six months, or sooner when we need to change course or re-evaluate options. My clients access their files online, where they can also leave me messages that include private notes and questions. I prefer in-person meetings (over telephone calls) to provide opportunities to grow our relationship and to have meaningful discussions. Max signals that he agrees with this format.

∼

LIKE MY OTHER CLIENTS, I'll check with Max, at least bi-monthly, to see how things are going. Usually, I send a message via the online portal. If a client responds indicating changing needs or concerns, we schedule an in-person meeting.

Restorative lawyering requires this type of frequent, consistent, and open communication. One client, Keith Younger, helped me to understand how important it is for the client to have this experience. Lawyers must have this form of communication to understand the client and the nuances of the legal conflict. A year before I met Keith, he hired two well-respected trial lawyers. "Good lawyers." His only contact with the office was his periodic calls to the paralegal, who reported that the attorneys were working on the case, without further detail. The attorneys finally called him one day to summon him to the office. At the meeting (the first since he retained them), the attorneys presented and then pressured Keith to accept a settlement. Keith became angry and left. He retained us a few weeks later. Several months later, we reached a resolution that Keith had participated in crafting and fully supported.

Don't be like Keith's lawyers. Communicate early and often. Establish shared benchmarks and projections. Mismatched expectations cannot result in an excellent attorney-client relationship. They will impair the client's satisfaction with the process and outcome. And the impact of the client's disappointment impacts lawyers. And by the way — we wound up settling Keith's case for four times what his prior attorneys pressured him into accepting — most likely because I listened and understood Keith's story well enough to convey it to the other side.

Back to Max. After our meeting, he left. I performed administrative tasks: opening a file, documenting it, calendaring deadlines, and developing the strategy to move the case, including incorporating the client's "done" statement into our analysis. But I wasn't finished. Recall Engagement Rule #7: Develop a Reflective Practice? The restorative lawyer examines their notes from that first meeting, ensuring that they feel confident in their attention to the client's needs and not the lawyer's ego. After a bit of reflection and perhaps a few modifications, it's time to get to work!

6.

Once I feel like I have a grasp on the case, I create a team to explore processes and outcomes. I've learned a lot about this from Collaborative Practice. In Collaborative Practice, we assemble the parties, their lawyers, and a team of professionals, including conflict coaches, financial experts, and child specialists, to help families create a resolution in a divorce case. The contributors to the team extend beyond the client and the lawyer and may work as a flexible, dynamic partnership.

The same dedication to collaboration can be built outside of formal Collaborative Practice. Building relationships with the client, their family, friends, the opposing party, their representative, or their counsel creates a less formal collaborative team. I usually think of the client and their families and friends as critical members of the problem-solving team. With expectations and time frames in place, the client may be more able to move forward despite being in the middle of a legal conflict.

Recall Sam Frost from chapter five—where his mother, Ellen, proved critical to our success. She drove Sam to appointments and quietly and respectfully participated in our meetings. She provided me with background on Sam, especially his difficulty in high school, which led to drug and alcohol abuse. Through these discussions, Sam gained an increased awareness of how his harmful acts had affected his family. As Sam's physical injuries healed, we worked together to develop life goals. He planned to get his driver's license back, return to school, and then pursue an alternative career. The collaboration between his mother, Sam, and myself created an excellent outcome for Sam. Sam's recovery provided him with new opportunities, beyond those that existed before his accident.

Ellen also helped Sam to understand my explanations about the law. While the law is only one factor we include in analyzing alternatives, the restorative lawyer strives to help the client understand options to make good decisions. Understanding the law can be difficult for clients. Having a support person familiar with the legal issues can help the client consider options involving legal questions outside of the meetings with the lawyer.

Managing the logistics of creating a team that includes family and friends creates challenges and questions for most lawyers. They may question how it might work. "How can we deal with this parade of folks coming through the office? All of these third parties? What about the attorney-client evidentiary privilege? If we allow them to participate, won't that eliminate the privilege?"

"Yes. And ..." We can explain the privilege and provide opportunities for private conversations alongside more expansive meetings. We can arrange our offices so the conference room is large enough to accommodate a team. We can be sure to create private spaces for breaking into smaller groups.

It's an additional challenge when children might be part of the team. "Little pitchers have big ears." Having children present can make communication with the client more complicated and can potentially harm or be traumatic for the child. If a child has a significant interest in the legal problem and a proxy cannot address the child's interests, the child's participation must be carefully and intentionally planned to facilitate a favorable process, potentially including help from a mental health professional. Children should rarely be involved in meetings due to a lack of childcare. There is no question that a child may experience trauma and stress when listening to most conversations that underpin a legal problem.

Another critical team member may be opposing counsel or, in the case of an insurance case, the claims representative. At some level, all participants share a common interest: to resolve a legal problem. Many lawyers issue a formal letter to the other attorney early in their representation. How can that letter be framed to invite collaboration? Can we place a call instead? I enjoy reconnecting with my old friends who we've worked with before and learning what has changed in their lives. A new grandchild? A move? Graduation?

When we don't know the other attorney, can we call them and introduce ourselves? We know we already have some things in common: We are both lawyers, usually in the same community, and are interested in the case or conflict. What else? Where are they from? Do they have children or grandchildren? What are their hobbies and favorite places to eat or visit?

Is this friendly introduction impossible? Sometimes, counsel may be confused by the kindness and be defensive. Others may not be naturally gregarious. Yet, we lawyers spend many of our days working at computers. Usually, my phone calls are warmly received, and I can hear a sense of relief that I've not called to threaten or badger but to connect and understand how we can work together.

I often reap intangible benefits through this relationship building, but sometimes, the benefit is concrete. Years ago, I was sitting at a continuing legal education program, and the presenter insisted to the participants that the insurance adjuster is not your friend. "Don't forget it." The presenter posed at the front of the room, his hands on his hips and head cocked to the side, he asked, "They don't call you on the day your statute of limitation is running out to help you, do they?"

I thought back to when I was in a horrible auto accident. A few days after the initial surgery, recovering at home and suffering from trauma and pain, I checked emails and made a few calls. (Just because I'm a restorative lawyer doesn't mean I'm not "Type-A!")

One adjuster from a large national insurance company called. He'd heard about the accident and wanted to be sure that I knew the statute of limitations on one of our cases was running out in two weeks. He wished me a speedy recovery. I don't rely on opposing counsel to remind me of the statute, but I share this story because I don't want us to lose the opportunity to recruit or at least invite the "other side" to our team.

At the beginning of Max's case, we start with a two-person team: Max and me. Without Will, Max does not want to include any family or friends on our team. I'm in solo practice. While I anticipate we'll find team members on the "other side" eventually, at this point, we do not have opposing counsel. No one signed off on the form letter for us to call. Eventually, we would create a fantastic team. But at the outset, it is just the two of us.

7.

I review my notes from our meeting and think about strategy — what will our representation yield to our client? Lawyers can misunderstand this step — it's not about drawing a road map for harming the other side or wreaking havoc, increasing the conflict. A restorative strategy begins by identifying goals that increase the potential for healing of the client's harm. Healing is found in identifying the problem, needs, and in creating the "done" statement.

A recent email from a mediation client demonstrates how effective a "done" statement can be at creating satisfaction in the resolution. During one of our first meetings, she described the life she hoped to create after the divorce.

Good Morning Brenda,

I just wanted to let you know the good news: We were able to get a court date of June 2nd. While we were supposed to be in court, it ended up being a six-minute conference call, and the judge signed off on it all Monday.

Once the QRDO goes through, he can move, which will be a good thing.

I already bought a house that will close in a week or so, and it's 14 minutes walking distance from my daughter in Washington. As soon as he is out, I have something to do at this house, and then I will head out to Washington by mid-October.

Thanks again!

This client got the divorce, satisfied her "done" by making the house available to sell and relocating near her daughter. The parties agreed to and accomplished the "done."

Once we can articulate where we are going, or the "done," we can create a road map or strategy for our representation. How will the healing occur? How can we meet needs? Sometimes, we rely on rights as our transportation. Rights do not drive the restorative lawyer, but we don't ignore them. Clients often want to better understand their rights to help them consider what is fair. But clients (and their lawyers) need not be bound, limited, or restrained by legal rights. Rights and needs are not the same things. Needs may exceed financial amounts and involve emotional needs. Sometimes the law helps (by enforcing rights) to meet those needs.

For example, I worked with a family representing Bruce Hampton after his extramarital affair resulted in the end of a thirty-year marriage. Cassidy Hampton felt betrayed and wanted Bruce to recognize the harm by paying a substantial sum in spousal support. He understood his legal rights might require less than she wanted in support, but he wanted to recognize his wrongdoing. After several meetings with both parties and their counsel, we arrived at an amount that gave Ms. Hampton financial security and Bruce peace of mind. (Bruce called me a few years later to say that she had asked him to terminate making payments, regardless of their legal contract, having arrived at a place where she no longer needed or wanted them.)

Developing a strategy to address the legal problem involves determining options for the "done" statement and examining ways to achieve it, including identifying and enforcing legal rights.

~

READING over the short unsigned letter from the insurance company as I prepare for a meeting with Max brings me back to some of Max's "done." He wants to be respected. He doesn't want to be treated like "garbage or an outcast." Max needs to have financial issues resolved — he fears losing the house he built with Will. Max's goal includes creating a sense that the systemic issues that led to his treatment by Will's employer and the insurance company would be resolved and others would not suffer the same harm. These are elements Max and I initially identified as necessary to finish the legal work, to be "done."

Max certainly enjoys a group of legal rights created by the insurance contract. Enforcement of those rights might meet some elements of his "done." Max could resolve the financial shortfalls. Max could feel respected by both Will's employer and the insurance company, who until now had not valued his loss. Working together, we created an evolving "done" statement when Max could live a happy, fulfilled life that Will would always be included in.

Max is late for this short meeting where I plan to review the "done" statement with him, my initial research into potential legal strategies, and the letters I have prepared to send to Will's employer and the insurance company. He explains that he's been rushing around all day and is exhausted. As soon as he sits down, I see he is holding back tears. Something happened today and despite Max's efforts, he can't contain his emotions.

~

I WANT to digress to discuss how lawyers deal with clients' emotions. When they come to see us, clients are often experiencing the worst time of their lives, and they may need to cry, scream, cuss, or sulk. For lawyers (including judges), emotional expressions often create discomfort, and the lawyers want the emotions to stop, especially when other counsel or parties are present. I've watched myself do it. If I'm mediating at the courthouse, I wonder if the bailiffs are worried I'm in the middle of a brawl or if the litigants waiting on benches in the hall can hear loud conversations or crying. My lawyerly impulse is to make it stop: I have many tools to try. I could minimize the clients' pain and tell them it's not so bad or look at the bright side. I could interrupt with a funny story. I could launch into a brilliant legal argument. I could tell them to tone it down.

But as a restorative lawyer, I'm learning to live with my discomfort when a client needs to display an emotion. I may work to change the pace, find the right physical environment, and create a relational space where clients can experience their feelings. I will check in to ensure that the client is safe and does not feel a power imbalance. But I want clients to know how it feels to be supported by their attorney, even when emotional. I try to understand how sharing deep feelings helps to create a critical building block in our relationship. I strive to avoid letting my discomfort limit the client's emotional responses. One of my colleagues in Collaborative Practice urges moving without fear toward the darkness. The darkness is the space where we experience the pain and loss. In the darkness, the resolution is not always visible. However, spending time in that unsecured, uncomfortable space may be the only way to create deep healing beyond superficially addressing a legal problem.

~

MAX FINISHES TELLING me a story about a trip with Will to Key West and smiles before he pauses, remembering it will always be the last one. Once centered, he encourages me to return to discussing the legal case. I take a few minutes and review his goals and confirm the "done" statement. I explain the law and what I anticipate happening once we request the files from the employer and the insurance company. We briefly discuss the legal issues. Having arrived at this point, it is time to get started. But for the restorative lawyer, the work is more nuanced than filing a complaint or preparing for trial.

Chapter 10

Navigating the Steps
WITHOUT BEING TETHERED BY TRIAL

Reach out to those you fear. Touch the heart of complexity. Imagine beyond what is seen. Risk vulnerability one step at a time.

— John Paul Lederach, *The Moral Imagination*

I.

MANY YEARS AGO, I enjoyed working with a friend as my co-counsel on several complex personal injury cases. While my friend James Kelsey enjoyed litigation, he also shared my enthusiasm for exploring early resolutions. We tried to resolve cases without filing suit while concurrently setting the case up for the adversarial process. Early steps included conducting investigations, obtaining records, and making a demand on the insurance company. We'd then negotiate, and when negotiations failed, we filed a civil complaint.

When James became ill and could no longer practice, his brother, who was out of state, took over. We worked as co-counsel, and I learned he had a different approach. In one of our first phone conversations, James' brother rejected my suggestion of making a demand, in hopes of negotiating an agreement. He found insurance adjusters so difficult to negotiate with that he filed suit in every case. I was surprised (and grateful) that he was willing to be flexible to expand the opportunities for early resolution of the cases we worked on together.

I wonder if a client's objective or "done" is typically met by immediately filing suit without attempting early resolution. When the lawsuit is filed, the story is recast into "x versus y;" the event becomes re-storied in terms of fault and blame. The participants become opposing parties, obscuring their shared interests. The complaint casts exclusive fault and blame, ignoring the potential for overlapping narratives, shared interests, and shared needs. Once filed, the parties (with their counsel's help) exchange long, compli-cated, often invasive lists of questions requiring formalized answers, often resulting in conflict over the questions. After they have exhausted the list of written questions, the next step is usually depositions. Often, the fault and blame are escalated by those oral interrogations. At this point, the parties are more at odds than at any point after the event. They cannot imagine sharing common ground. Their attorneys resolve the case (often close to a trial date) with a number that no one is happy with. This entire dispute resolution process centers on preparing for a jury trial, which most likely will never occur.

A restorative approach to developing the case provides an alternative process that centers on something other than an imaginary trial date. I call this approach, "sansatrial." When I was growing up in the 1970s *Life* and *Time* magazines carried advertisements for Sansabelt pants — pants that "stayed up" without a belt, all due to a patented rubber waistband. How liberating! Goal met — with a flexible and integrated option!

In the restorative practice of law, a trial is not viewed as the inevitable destination. The restorative lawyer may take steps to prepare for trial but remains mindful of the fact that the case will most likely not go to trial. The *sansatrial* period retains a focus on the client's overriding goals and creates opportunities for collaboration with the opposing parties. The lawyer develops a peaceful and resourceful zealousness to advocate for meeting the clients' needs without harming the other side, mindful that the points of intertwined narrative and shared interests may create opportunities for a collaborative resolution. The restorative lawyer embraces almost any available process that may reach the client's needs, whether it is early neutral case evaluation, mediation, or a settlement conference. The restorative lawyer trusts the client to define their subjective experience of justice.

Sometimes, attorneys challenge me on this engagement and exploration of early available alternatives to meet the client's goals. What if the other side thinks we are weak? Shouldn't we do everything we can? These questions are often not motivated by meeting clients' needs but are driven by the fear of the attorney of appearing weak to their peers. Lawyers may feel the fear quelled only when they prove that they march down the litigation highway, boasting about skills, and feeling confident that they have done everything the law permits them to do.

2.

During the *sansatrial* period, a challenge that many conventionally trained lawyers face is their fear.

~

I HATE SITTING in the conference room of this big law firm I'm working with. It has a huge wooden table with a big piece of glass on it, but for some reason it still feels like Formica. The chairs pretend to be formal, but they are made of vinyl. Even the wallpaper seems to have plastic interwoven into the pattern. Of course, it has the requisite fluorescent light overhead. I'm working with co-counsel from the firm.

My co-counsel, a young lawyer without much litigation experience, arrives at our meeting to discuss strategy. I'd met with the client a few days earlier and reviewed the complaint. The case is complicated, and the complaint is over twenty pages long. It involves estranged family members, and all lawyers are paid by the hour. During the first hour, we finish drafting the answer, outline discovery objectives, and assign tasks between us. We even discuss depositions, but that's a way off. Looking over the long list of tasks, I think about the financial and emotional costs to the client. I decide to propose a shortcut.

"Have you thought about early mediation?"

"What?"

"Early mediation."

"That'll be in the court scheduling order. Once we get to that, we can do mediation."

"I was thinking we might want to try early mediation, like just after we file the answer. I've had some PI cases where we mediated before we filed the complaint, and it worked out in a few of them."

"No. We are not going to approach them to mediate. Are you crazy?"

"Why not?"

"They'll think we have a weak case — if we approach them now. Or that we are afraid to go to trial." That comment, to me, smells like fear. Fear of looking afraid. Fear of insecurity in the case, the clients, or their positions. "We can do mediation after discovery, if you want."

~

WHAT IS FEAR? And who should be afraid of trial? What might they fear?

Let's start by considering the client's fear. Do clients experience fear of being engaged in legal processes, particularly going to trial? Do they fear the outcome? Clients have no control over the outcome when a judge or jury makes the decision that may entirely change or destroy their lives. Clients often fear much of the traumatizing process of going from initiating a lawsuit to defending an appeal, even when they win. My teachers—the clients I've described in these stories, taught me about their fear. Kate was afraid. She told me she never wanted the experience of being a victim in a trial again, after surviving the humiliation as a rape victim. For Anna's uncle, going to court was worse than going to a funeral. Living the consequences and outcome of the trial, are terrifying for clients. In our pursuit of justice, lawyers may create unintended consequences, causing clients to experience further trauma and suffering.

The term "unintended consequences" stands for the concept that we may have good intentions, but our actions have effects that are unanticipated. American sociologist Robert K. Merton applied the term and cites "ignorance" and "error" as two sources.[1] A good example followed the Haiti earthquake in 2010. Caring donors provided an influx of foreign food aid, which hurt rice farmers' livelihoods.[2] The restorative lawyer knows their client well enough to be able to walk in their shoes and begin to comprehend the impact the litigation has on them. The lawyer knows that pursuing what they may perceive as justice for a client, by scheduling a deposition or going to trial, may create unintended adverse consequences. The restorative lawyer works to identify and mitigate those consequences by locating potential opportunities for healing, even in adversarial situations.

What about the lawyers, are they afraid? What do they fear?

I'm not willing to speak for all lawyers, but I'll admit, I have known fear. I've been scared when kayaking class four rapids, scuba diving without certification, hang gliding, biking on a busy highway, running the last two miles uphill in a marathon, giving birth at home, picking up my teenager from the police....

But as a lawyer, the anxiety I've experienced arguing a case at the Supreme Court, making an argument before a jury, or cross-examining a witness, pales in comparison to the real fear of serious danger and consequences possible as I faced those personal experiences. Of course, I've felt stressed, anxious, and worried I wasn't doing a good job. But not afraid. However, as I've become a restorative lawyer, I have new fears. I am afraid that my pursuit of justice creates unintended consequences for my client and my community. I am afraid that I won't see the harm I'm creating. I fear that in pushing a case through the litigation meat mincer, we destroy familial, communal, and professional relationships. I fear that we misallocate resources when we spend time working to prepare for a trial, potentially draining time and resources available to meet the parties' needs.

Often, cases settle on the eve of trial. The money is already spent. More significantly, the parties are already emotionally torn. The harm we set out to repair has compounded. Fear of appearing weak cannot create the agenda for the *sansatrial*. Our client's legal situation is not about our ego, and it's not about trying to prove that we are not afraid. The restorative lawyer keeps focused on meeting the client's needs — of healing the harm. The restorative lawyer remains attentive to the potential of causing more damage to the client, their relationships, and their happiness. In doing so, the lawyer is willing to be tethered to values and principles that create healing and move away from those that center on adversity.

3.

My work in the *sansatrial* period in Max's case took several steps once we developed the "done" statement. This work took two primary forms: uncovering and developing the multiple narratives and increasing the number of participants in our collaborative team.

To develop the stories without moving towards trial, I researched the law and other cases against this insurer to help locate support to enforce Max's rights to meet his needs. I requested the insurance and employer's files. Initially, the insurance company (I'll call them Pillars Insurance) responded to our request for the file with a letter signed only by "Group Life Claims Operation." It read: "With that respect, we must point out that Pillars Insurance previously provided you with our entire claim file in this matter accompanied by our letter ... the letter also explained how to obtain a copy of the plan ... The claim file that you now possess also contains our previous letters to your client which explain the basis for our denial." After several more letters, complete with legal arguments about the duty to provide the file, Pillars sent the full file.

As we received more information, I did not try to create a dominant narrative to eliminate other stories. I did not engage in game playing with factual development. I did not craft lists of cumbersome questions. I did not restrict our ideas to legal analysis or trying to support our theory of the case. In the *sansatrial* period, I worked to uncover multiple narratives and locate commonality.

In restorative lawyering, we work to be an open book and request the same from our clients. Clients provide factual background. The lawyer creates a legal analysis to help the client understand their rights and duties, and consider their hopes, dreams, and fears. Information may also be available from third parties, such as the insurance adjuster, an investigating police officer, or a family member. Regardless of the source, a transparent, collaborative process requires open communication and free disclosure of information between attorney and client. The best decisions are informed decisions.

Getting the stories out in Max's case took a year filled with many letters, research, and a few threats. During this time, Max and I decided to expand our team. Max did not have family members he wanted to be part of our team at this stage. In complex cases, I often prefer to work with co-counsel and once Pillar failed to cooperate in any way, we recruited a young attorney, Seth Woodley to work with us. We continued to search out the folks who would conventionally be described as "the other side" who could potentially work with us to find a way to resolve Max's legal problem, to help him heal, and to meet his needs. Most of those efforts resulted in receiving no more than an unsigned form letter.

However, once we had sufficient documents to understand each side's story and interests, Seth and I sent a letter summarizing our legal arguments and requesting to settle the matter. That letter triggered a response, and a few top executives agreed to meet and independently discuss the situation with us in a telephone meeting. We were hoping to expand our team. But first, we needed to meet with Max and be sure we were still working towards his goals.

⌒

WE ARE MEETING in Seth's office. Max tells us he is really having a hard time. He misses Will terribly, and they bought the house with both of their incomes — he's far behind in payments. However, Max explains that he wants to be active in his case. He wants to understand the legal arguments and participate as much as he can in reaching a resolution. Seth explains the legal argument in some detail. He summarizes his assessment. "... What is at the bottom of the case is this — Will's employer didn't give him the form to enroll in the expanded benefit program providing his full life insurance benefit. Will submitted all the papers they gave him, but they didn't give him this one."

Max interjects, "They took the premium out of his paycheck. Where did that go?"

Seth responds. "That's what we all want to know. It was deducted. The policy provides for a domestic partner to have coverage — so I think they are on the hook. They say since Will didn't return the form, they aren't paying out. But that's why the employer is also involved in this case. They should have returned the form."

After a while the subject shifts — we turn to the next steps.

"We have a phone meeting scheduled with executives from the insurance company and the employer. That's what we want to talk about today." I pick up here. "We don't think these guys will resolve this. But they are agreeing to talk with us, so we'll do that. We want to get as much information from them as we can to increase our ability to evaluate the case and negotiate." Before the meeting, Seth and I had discussed our negotiation strategy, deciding that it would start by gathering facts and assessing needs and interests of all parties. Our meeting with Max was to be clear on his needs, interests, and to approach the WATNA and BATNA for the first time.

"Max, can you tell me about what you are hoping will happen here? What outcome would be best?" Max easily identifies his goals.

"Of course, I want them to shell out the full policy amount. Will paid for it, and it feels like I'm betraying him if I don't get the policy paid — but most of all I need to keep the house and as hard as it is, I need to move on." I review the work I'd undertaken to contact the lender and that we had a short-term resolution to prevent foreclosure. But that wasn't going to be enough.

"I mean, I appreciate that they aren't going to foreclose, but what about next year ... and the next one. I don't want to worry about it anymore. I would really just like this to be over, for me to be sure in the house and to do what I can so that this doesn't happen to other people. Is that even possible?" Max quickly moves past the idea of getting as much money as possible into articulating priorities. Identifying the client's interests and needs must be undertaken before negotiation. It is also a significant challenge. Clients often meet a lawyer only after spending lots of time thinking about how they have been wronged and how legal rights may remedy that wrong. They are often unprepared to think about their needs or long-term goals. We can often help the clients move away from ruminations about legal rights and processes and locate the interests and needs that will form the foundation of an acceptable resolution.

"I don't know, Max. But we'll see what they say and then determine the next step. We have a call scheduled next week. Do you want to participate in it?"

"Would it help?"

I shrug. "I don't know, but I doubt it at this point. I think mostly we'll be getting information and while we are happy to have you participate, it's also okay if you prefer not to."

"Good. Even coming in here stresses me out. Just do the call, and if there is anything good to report, let me know." His cell phone was beeping. He looked at the screen. "There's something urgent at work ... are we finished? Can I go?"

"Of course. Call or email if you need anything."

"Thanks." He rushes out. I got the sense he'd had enough and just wanted to leave. Seth and I decide to take the time to continue to plan the negotiation — to assess everyone's WATNA and BATNA to be prepared for the phone conference.

∾

INTEREST-BASED negotiation is usually a superior approach to the zero-sum process many lawyers intuitively rely on in discussing resolutions. In zero-sum negotiation, for one party to gain, the other loses. It's also called "fixed pie" negotiation because we assume that the pie holds the total amount of value we have in a negotiation and our job is to cut it up and get a larger piece of pie. In Max's case against Pillar Insurance, a purely fixed pie negotiation would look at the fact that there is $100,000.00 at stake and nothing else. We want to get as much as we can, and the insurance company wants to pay as little as they can. The more one gets, the more the other loses.

In interest-based negotiation, we look to add value. What, besides dollars, is important to the parties in this case? To do that we look at what would happen if we don't reach an agreement. Max has an overriding interest in keeping his home, best facilitated by a faster resolution. (During this period of the *sansatrial*, Max's lender agreed not to foreclose in exchange for partial payments while we pursued all options.) The employer's interest was primarily to preserve their reputation, both as a retailer and an employer. Similarly, the insurance company wanted to ensure that the public and industry would perceive them as fair, and unlikely to deny claims to cause unnecessary hardships. With the interests identified, the analysis turns to the WATNA and BATNA. What happens if we don't reach an agreement? How might these intangibles be impacted?

We approached the phone negotiation clear about Max's interests and goals. Max's WATNA (worse alternative to a negotiated agreement) meant losing at trial and created a financial disaster. Waiting one or two years before realizing any money may result in him losing the home. His BATNA (best alternative to a negotiated agreement) would be recovering the full policy. The WATNA for Pillar Insurance and the employer meant a damaging public trial and public judgment. Even reaching their BATNA and winning at trial would nonetheless create adverse publicity.

The phone negotiations between my co-counsel, Seth, and the employer and insurance company representatives did not result in a resolution. Unfortunately, they continued to be inflexible, focusing on the validity of their narrative and failing to consider the potential poor outcomes without a negotiated resolution. To locate overlapping interests, create more value, and expand the potential for a mutually beneficial outcome, Seth and I agreed that a successful resolution would require better-skilled negotiators for the insurance company and employer. These company representatives weren't cutting it. We needed someone proficient at negotiation and who better understood our assessment of Max's legal rights and the company's duties. We proposed that we engage in pre-suit mediation, but both defendants declined. We had to file to maximize the potential for a satisfactory negotiated agreement.

4.

When I graduated from law school in 1987, we often began representation by filing a complaint without considering options such as mediation or structured negotiation with our clients. We believed it was just that simple. But it is not that simple. Filing a suit without exhausting other options may subject clients to unnecessary delays in resolving their legal problem. Clients are instantly involved at some level in an adversarial process that tends to produce emotional strains on their well-being.

How does the restorative lawyer decide when to file a suit? What questions do we ask ourselves, and our clients? Are there factual differences that might be resolved by a court proceeding? Have we exhausted negotiation and efforts to mediate? Are there time deadlines? Does the client have unmet needs that cannot be satisfied without initiating litigation? Does the client have rights that may need to be enforced to meet their needs that are not being recognized? Can filing suit increase the collaborative team members in a way that moves the resolution in a beneficial direction?

Involving litigation counsel prematurely can complicate efforts to resolve the case. Some lawyers who focus their practices on litigation are not skilled in collaboration and may have poor communication skills. These lawyers may communicate only through legal pleadings, convincing the client that this approach is doing all that can be done. They may be unaware of their client's needs and file motions without deciphering the client's long-term goals and creating a strategy to meet them.

We viewed filing suit as a way to improve opportunities for negotiation, perhaps expediting resolution to eliminate the increasing stress and anxiety Max experienced. Sometimes impasse in negotiation can be broken by locating new frameworks, or alternative negotiators. Filing suit against Pillar Insurance and Will's employer provided more options for negotiation. After filing suit, we returned to negotiations as soon as possible. We were forthright that we would not serve the complaint immediately to provide an opportunity to resolve the matter without formal legal discovery processes. Both defendants retained counsel.

The lawyers were as different as night and day. Pillar Insurance's lawyer had poor negotiation and communication skills. He continued to be terse and only understood positional bargaining. However, the employer's counsel, Jacklyn, was well-educated, talented, skilled, and appeared ready to represent her client equally well in collaborative and adversarial processes.

Jacklyn reached out immediately and set up a phone call with Seth and me. She willingly recognized Max's experience of harm without volunteering resolutions. She assured us that she wanted to understand our legal analysis fully. After the call, she emailed me.

Seth/Brenda, good talking to you. We appreciate your offer of sharing the claim file with us. To facilitate that, I am copying my admin, as she can email a FedEx airbill for your

use in sending the claim file. I understand that you still
need to visit with your client about this.

In the meantime, please call me if you have any questions. I
will visit with our client about your request for certain policies. Thank you

While we continued to attempt negotiation, the logistics of
getting the lawyers and parties together created challenges. It
seemed like we were moving closer to resolution. The employer
seemed willing to accept some responsibility for not processing the
paperwork, but they wouldn't concede all responsibility for the
error that deprived Max of coverage. They continued to seek more
information from Pillar Insurance, their client, and from us. By
July, we pushed up against the service deadline. Both defendants
agreed to accept service of process, and we continued to exchange
information informally.

Six months later, we had exchanged most of the information
and were hopeful that we were getting closer to serious negotiations. We were still working together, even if we disagreed. Jacklyn
checked in with me to discuss options, and used a tone in her
emails that continued to encourage cooperation and discussion.

Seth, ok, thank you. We figured you guys were probably
still working on the demand, but I just wanted to be sure I
hadn't missed it. The creative option we discussed would
be atypical, but not impossible, and I appreciate your
approaching us with ideas. I would be happy to discuss
further at some point.

That said, when you can, it would be good to get an official
demand from you guys. I know that we have verbally
discussed numbers, but as you can imagine, our client

wants to see something in writing, directly from you all (which I can pass on).

Again, this is for settlement purposes only. Thank you

We continued to build our relationship with Max. A television producer contacted me to feature Max's case on a program as a David vs. Goliath story. After we discussed it, Max thought about it and emailed me.

"I'm not sure how I feel about it. I am interested because I definitely don't ever want this to happen to anyone else, especially not to one of Will's friends who still works there. But I don't want to cause a bunch of trouble with the employer and then have them not go through with this. I trust you and the role you feel best I agree with ..."

5.

In August, the federal court issued a scheduling order requiring us to have our initial planning meeting, provide the report, and attend a scheduling conference. These tasks became opportunities to create relationships and discover the obstacles in resolving the dispute. Intrinsic to the planning, was formal discovery.

Formal discovery wasn't likely to change the outcome, we had already engaged in informal discovery. Both Collaborative Divorce and Strategic Negotiation recognize informal discovery often generates sufficient information for the parties to be well-informed for negotiation or mediation early in the litigation process. Pillar's attorney was less comfortable with the informal information sharing and insisted on formal discovery. However, we worked strategically, mindfully, and intentionally. We figured out where we were going with the discovery and then created a discovery plan to go there. No fishing expedition. No useless forms.

For discovery to be mindful, questions seek information strategically to help resolve the conflict, settle the case, and not just generate paper or billable hours. Questions that irritate the other party or nail them down to a point that has no impact on the bigger picture are avoided. In the 30-plus years that I've practiced, I've sent and received broadly drawn, blaming, and blustering discovery. Does this move the parties towards being made whole? Does it allow for the weaving of multiple narratives? No. It creates animosity and often generates more needs. Implicit blaming is destructive.

During discovery in a personal injury case, many plaintiffs feel like fault is being attributed to them or that the injuries are not perceived as significant. The lack of validation of injuries and the lack of acceptance of responsibility often stalls potential for settlement. It often reignites anger stemming from unmet needs. This does not move either party closer to meeting long-term goals.

When I first meet with clients who have been injured, many are not angry. Some see the event as an accident — anyone can make a mistake. After being scrutinized by opposing counsel in discovery (and especially during the deposition), they grow defensive and angry. The opposing attorney's questions often invalidate their suffering. Victims feel as though the other side believes it was the victim's fault, or that they exaggerate their pain and injuries. The plaintiff often feels like the defendant is failing to accept responsibility for their wrongdoing and blaming the victim.

As a restorative lawyer, depositions and formal discovery are not off the table — but we are careful and strategic to be sure that we are not just checking a box or needlessly inflaming the "other side." Discovery functions to get the information we need to understand both sides, making it possible to resolve the legal conflict through negotiation.

6.

Freely exchanging information and reviewing it, creates opportunities to explore ways to resolve factual disagreements. During discovery, the restorative lawyer discloses information freely and as early as possible. Early disclosures of crucial facts and legal guideposts permit a broad evaluation of options that may speed up a client's goal to "move on." When the other party seems to be far from resolving the case, we try to identify what information we have that may be useful in changing their mind. Why do we see the case so differently? Understanding both sides' perceptions and needs creates an opportunity for a win-win negotiation.

As information comes in, we identify more shared facts. At the same time, we find more disputed facts. Synergetic, joint discussions may help determine ways to address a disputed fact. Does the factual disagreement have to be reconciled? Can the two stories coexist without reaching agreement on the fact? Is it a fact that doesn't affect the outcome in meeting the parties' needs?

In a restorative practice of law, the attorney rejects the "single story."[3] All factual issues may not be able to be reconciled and having them resolved by a judge or jury (who are often referred to as the "finder of fact") may create additional conflict. As a matter of practice, lawyers often overestimate the necessity to adjudicate every fact. The question for the restorative lawyer is whether or not the parties will benefit from having a third party adjudicate this fact. Independent of legal findings, why does the resolution of the disputed fact matter? What are the parties' needs relative to the disputed fact? Can those needs be addressed without reconciliation of the point of contention?

In some cases involving accidents, fault can be a close call. If all of the parties' needs can be met, it may not be necessary for anyone, much less a third party, to decide which factual account is most credible. It is not unusual for liability or causation to be disputed. In restorative lawyering, the focus is less on the unresolved fact and more on the resulting needs of the parties. Once met, the need for a contested adjudication often disappears.

In Chapter Five, Kevin, the child injured by the light fixture at the military base, involved a situation that created two distinct narratives, specifically about what caused the child's brain injury. Despite that difference, we reached a resolution that provided for the child's maximum gain through eligibility for special services and government services to address his needs. The narrative that the mother developed conflicted with that of the defendant. We could reconcile them to our mutual satisfaction only by allowing for ambiguity, not by allowing one story or narrative to be the dominant narrative, extinguishing the other.

In Max's case, the disputed fact involved the absence of a request for an insurance supplement in the insurance file, and it seemed impossible to reconcile that fact. As we continued in the *sansatrial* period, we found that most of the stories were consistent, but that dispute continued. As the date for our mediation moved closer, we increased opportunities to meet and negotiate.

On January 22, I emailed both attorneys, interested to inquire if we might be able to settle all issues since the mediation was just over a week away. We had just received 17 inches of snow, and we were all hoping to resolve the case without traveling in the blizzard.

During this period of active negotiation, the biggest obstacles were the disputed facts, the lack of negotiation skills with Pillar's lawyer, and Max's need to have sufficient financial resources to be able to get his house payments caught up and other debts paid.

Jacklyn, the employer's lawyer, taught me a way to think of communicating an offer to a client that may be a tool for the restorative lawyer. When I proposed an offer, she'd say that she needed to "visit with the client about it." I liked that. "Visit" means to go or see for a particular purpose, but it also means to pay a call as an act of friendship or courtesy. I found this term much more respectful than what we usually say, "I'll pass it along to my client."

As the snow piled up to a record 40 inches, Seth and I discussed agreeing to postpone the mediation. We wanted to be agreeable. But couldn't delay resolution; Max's delinquent bills continued to pile up. A few days later, the roads had thawed out. Jaclyn flew into the city and took the two-hour drive to the mediator's office. The insurance company lawyer made a short drive from his home in the city. We were ready to mediate.

~

SETH and I arrive at the mediation session a little early. The mediator employs an evaluative mediation style. He typically would place each side in different rooms and usher offers back and forth. He seats us in the first conference room. A few minutes later we hear the other attorneys arrive, separately, and they are escorted up the steps to another conference room. The door opens and Max and a young woman walk in. Max hugs both Seth and me.

"This is Amber. She's a BFF. I hope it's okay that I brought her."

"No problem. We are happy to have you here and please let us know if you need anything or have questions. Everything in mediation is confidential — but if Max wants to talk to us in a way to preserve the attorney-client privilege, we may have to have Amber sit out for a minute. I don't think that'll happen, but Max, let me know if you have any questions, and we can speak privately first."

Max smiles. "Sure."

The mediator comes in and does a long-winded opening statement about mediation, the layout of the office, and coffee. We summarize the negotiations thus far and he goes upstairs. We visit for a while, talking about our dogs, the snow, and the holiday.

"I think I'll go to work, now. You are clearly in good hands." Amber stands up and smiles at us.

"That's fine with me. I'll text you if I need anything."

Amber leaves and a few minutes later the mediator returns

with a counteroffer. We continue to throw numbers back and forth over the next three hours and arrive at a number that will work. It's not 100 percent of what we are seeking, but it's close and most importantly it's high enough to cover the bills and past due mortgage payments. We have enough money on the table to arrive at Max's "done" statement. However, Max wants an apology and an assurance that the employer has taken action to remedy their error in processing paperwork.

We are surprised when the mediator returns quickly and opens the doors. Jacklyn walks down the steep steps into the conference. She doesn't sit down, at first. Rather she looks Max right in the eye.

"Mr. Stallard, I'm so sorry about this. First of all, I'm sorry that Ben Woods, the president of the company couldn't be here today. He cleared his schedule, but he's snowed in and couldn't be here. I have spoken with him, and I understand his position. We are sorry he's not here, but we are also so sorry for everything you've suffered from your loss. Losing Will must have been one of the most difficult things a person faces in their lives."

Max is tearing up, and of course, I start to tear up.

"We are also really sorry that you've had to go through all of this court proceeding to get what you are entitled to. Our company made errors in the paperwork, and they were significant since they are behind the problems you've faced. And I am also so sorry that it took so long and so much effort on your part to resolve it." Jacklyn does not try to shift the blame to Will for having overlooked the paperwork or to Pillar for taking the payments. She focuses on her apology.

Max is no longer tearing up. "Thank you, I accept that apology. But I really want more. What's to say this is not going to happen to someone else, even one of Will's friends? I can't live with myself unless I know I 've done everything I can do. I don't want anyone to go through what I've been through the last two years."

Jacklyn looks at us all, "May I sit down?" We all nod, and she does. She pulls out a folder full of documents, policies, and forms.

She carefully shares outlines, details, and paperwork to demonstrate their remedial efforts to correct their procedures. She explains details and answers questions. After about 45 minutes, the mediator's assistant returns with the typed agreement. We sign the agreement.

∾

A FEW WEEKS LATER, we signed the releases, dismissal orders, and received the check. But we were not "done" yet. Max needed to move past his financial difficulties. But before we review those steps, it's helpful to consider what happens with opposing counsel in the *sansatrial* period, particularly when it begins to move closer to trial, goes to trial, or is appealed.

7.

What might have happened if the attorney representing the employer was not skilled, like Jacklyn? What would our next step be if we couldn't resolve the case at mediation? Sometimes cases, such as those significantly impacting public policy or communities, can only be resolved at trial. In Max's case, the restorative approach led to resolution during the *sansatrial* period. Where does the restorative lawyer start when, for any reason, the case proceeds to an adversarial process for resolution?

The lawyer should first engage in diligent and critical introspection to examine their assumptions, thoughts, strategies, and impulses. Is the lawyer certain that the adversarial processes provide the only tools to meet the client's goals? The lawyer should determine that the case is truly one of the two percent that will go to trial. One of the few cases in my career that was indeed a two-percenter involved a young software engineer charged with a crime.

Chris White hired me to represent him on criminal charges.

Chris funded his college by joining the National Guard. After graduation, he, like many guardsmen at the time, skipped drills, typically scheduled on weekends or breaks from his job as a computer engineer. The state passed legislation to criminalize missing drills, and the district attorney charged him with ten misdemeanors, a separate charge for each missed drill. They were playing hardball.

I took his case, confident that we could work something out. I called the district attorney and proposed that Chris make up his drills. The response was an unequivocal "no" and confirmation they sought "mandatory jail time." Chris reported that other guardsmen, including a single mother, were convicted and serving their jail time on weekends. We did not give up. Chris spent his summer vacation making up his missed drills. I called the district attorney again. Ten separate misdemeanors. One day per charge. No deal.

We filed a Writ of Prohibition to stop the prosecution on the grounds that the state action was an unconstitutional violation of the supremacy clause. We won in Circuit Court. The Guard appealed and we won when the State Supreme Court declared the statute unconstitutional. Chris never went to jail, and the state stopped sending guardsmen to jail.

This case was a two-percenter for at least several reasons:

1. The other side refused to talk.
2. The client had resources and unmet needs that could withstand a protracted litigation period.
3. Other people were impacted by the resolution.

Once the lawyer determines that the case is genuinely a two-percenter, the restorative lawyer may look at each process along the route and consider how to work more consistent with restorative principles and values. Every legal process in a conflict can be placed on a continuum to assess how restorative or destructive the practice may be. Every restorative lawyer can explore how to move it closer to the restorative end of that continuum.

Even within adversarial procedures, the restorative lawyer can find ways to make the process more collaborative, problem-solving, and restorative. In the last chapter I described my work with Bruce Hampton when he agreed to pay more spousal support than required by the statute. At the hearing to adopt the agreement, I had the opportunity to make a court proceeding more restorative by prioritizing Bruce's goal to create as amicable a process as possible. In this jurisdiction, the parties attend the final hearing, swear under oath, and provide the court with a reason to adopt their agreement. When we arrived for the final hearing, we found Bruce's wife, Cassidy, sitting with her counsel in a private conference room, adjacent to the courtroom. As we exchanged pleasantries, she struggled to speak.

I understood, that as the petitioner in the case, Cassidy would testify first to provide information for the judge to review the agreement. I asked her if she'd prefer that I conduct a direct examination of Bruce, and she accepted my offer. I led Bruce through the requisite testimony, and Cassidy agreed with a sufficient few words, for the record. In a few minutes, the hearing was over. A week later, I received this note from Cassidy.

Hi Brenda,

I just wanted to thank you for your kindness and support during the hearing on Tuesday. Your suggestion made the process much easier for me.

Take good care,

8.

Could restorative justice also impact a jury trial? Lawyer and restorative justice colleague, Fred Van Liew, now works as a coordinator for a restorative justice program in Maine. Years ago, he ran a restorative justice project within a district attorney's office.

When Fred prosecuted a case that involved political issues resulting in the defendants being charged with crimes consistent with civil disobedience, he felt sure that the case would go to trial and worked to find the least destructive way to proceed to trial. Both the defendants and Fred agreed that justice required both sides to have the opportunity to put on their full case. They wanted the best format possible to tell their stories and to have the chance to explain their interests to the jury. Fred did not object to evidence regarding the motivations behind their civil disobedience, allowing their full story to be told in open court. The week-long trial resulted in a conviction. When I discussed this case with Fred, he described how he felt informed by restorative justice as he prosecuted the matter. He said he proceeded so that he could "let the people tell their story. ... RJ is so much about storytelling."

I've spent enough time discussing the two percent — when we must litigate a question of fact or law. Let's return now to a more typical situation when a jury trial is unlikely— Max's case. I left off after we settled with the employer and the insurance company. One of the defendants had made an apology and provided adequate assurances about remedial actions to prevent the reoccurrence of the wrongdoing. But the case wasn't over. What about Max's goals — his "done"?

During my first meeting with Max, we defined that goal. He needed to resolve his financial situation and bring the house payments current. He believed that relieving the financial anxiety would help with his depression. He wanted to be treated respectfully. Max wanted to re-story his experience to create peace with his loss while establishing financial security. He wanted to retain the home that represented his shared life with Will. Max wanted to feel like his efforts could prevent others from suffering from the careless acts of the employer and the insurance company. He wanted to be able to both hold on to and move on from the life he shared with Will.

~

I SIT down to review the file one afternoon before Max comes in for an appointment. I look at the numbers — Max now has sufficient funds to bring his mortgage current. But I still have some questions. I want to talk with Max to be sure he feels respected. I want to confirm that he's satisfied with the company's remedial efforts to fix the deficiencies that generated his legal problem. I also want to see if he is coming out of the depression he's been in since I met him. We have a few concrete items on our "to-do" list. Primarily, we need to finish up with credit repairs, to work within his rights under consumer laws to pay off balances and have negative credit references removed.

Max arrives. He seems different, calmer and more energetic. He focuses quickly as we set up piles of papers — one for each creditor. We methodically approach each stack, lined up along the edges of the table. It's clear most of them are paid. We are close to the "done."

"Guess what?"

I don't look up, feeling pulled into my Excel spread sheet as I attempt to sort out late fees and Fair Debt Collection Act claims. "What?"

"I'm seeing someone." I stop and look up at Max. He is so cute, smiling with a hopeful glimmer in his beautiful blue eyes. He speaks with the same compassion, but with new insight. "I miss Will. I'll never stop loving him. But Jacob may be a keeper."

I moved two more of the bills from the *contested* stack to the *resolved* stack. "Tell me about him."

~

I FINISHED his case a few months later, confident that we had reached his goals. Max now shares his life with Jacob and the latest addition to their family: a chestnut filly named Kenzo, born on February 19.

Chapter 11

My Heart Is Healing

COMPASSIONATE PATIENCE – SITTING IN SILENCE

Restorative justice can produce ongoing transformation. However, the transformation must begin with ourselves, for we too have recompense to pay, reconciliation to seek, forgiveness to ask, and healing to receive.

— Dan Van Ness, *Restorative Justice*

I.

As I AM BECOMING a restorative lawyer, I find the same potential for growth in relationships, mutual healing, and community strengthening that I found in my work with Max. Something else accompanies this change: moments while I'm working when I feel whole or complete. Not that elated feeling when I win a ruling, a trial, or an appeal. It's not that sense that I can walk on clouds because I rocked a cross-examination and made the ass on the other side look like a fool. Not the thrill of sitting at the counsel table and having the judge read the verdict — in our favor.

The restorative lawyer is at peace, sitting quiet and still beside a client.

It's like walking on the beach with someone you love or playing with a child at the park. We are not thinking about where we are walking to or if that trip to the park will make the child like us more or make us more money. This peaceful stillness is what I seek in my time with my clients. Being able to stand with them, walk with them, and share moments of our intertwined lives. In this space, this stillness, I may find the place for restoration, where the healing sits.

In this calmness dwells the place where peace meets justice in the restorative lawyer's work. The agony of failing to attain a certain resolution for a client—an acquittal, a good verdict, retention of custody—gives way to satisfaction from the healing capacity we create within the lawyer-client relationship. Here is the moment we let go of the external outcome far beyond our control. Standing in its place, we embrace a moment of contentedness.

The moment is the opposite of sitting at counsel table, hearing your client's testimony, intuitively knowing that things will end badly. I have suffered through more of those moments than I can count. Belinda Pierson will never see her children again once she loses custody of Tasha and Steven to her abusive husband. Micky Powell is going to spend the rest of his life in prison. Mary Baker will never know how her son wound up on a roadside in a strange city with bullet holes in his chest. Tish Hoover dies in a hospital bed while her ex-husband golfs with his new girlfriend, financially supported by the proceeds from Tish's malpractice award following a delayed uterine cancer diagnosis.

How did I move here? How have I found my way to becoming a restorative lawyer? How did I learn that I could have a life as a lawyer with this level of significance — transcending the daily practice?

Simple. I've been honored and blessed with the most competent teachers.

And healers.

2.

Who was your first teacher? As a lawyer? As a restorative lawyer? As Rachel Naomi Remen observes, "Perhaps the world is one big healing community, and we are all healers of each other. Perhaps we are all angels. And we do not know."[1] I've had many great teachers, but three specific ones helped me find that space where peace meets justice in our everyday work. It was easy to overlook them, but their message became imprinted in my soul — there for me to read when I was ready. Initially, I had no idea that Lydia Sharp, my very first client, was also my very first teacher. And yes, there are angels at the jailhouse.

After studying the law for three years, I became a lawyer. A few days later, I received a call notifying me of my client: a court-appointed criminal defendant. I put on my new lady lawyer suit I'd bought for the swearing-in ceremony and drove to the jail. In those days, we had no private space to talk. I pulled my chair up on the other side of the bars as my first client, Lydia Sharp (seated in her chair on her side of the bars), told her story. She was charged with forging prescriptions. She showed me scars on her arm from wounds inflicted by her husband.

Lydia told me a story that sounded like a movie I'd just watched starring Farrah Fawcett, *The Burning Bed*, so much so that I wondered if she was telling the truth. I left the jail and drove home. I knew that my life would never be the same. My life as a lawyer was not going to be the way I'd imagined it. I had just witnessed pain I'd only seen on television. I could never return to a naïve world where I could imagine a lawyer having the capacity to *fix* injustices. I could work for social justice, but I wouldn't be the hero. I was eventually going to be the student, and I was going to be healed.

Lydia taught me what it looked like to be a woman who had survived a lifetime of trauma and abuse. She taught me what it looked like to become addicted in order to survive. In listening to her through the bars, I dedicated myself to trying to halt the parade of abuse she suffered, even if only in our relationship. Lydia taught me how to do that. She taught me what it means to listen deeply and with compassion. She taught me what it feels like to tell the district attorney you won't take a guilty plea because this client needs treatment and to keep asking for it. Even as opposing counsel laughed and mocked my naiveté, optimism, and hope, I rededicated myself to my work as a healer. I visited Lydia at the out-of-state hospital after they dismissed the charges. That was decades ago. I don't know what happened to her. I only know what happened to me.

And what happened to me during the next 30 years is this: my heart breaks over and over by the tragedy that brings people to me seeking representation, conflict resolution, and healing. I work with them, searching for the power to heal. We look within the fabric of their being to create a new scar that will forever be a part of them, a reminder of the hideous event that came into their lives that they did not invite. As I do, they heal. Like the silk that sutures together skin pulled apart by an accident, these friends, clients, and cherished ones suture the wounds on my heart.

Clients create opportunities for relationships — and a chance for healing and justice.

Somehow, between the clients providing me with the guts to suture our wounds and the love that emerges when we place relationship over procedure, the practice becomes more healing and less destruction. When we change the question from, *What law was broken?* to *Has there been harm? How do we meet needs?* the space for healing emerges. When we pay less attention to the outcome — who wins and how much — and more attention to how we get there, all participants win. We become part of the restorative process.

Our work alongside our clients heals our broken hearts. I met another teacher sharing the lesson of the reciprocal capacity of healing within our work as lawyers while I was a young assistant district attorney. A few days before Christmas, Human Services wanted to remove a young child, Tia, from her parents, Maggie and Marcus James, due to Tia's "failure to thrive." The court found that Human Services had not made "reasonable efforts,"[2] therefore; the child remained with her family — with services and frequent meetings between the attorneys and service providers. The parents had numerous learning disabilities, and the child suffered from a physical disorder that made it difficult to swallow. This family both broke and healed my heart.

Broken by seeing the obstacles they faced. Healed by being allowed to be part of their lives. One afternoon, I went shopping with two of my children, both under six. We drove to a small shopping center in our mini-station wagon. Finishing our shopping, we saw Marcus, Maggie, and Tia sitting on a bench, and stopped to chat. I offered them a ride home; it wasn't far from my house and would be easier for them than the bus. We squeezed into our car. In my mind's eye, I can still see my two children, with Tia and her mom, sitting in the car's back seat. They got out at their apartment development, and we drove away. We were not opposing parties seated across from one another in a courtroom. We were two families sharing a tiny space. While driving across town, we discussed our shopping trip, school, and birthdays. I think we even sang a few short songs, mending my heart.

3.

Clients are our teachers: They understand that justice is more than getting money, getting revenge, or getting even. Justice is more than the law. Embracing the ambiguity of justice centers on love and creates healing. Another teacher who showed me how our intertwined journeys of discovery and compassion contain the capability to heal, was Mary Barker. Mary became a victim when somebody shot her son and shoved his dead body out of a car in a faraway city where he attended college. In all her suffering, Mary healed my heart. She didn't know what to do when the police and the district attorneys couldn't identify any suspects. They ignored her requests. When she contacted me, I accepted her case to see if I could do anything. I set out to be a good lawyer. I requested the police report and shared it with her. I consulted with two excellent litigation attorneys about liability for the university where her son attended or the hospital that failed to resuscitate him. Nearly empty-handed, I applied for burial expenses from the state's crime victim's fund. This, too, was denied; they declared that Mary's son was "not an innocent victim of crime."

I persisted. I gathered what information I could, shared what scant facts I could uncover, and listened to Mary when no one would listen. But I felt like I failed. My heart felt more broken and defeated as I sent her a letter closing her case. But the case wasn't over.

Mary wrote back. She described the lack of justice from the police, the crime fund, and the district attorney. "I feel that your time has been wasted. But remember, you pulled me through my grieving time. You were there for us."

Mary taught me that my failures with the institution did not solely define our work. Did I create healing for us both by removing the cloak of invisibility the institutions had draped over Mary? Did receiving compassion from a helpless advocate help Mary? Anthropologist Julienne Anoko describes her work in the Congo fighting Ebola; she says, "What I'm trying to give people is the kind of compassion I have looked for in the difficult moments in my own life."[3]

It takes more than a moment, more than a week, more than a month to heal a lawyer's broken heart. Recall Ella Riley, the grandmother who lost custody of her grandchildren after her daughter was murdered? Ella's suffering caused my first heartbreak. My healing began immediately, but I did not see it. One day, I went to work and realized that my teachers (my clients) had been providing healing for years. And once I recognized what was happening and the capacity within the relationships, everything changed. My restorative approach to practicing law meant my days had become very different.

4.

In Thornton Wilder's play *Our Town*, the stage manager reminds us, "Choose the least important day in your life. It will be important enough." Yes, our ordinary days are precious and contain our teachers' lessons — if we take the time to recognize, understand, and appreciate them.

∽

TODAY, I start online with a few free consultations with prospective clients. One of them wants to know her options in a divorce. She says, "We don't agree on everything, but we don't want to get involved with lawyers and courts." Another is a former client, Sasha. She fell into a big hole in a big box store and now can't continue in her daily life with the pain she suffers in her back and knee. Others have questions about employment discrimination, contractors, and eviction. I make referrals, open files, or provide suggestions then finally turn the computer off. I drive to my colleague's office for a four-way meeting in a collaborative divorce case. The financial neutral has just produced reports, and we plan to integrate them into a property settlement agreement.

Lunchtime rolls around, and I dash off to lunch with a former client who suffered a severe brain injury. Her case has been closed for a few years, but we are getting together to visit today. I enjoy catching up with clients long after their cases are over. It is particularly satisfying today since Sabrina's recovery is nearly complete and she is enjoying her life.

After lunch, I make three calls. Two of them are short, and I'm looking forward to touching base with a few insurance adjusters I haven't spoken with for a while. One has been assigned a case we just accepted involving a child who was injured in a car accident. I don't know the adjuster on the other case, a homeowner's insurance claim, but I'm hoping one or two calls may resolve it. The complaint is straightforward, and the client wants the matter to be concluded quickly.

The tough call is to a family who lives out of the area. I'm representing their daughter in a crime victim's fund case, preparing for a hearing in a few months. I was finally able to subpoena the police records and need to schedule an appointment to review the reports with them. It will be challenging since the records don't support their daughter's recollection of the evening when she was sexually assaulted. They will need plenty of time to emotionally prepare for the meeting. They will also need plenty of time to review the records with me, so that they might comprehend them.

I hang up and answer emails, mostly about scheduling, phone messages, and obtaining records. It's time for my last meeting of the day.

It's drizzling, so I decide to drive the short distance from my office to my client's house. Perrietta White is a beautiful woman in her early 70s. We got to know each other last fall after she was a passenger in a car coming home from the senior center. The driver hit the gas rather than the brake, and the car ran into a brick rancher. Perrietta suffered from severe shortness of breath and was transported to the emergency room of the local hospital. When her condition couldn't be stabilized, medics airlifted her to a nearby trauma center.

Physicians at the center discovered her undiagnosed heart disease. She underwent extensive heart surgery. Her son scheduled my first meeting with Perietta at her house soon after she came home. I remember it as being a bit chaotic, with medical equipment crammed into the tiny kitchen, along with Perietta and a physical therapist supervising exercises while we talked. Initially, Perietta was most afraid of her mounting bills. Medicare paid most of them, others could be covered by her auto insurance company.

Today I am stopping by her house to have her sign several checks issued to cover medical bills. I park in front of one of the 19th century houses lined up along the narrow street.

Perrietta is sitting in a plastic Adirondack-style chair on her porch. Her hands are folded neatly in her lap, holding her purse and several envelopes with open flaps containing unpaid bills. We visit for an hour. We talk about her being raised in that house, her brother who doesn't stop to say "hello" when he passes by us, and she asks about my son's upcoming wedding. Sometimes, we pause and watch the rain fall. When it's time to go, she asks me to drive her to the senior center for lunch. She endorses the back of the med-pay checks so that we can deposit them to pay her bills. I drop her off. She smiles and waves as she goes into the building.

⁓

FROM PERRIETTA, I learn the simplest and most important lesson in becoming a restorative lawyer. Being a restorative lawyer means having the capacity to sit still beside a client for a few minutes on her porch, watching the rain — not talking about anything.

I learn to enjoy this moment in time. Justice.

Peace.

Many clients have taught me the lessons that deliver me to this moment, ready to learn. My first client, Lydia, taught me that trauma is real and that healing for clients concurrently creates healing for the lawyer. The young family, Marcus, Maggie, and Tia, taught me that relationships create far more opportunities for repair than statutes and rules have the capacity to initiate. And the grief-stricken mother, Mary, who showed me how my meager, sincere efforts to provide healing (that felt like pure failure) could be the only fragment of justice to show up after a tragedy.

But today, it's Perrietta who, by example, teaches me to slow down, to sit in silence--to enjoy our mutually shared compassionate patience with one another. We visit, deeply yet briefly, in the world that each of us occupies through that silence. Perrietta, along with all those who have generously interwoven their lives into mine, demonstrate the potential for relationships and partnerships, when we gracefully and with open hearts, seek resolutions together.

We can sit in stillness, feeling a peace alongside clients.

We can comprehend experiences we'll never know, even with complexities and divergent fragments of stories, woven but frayed.

We can create environments to locate internalized, expansive, subjective justice. We have the teachers, the tools, and the opportunity to learn.

We can all be taught to create a new way of being a lawyer, if we can embrace our fears and vulnerabilities long enough to let the healing begin.

Yes, we can all become restorative lawyers.

Acknowledgments

Somewhere along the way, some of us become fortunate to find ourselves in a community that supports, encourages, and loves us. I am grateful to have fallen in with the right crowd, who has made it possible for me to find my way to becoming a restorative lawyer. Thank you to everyone in this community, including my family and friends, who created space for me to explore this practice and find time to write about it.

I want to thank thousands of unnamed clients, opposing parties, lawyers, judges, bailiffs, witnesses, receptionists, legal assistants, administrative assistants, secretaries, and countless others who taught me the importance of respect, responsibility, and relationships with those who work with legal conflicts daily. I also want to thank my spouse, Chris Quasebarth; we launched our legal careers together in 1984. Despite decades of challenges, we have supported one another as we persisted in our struggle to work for justice and peace.

Thank you to friends, family, and colleagues who read this book and provided valuable insight and guidance, including Michael John Aloi, Jane Buchbauer, Lee Ann Dransfield, Karina Echazú, Taylor Graham, Lori Hovermale, Denise Hughes, Teresa McCune, Debra McHenry, Elexa Waugh-Quasebarth, Laura Partington, and Paul Marshall Yoder.

I'm deeply grateful to the Center for Justice and Peacebuilding for providing the education to expand my understanding of the law beyond critical legal theory. Within this setting, I've been able to explore and search for answers to address a legal system that, while it may sometimes create opportunities for healing, is embedded with a potential to create harm.

I want to extend my heartfelt thanks to Robyn Short for her patience and skill in guiding this book through the publishing process. Her dedication and expertise have been invaluable. I also want to express my gratitude to the Longevity Marketing team who designed the book, with a special mention to Ifraz Khan for the cover design.

About the Author

Brenda Waugh is a lawyer-mediator who has practiced law since 1987 as a legislative lawyer, assistant district attorney, legal services attorney, and in private practice. Brenda has included mediation, collaborative law, and restorative justice facilitation in her practice since 2010. While *Becoming a Restorative Lawyer* is her first book, she has published several law review articles on restorative justice and critical legal theory. She has taught courses at the West Virginia University College of Law and Eastern Mennonite University's Center for Justice and Peacebuilding and has conducted workshops throughout the United States and Canada.

About the Photographer

Howard Zehr is a distinguished professor of restorative justice at Eastern Mennonite University's Center for Justice and Peacebuilding and director emeritus of the Zehr Institute. He is the author of *The Little Book of Restorative Justice, Changing Lenses*, and *Critical Issues in Restorative Justice*, among other titles. He lives in Broadway, Virginia. His photographic books include *Still Doing Life: 22 Lifers 25 Years Later* and *Transcending: Reflections of Crime Victims*.

Notes

Introduction

1. See, i.e. Gerry Johnstone and Daniel W. Van Ness, *Handbook of Restorative Justice* (Devon: Willian, 2007). More specifically, this practice is shaped by the principles and values first clearly articulated by Howard Zehr in Howard Zehr, *Changing Lenses, A New Focus on Crime and Justice*, (Scotsdale, PA: Herald Press, 2005).
2. "The Story Behind the Song, Dolly Parton, You'd Better Get To Living," *The Boot*, September 18, 2015, https://theboot.com/story-behind-the-song-better-get-to-livin-dolly-parton/ (accessed October 30, 2020).
3. Annie Duke, *How I Raised, Folded, Bluffed, Flirted, Cursed, and Won Millions at the World Series of Poker*, (New York: Hudson Street Press, 2005), 142.

1. My Heart Is Broken

1. Heiner Kipphardt, *In the Matter of J. Robert Oppenheimer*, directed by Frank Condon, Odyssey II, Los Angeles, CA, April 19-June 19, 1983.
2. Scott Turow, *One L* (New York: Penguin Group, 1977), 7. (*Describing first year law students*).
3. *Pierson v. Post*. 3 Cai. R. 175 (1805). This appellate decision included in the first year of study for most American law students involves a dispute about the ownership of a fox by two hunters in pursuit. The appellate court's reasoning in defining property is a pivotal case in American jurisprudence.
4. Duncan Kennedy, *Legal Education a Reproduction of Hierarchy*, (Cambridge: Harvard,1983), 54.
5. Camden County, like all locations and names in this text are fictitious.
6. Tracy Chapman, "All That You Have is Your Soul," on *Crossroads*, Electra Entertainment, 1989.
7. Rachel Naomi Remen, *Kitchen Table Wisdom* (New York: Penguin, 1996), 252.
8. *Ibid.*, 252.

2. My Jealous Mistress

1. Howard Zinn, *You Can't Be Neutral on a Moving Train: A Personal History of Our Times* (New York: Beacon Press, 2010), 43.
2. I explored my experience with this tragedy, comparing restorative responses in a law review article published after the tragedy. Brenda Waugh, "Who Will

Choose the End Words? Structuring Justice Amid Tragedy, *Washington University Journal of Law & Policy* 36, (2011): 141-177. https://openscholar ship.wustl.edu/cgi/viewcontent.cgi?article=1045&context=law_jour nal_law_policy (accessed April 22, 2021).

3. Nikki Giovanni, "Convocation," (speech, Blacksburg, VA, April 17, 2007), https://www.archive.vtmag.vt.edu/memorial07/VTMagazinePDF/convoca tion.8.pdf (accessed September 29, 2024).

4. Lucinda Roy, *No Right to Remain Silent* (New York: Harmony Books, 2009), 302.

5. David Orr, "The Most Misread Poem in America," *The Paris Review*, September 22, 2015, https://www.theparisreview.org/blog/2015/09/11/the-most-misread-poem-in-america/ (accessed April 7, 2021).

6. Daniel W. Van Ness and Karen Heetderks Strong, *Restoring Justice: An Intro-duction to Restorative Justice* (New York: Routledge, 2015) 23-24.

7. Van Ness suggests that restorative justice and indigenous justice share a focus on repairing harm rather than inflicting retributive harm and in practices such as the talking circle. *Ibid.*, 16.

8. *Ibid.*, 25.

9. *Ibid.*, 28.

10. Zehr, *Changing Lenses*, 270, 278-279.

11. Johnstone and Van Ness, *Handbook,* 48. I say "roughly" since some scholars argue that inclusion, encounter, amends, and reintegration are elements of restorative justice.

12. Throughout this text, I use the term "offender" to describe a person accused of wrongdoing. Lawyers are accustomed (and comfortable) with term "defendant". "Defendant" describes the position of the person accused of wrongdoing inci-dent to the legal process of prosecution. It does not describe the more complex relationship as does the term "offender." The term "offender" is far from perfect for many reasons. It narrowly describes a person in one context in one point in time and does not account for the more complex, deeper story. It also is a noun, a label, that may be incorrect, incomplete, and be more proscriptive than descriptive.

3. Being a Good Lawyer

1. Shenandoah University Films, Paulette Moore and Brenda Waugh, "Pillars of Justice," 2009, https://vimeo.com/2789213.

2. James Willard Hurst, "Lawyers in American Society 1750-1966," *Marquette Law Review* 50, (1967).

3. Richard K. Neumann, "Comparative Histories of Professional Education: Osler, Langdell, and the Atelier," *Hofstra Univ. Legal Studies Research Paper*, No. 12-10, 40, https://papers.ssrn.com/sol3/papers.cfm?abstract_id= 2016462 (accessed April 8, 2021).

4. For a discussion of civil cases in federal court, *see* William P. Lynch, "Why Settle for Less: Improving Settlement Conferences in Federal Court," *Wash-*

ington Law Review 94, (2019):1233, https://digitalcommons.law.uw.edu/cgi/
viewcontent.cgi?article=5079&context=wlr (accessed April 28, 2021). For a
discussion of criminal cases, *see* John Grimlich, "Only 2% of Federal Criminal
Defendants Went to Trial in 2018, and Most Who Did Were Found Guilty,
"*Pew Research Center*, June 11, 2019 https://www.pewresearch.org/fact-tank/
2019/06/11/only-2-of-federal-criminal-defendants-go-to-trial-and-most-who-
do-are-found-guilty/ (accessed April 28, 2021).

5. Throughout the text, I have critiqued the adversarial process, which pits two
   sides against each other to battle for a singular cohesive and acceptable factual
   account and interpretation of the law. My legal experience is limited to this
   system, with roots in English Common Law, standing in contrast to the inquisitorial system used in civil law countries in Europe and Latin America. While I
   am critical of the adversarial process's defects, especially its reliance on competition to determine the "truth," it is beyond my experience (the scope of this
   book) to explore the inquisitorial system in depth or to conduct a comparative
   analysis.
6. Scott Turow, *One L*, 10.
7. William M. Sullivan, Anne Colby, Judith Welch Wegner, Lloyd Bond and Lee
   S. Shulman, *Educating Lawyers: Preparation for the Profession of Law* (San
   Francisco: Jossey-Bass 2007).
8. Van Ness and Strong, *Restorative Justice*, 164.
9. Robert J. Sternberg, *Beyond I.Q.* (Cambridge: Cambridge University Press,
   2009).

4. Thinking Like a (Restorative) Lawyer

1. While I now view working for peace to be part of a lawyer's work, before
   attending graduate school at the Center for Justice and Peacebuilding, I did not
   consider lawyers to be peacebuilders. John Paul Lederach, a founder of CJP,
   describes peacebuilding as "understood as a comprehensive concept that
   encompasses, generates, and sustains the full array of processes, approaches,
   and stages needed to transform conflict toward more sustainable, peaceful relationships. The term involves a wide range of activities that both precede and
   follow formal peace accords. Metaphorically, peace is seen not merely as a
   stage in time or a condition. It is a dynamic social construct." John Paul Lederach, *Building Peace: Sustainable Reconciliation in Divided Societies* (Washington, D.C.: U.S. Institute of Peace Press, 1997), 75.
2. Some lawyers suggest that the law is objective and, therefore, devoid of values.
   For a discussion of the relationship between values and objectivity in the law
   see Neil McCormick, *Institutions of Law: An Essay on Legal Theory* (Oxford:
   Oxford University Press, 2007), 305.
3. Maya Angelou, Facebook Post, Last modified November 11, 2011, https://
   www.facebook.com/MayaAngelou/posts/if-we-lose-love-and-self-respect-for-
   each-other-this-is-how-we-finally-die/10151446619889796/ (accessed April
   9, 2021).

4. William Aiken, "Respect," *The CPA Journal*, February 2002, "http://archives. cpajournal.com/2002/0202/nv/nv14a.htm (accessed April 9, 2021).
5. Ury, William, *The Third Side* (New York: Penguin, 2000).
6. American Bar Association. *Model Rules of Professional Conduct*. https://www. americanbar.org/groups/professional_responsibility/publications/ model_rules_of_professional_conduct/. (accessed April 9, 2021).

5. Thinking Like a Restorative Lawyer

1. Oliver Wendell Holmes, "The Path of the Law," Harvard Law Review 10 (1897): 457, http://moglen.law.columbia.edu/LCS/palaw.pdf (accessed April 21, 2021).
2. I am intrigued by comparing the philosophical underpinnings of restorative justice with the jurisprudence of our conventional American legal system and plan to explore the topic in more detail in a future article. Some of the "lost saints" informing our assumptions about rights and the law could include Jeremy Bentham, H.L.A. Hart, Ronald Dworkin, Lon Fuller, Karl Llewellyn, and John Rawls.
3. Howard Zehr, *Changing Lenses*, 270.
4. J.K. Phillips, M.A. Ford, and R.J. Bonnie, eds. *Pain Management and the Opioid Epidemic*. Washington DC: National Academies Press, 2017. https:// www.ncbi.nlm.nih.gov/books/NBK458660/(accessed September 10, 2024).
5. A group of lawyers working in restorative justice gathered several times with Howard Zehr between 2010 and 2019 near Harrisonburg, Virginia to thrash out concepts, critiques, and approaches in restorative justice. In attempting to leave no stone unturned, we adopted the term "palaver" for the event—since it refers to discussions that go on too long and perhaps exhaust a topic.
6. For the restorative lawyer, collaboration requires the following: at least two committed people, common interests, articulable shared goals, developed communication skills (or a skilled facilitator), a desire to build or at least sustain relationships, a growing level of trust, complete equity in participation and decision making, active engagement with the process, and transparency in emotional and factual information.
7. Lujan v. Defenders of Wildlife, 504 U.S. 555, 560-61 (1992); see also Summers, 555 U.S. at 493.
8. Lorraine Stutzman Amstutz, "The Relationship Between Victim Service Organizations and Restorative Justice," in *Critical Issues in Restorative Justice,* ed. Howard Zehr and Barb Toews (Monsey, New York: Criminal Justice Press, 2004), 85.
9. Stephen Levy, *Legal Project Management* (Day Pack Books, 2009), 281.

6. Rules of Engagement

1. Lainey Feingold, *Structured Negotiation: A Winning Alternative to Lawsuits* (Chicago: American Bar Association, Section of Dispute Resolution, 2016), 74.

2. John Lande, *Lawyering with Planned Early Negotiation: How You Can Get Good Results for Clients and Make Money* (Chicago: American Bar Association, 2015), 53.

3. Michele Leering, "Conceptualizing Reflective Practice for Legal Professionals." *Journal of Law and Social Policy* 23 (2014), 100.

4. Stephen J. Meyer, "A Poker Champion Explains Why You Make Bad Business Decisions," *Forbes*, June 3, 2014,https://www.forbes.com/sites/stevemeyer/2014/06/03/a-poker-champion-explains-why-you-make-bad-business-decisions/#1e44236a430f.

5. Meyer, "Poker Champion."

6. Remen, *Kitchen Table Wisdom*, 219.

7. Chimamanda Ngozi Adichi, "The Danger of a Single Story," *Ted Talk*, July 2009.https://www.ted.com/talks/chimamanda_ngozi_adichie_the_danger_of_a_single_story?subtitle=en Throughout this text I have referred to "single story" to describe two opposing stories wrangling for dominance within the legal setting. Ngozi Adichie's concept of the single story tended more to emphasize how stereotypes are supported by single stories. She says, "The consequence of the single story is that it robs people of dignity. It makes our recognition of our equal humanity difficult and it emphasizes that we are different rather than how we are similar...The single story creates stereotype and the problem with stereotype is not that they are untrue but that they are incomplete, they make one story become the only story." In my experience, I find the notion of the dominant single story in a legal dispute to pose similar obstacles by creating incomplete stories that focus on differences, not shared experiences, needs, and outcomes.

8. Binny Miller, "Give them Back Their Lives: Recognizing Client Narrative in Case Theory." *Michigan Law Review* 93 (1994): 485, 494.

9. This is a standard trial advocacy training case that has been around since 1979, *See* Seth W. Moscowitz, "Legal Exhibits, Mock Trials, Music Draws Visitors to Fair," *Washington Post*, May 10, 1979. https://www.washingtonpost.com/archive/local/1979/05/10/legal-exhibits-mock-trials-music-draw-visitors-to-fair/559cc9a9-a397-4d90-b05d-ofae2c509e0e/(Accessed October 4, 2024). Blogger Clint Frizzel reported it was still being used in his law school in 2012. Clift Frizzel, *Just Another Wordpress.com site.* https://clintfrizzell.wordpress.com/2012/03/02/state-vs-diamond/ (Accessed September 24, 2024).

10. Lode Walgrave, *Restorative Justice and the Law* (New York: Routledge, 2002).

11. Adichie, *Danger.*

12. Robert M. Persig, *Zen and the Art of Motorcycle Maintenance* (London:Vintage, 1974).

13. Donald A. Schon, *Educating the Reflective Practitioners* (San Francisco: Jossey-Bass, 1987).

14. Leering, "Conceptualizing."

15. Leering, "Conceptualizing," 102.

16. Leering, "Conceptualizing," 97.

17. In one often-cited study, almost two-thirds of the participants (both men and women) reported at least one childhood experience of physical or sexual abuse,

neglect, or family dysfunction. More than one in five reported three or more such experiences. Vincent J. Felitti, M.D., F.A.C.P., Robert F. Anda, M.D., M.S., Dale Nordenberg, M.D., Valerie Edwards, B.A., Mary P. Koss, Ph.D., James S. Marks, M.D., M.P.H., "Relationship of Childhood Abuse and Household Dysfunction to Many of the Leading Causes of Death in Adults," *American Journal of Preventative Medicine* 14 (May 1, 1998): 245-258.

18. Laura van Dernoot Lipsky and Connie Burk, *Trauma Stewardship: An Everyday Guide to Caring for Self While Caring for Others* (San Francisco: Berrett-Koehler Publishers, 2009). Tesler's perspective is apparent in her article, Pauline H. Tesler, "Informed Choice and Emergent Systems at the Growth Edge of Collaborative Practice" *Family Court Review* 49 (April, 2011): 239-248.https://onlinelibrary.wiley.com/doi/abs/10.1111/j.1744-1617.2011.01367.x. (accessed April 12, 2021).

19. Bria Samoné Henderson comment from panel discussion, "Perhaps my Protest Looks Different," June 19, 2020, American Shakespeare Theater. https://www.facebook.com/12852193346/videos/735219157288904 (accessed April 22, 2021).

20. For a discussion of lawyer discipline and potential restorative responses *see* Rachel Hott and Brenda Waugh, "Discipline Does Not Make an Ill Lawyer Well... but Can It?: Creating Effective, Consumer Friendly and Humane Lawyer Discipline Systems by Adopting Principles, Values and Processes Rooted in Restorative Justice," *Richmond Public Interest Law Review,* 23 (2019-2020): 243.

21. Information is available on our website, lawyer-wellness.com.

22. Tesler, *Informed Choice.*

23. Louise Phipps Senft, *Being Relational: The Seven Ways to Quality Interaction and Lasting Change* (Florida: Health Communications, Inc., 2015).

24. Jane Cohen Barbe, "Open Letter from Denton Partner, July 19, 2019," accessed April 10, 2021, https://www.lawfuel.com/blog/open-letter-from-dentons-partner/. During the last few years, I've noticed a growing awareness of the absence of wellness in lawyers. A 2016 study sponsored by the American Bar Association Commission on Lawyer Assistance Programs and the Hazelden Betty Ford Foundation surveyed nearly 13,000 currently practicing attorneys and found higher than average instances of alcohol abuse and depression. Patrick R. Krill, J.D., L.L.M.; Ryan Johnson, MA; Linda Albert, M.S.S.W., "The Prevalence of Substance Use and Other Mental Health Concerns Among American Attorneys," *Journal of Addiction Medicine* 10 (January/February 2016): 46-52. https://journals.lww.com/journaladdictionmedicine/Fulltext/2016/02000/The_Prevalence_of_Substance_Use_and_Other_Mental.8.aspx. (accessed April 20, 2021).

7. Approaches and Methods for the Restorative Lawyer

1. Marshall Rosenberg, *Nonviolent Communication A Language of Life* (California: Puddle Dancer Press, 2015) 2.
2. Rosenberg, *Nonviolent Communication.*
3. "Course Catalog," Lewis and Clark Law School (accessed September 29, 2024) https://law.lclark.edu/courses/catalog/law_050.php.
4. Levy, *Legal Project Management*, 207.
5. Levy, *Legal Project Management*, 216.
6. Levy, *Legal Project Management*, 46.
7. Levy, *Legal Project Management*, 24.
8. Levy, *Legal Project Management*, 45.
9. Lawyers often refer to counsel for the other party as "opposing counsel" who is on the "on the other side." Collaborative law has taught me to avoid these terms, since in collaborative (as well as most cases) the counsel often does not oppose the goal that my client seeks but rather opposes a position. Similarly, the "other side" accepts a theory that there are two sides of the dispute when most disputes are multifaceted with diverging and overlapping interests intertwined.
10. Roger Fisher and William Ury, *Getting to Yes: Negotiating Agreement Without Giving In* (New York: Penguin Books, 2011).
11. This fictional fact pattern is modeled after the lower court decision in *Kelo v. New London*, 268 Conn. 152, 843 A.2d 500 (2004), reported at https://www.jud.ct.gov/external/supapp/Cases/AROcr/CR268/268cr152.pdf (accessed September 26, 2024).
12. Levy, *Legal Project Management*, 206.
13. Levy, *Legal Project Management*, 181.
14. Fisher and Ury, *Yes*. One of the most effective approaches to mediation requires the negotiator to determine their underlying interest and to detail the means of determining the BATNA (Best Alternative to a Negotiated Agreement) WATNA (Worst alternative to a negated Agreement) and MLATNA (Most Likely Alternative to a Negotiated Agreement.).
15. John Burton, *Conflict Resolution and Prevention* (New York: St. Martin's Press, 1990).
16. A more modern approach to parenting children in separate households avoids terms such as "sole" and "custody" in favor of "shared" and "custodial responsibility." The latter implies the important role and duty of both parents as well as naming the legal relationship in accordance with the way we describe relationships between people rather than people and personal property.
17. Sara Cobb, interview by Julian Portilla for *Beyond Intractability*, http://www.beyondintractability.org/audiodisplay/cobb-s (accessed May 30, 2017).

8. Techniques, Skills, and Strategies For the Restorative Lawyer

1. Talking circles provide an excellent opportunity to practicing listening. Participants speak one at a time, guided by an object—a talking piece. With a talking circle, listeners are required to "hold that thought" until it is their turn. This format tends to create more attentive listening when we are not preparing a response. I rely on Kay Pranis for direction and coaching in being a keeper of the circle. Kay Pranis, *A Circle Keepers Handbook*, 2017. https://livingjustice press.org/wp-content/uploads/2019/04/Circle_Keeper_Handbook_2017.pdf (accessed September 26, 2024).
2. Tesler, Pauline, "Neuroliteracy for Collaborative (and Other) Lawyers," *New York Dispute Resolution Lawyer* 4 (2011).
3. As early as the 1990s, CLS critical race theory scholar, Patricia Williams noticed that legal language takes away the complexity and nuances in the analysis of legal disputes. Patricia Williams, *The Alchemy of Race and Rights: Diary of a Law Professor* (Cambridge: Harvard University Press, 1991). In her lectures that I attended as a student at George Mason University's School of Conflict Resolution in 2010, Professor Sara Cobb used the language of rehydrating a story to provide for the nuances that are lost.
4. William Ury, "On Building a Golden Bridge," https://www.littlefallsmedia tion.com/blog/william-ury-on-building-a-golden-bridge, (accessed September 26, 2024).
5. Patricia Lee Brown, "What Would a World Without Prisons Look Like," *New York Times*, March 6, 2020, (accessed November 23, 2020). https://www. nytimes.com/2020/03/06/arts/design/prison-architecture.html
6. Henry David Thoreau, *Walden; or Life in the Woods*, (New York: Thomas Y. Crowell, 1910) 194.

10. Navigating the Steps

1. Robert K. Merton, *Sociological Ambivalence and Other Essays* (New York: Free Press, 1976).
2. Adam Davidson, "How Foreign Aid is Hurting Haitian Farmers," *NPR, Morning Edition*, June 11, 2010, https://www.npr.org/sections/money/2010/ 06/10/127750586/how-foreign-aid-is-hurting-haitian-farmers, (accessed January 2, 2021).
3. Adichie, "Danger."

11. My Heart Is Healing

1. Remen, *Kitchen Table Wisdom*, 248.
2. The term "reasonable efforts" was introduced to the child protection system in 1974 through the Child Abuse Prevention and Treatment Act (CAPTA).

CAPTA aimed to reduce the number of children in foster care and shorten their time in state custody by requiring plans to address issues that prompted the removal of a child from parental custody, appointing a Guardian Ad Litem (GAL) for each child, and assigning judicial oversight. CAPTA focused on preventing out-of-home placements, promoting family reunification, and ensuring timely permanency. Further legislation, such as the Adoption Assistance and Child Welfare Act (1980) and the Adoption and Safe Families Act (1997), defined "reasonable efforts" by establishing federal reimbursement for agencies, documenting judicial oversight, and outlining exceptions where efforts weren't required. In my experience in child welfare litigation, the courts typically include this finding to ensure the federal funding is received without necessarily hearing sufficient evidence to support any factual finding related to this conclusion.

3. Ryan Lanora Brown, "Congo Ebola Crisis: To Fight Disease an Anthropologist Heals Distrust," Christian Science Monitor, January 3, 2020, https://www.c-smonitor.com/World/Africa/2020/0103/Congo-Ebola-crisis-To-fight-disease-an-anthropologist-heals-distrust? (accessed July 30, 2020).

Index

www.ingramcontent.com/pod-product-compliance
Lightning Source LLC
Chambersburg PA
CBHW022046210326
41519CB00055B/845